ZERO

TO

HERO

The Single Entrepreneur's Guide to Building Billion-Dollar Businesses with AI

Editor

Aditya Basu

Copyright Information

Title: ZERO TO HERO: The Single Entrepreneur's Guide to Building Billion-Dollar Businesses with AI

Editor: Aditya Basu

Published by: Aditya Basu

Publisher Website: www.adityabasu.com

Edition: Print First Edition (Global Distribution)

Imprint: Aditya Basu - Non-Fiction Books

ISBN: 978-93-343-7186-4

Disclaimer

This book, "Zero to Hero: The Single Entrepreneur's Guide to Building Billion-Dollar Businesses with AI," is the result of human creativity and critical thinking, with AI serving as a supportive tool in the workflow. This book has been meticulously reviewed and fact-checked by the Editorial Team, with great care taken to ensure the accuracy and relevance of its content as of July 2025.

All Strategic Scenarios mentioned in the book are Fictional Competitive Scenarios.

By engaging with this material, readers acknowledge their responsibility to evaluate the content's relevance and applicability to their specific circumstances, recognizing that this work represents a foundation for further exploration.

Readers should note that this is a forward-looking work. The central thesis—the emergence of a solo-founder billionaire—is a forecast based on the analysis of powerful, observable trends in technology, business, and capital markets. As of the time of publication, this historic milestone has not yet been definitively achieved. This guide, therefore, presents a potential roadmap toward that future, not a reflection of a well-trodden historical path.

There is no guarantee, express or implied, that you will become a billionaire by following the methods outlined in this book. Entrepreneurship is an inherently risky endeavor, and success is dependent on a multitude of factors including skill, dedication, market conditions, and a degree of luck. The frameworks and strategies within are presented as an educated exploration of a possible path, not a guaranteed formula for wealth. Should you fail in your quest, we encourage you to analyze the reasons, learn from the experience, and try again, as resilience is the true hallmark of any great entrepreneur.

The publisher, author, and editor will not take any financial or legal responsibility for any business losses, damages, or other consequences that may result from following the guidelines or concepts presented in this work. This book is for informational and educational purposes only.

You are strongly advised to conduct your own independent research, perform thorough due diligence, and consult with qualified legal, financial, and business professionals before making any significant business decisions or investments.

Our primary goal is to expand your perspective on what is possible in this new era of individual leverage. We are just planting a seed in your head so that you can think big, build systems, and use the incredible power of AI to become bigger, more impactful, and maybe, just maybe, a billionaire someday.

Dedication

To My Beloved Father, Late Mr. Puskar Basu

In the quiet corners of my heart, your memory resides—like the warmth of sunlight on a winter morning. You were my guiding star, my unwavering support, and my confidant. Your love and wisdom continue to inspire me every day. Though you're no longer here, your presence lingers—a comforting whisper in the wind, a star that guides me through the night. Thank you for being my father, my friend, and my hero. Until we meet again, know that you are cherished, always and forever.

Aditya Basu

Contents

Foreword

We live in the shadow of an explosion. In late 2022, the public release of ChatGPT was not merely the launch of a new product; it was a Cambrian explosion for intelligence itself. The shockwave of that event is still reverberating through our economy and our society. Here, in mid-2025, we have moved past the initial novelty and are now standing at the dawn of a profound and irreversible restructuring of how we work, create, and build. We are at an inflection point as significant and as vertigo-inducing as the birth of the commercial internet in 1995 or the launch of the first iPhone in 2007. The rules of the game are being fundamentally rewritten.

Yet, in observing the response to this revolution, I have been struck by a collective failure of imagination. The vast majority of established corporations are attempting to simply bolt AI onto their legacy systems and bureaucratic processes. They see this awesome new power as a tool for incremental efficiency—a way to write marketing copy slightly faster, to summarize meetings, to make their existing, bloated structures marginally less inefficient. Many entrepreneurs, too, are thinking in terms of "AI features," not "AI-native" companies. They are building products *with* AI, but not businesses that are fundamentally *of* AI. This is akin to the first automakers trying to design a "faster horse" instead of envisioning the entire system of highways, supply chains, and suburbs that the automobile would eventually create.

This is why the book you are holding is so critically important. *Zero to Hero* is the first work that truly grapples with the deepest, most radical implication of this technological shift: the unprecedented empowerment of the individual. It correctly posits that the fundamental unit of economic value creation is no longer the funded "team" or the hierarchical "firm," but the highly leveraged solo founder.

The core premise of this book—that a single person can now architect and orchestrate a symphony of AI agents and automated systems to achieve the output, scale, and valuation of a thousand-person organization—would have been science fiction five years ago. Today, it is an engineering reality. This book is not a philosophical treatise on the future; it's delivers a detailed, practical, and actionable blueprint for building it.

From the psychological rewiring required to shed the "freelancer mindset" to the tactical details of building an automated, self-running operational stack, this book provides the complete operating manual for a new generation of entrepreneur. It recognizes that the coming decades will be defined not by those who can manage large teams, but by those who can design intelligent systems.

The next wave of market-defining, world-changing companies is about to be built. They will not be born in sprawling corporate campuses or born from massive Series A funding rounds. They will be launched from the laptops of quiet, focused, and relentless individuals. They will be hyper-efficient, wildly profitable, and run by a new archetype of founder. This book is their guide. The playbook for the next generation of titans is in your hands. The question is no longer who will let you, but who can possibly stop you.

Aditya Basu
Editor

Part 1: The New Landscape

The "Why": Establishing the paradigm shift that makes the solo-founder unicorn a realistic possibility

Chapter 1: The Paradigm Shift

Introduction

Imagine the birth of a billion-dollar company. The image that springs to mind is likely a garage packed with brilliant engineers, a whiteboard covered in frantic scribbles, and a room buzzing with the electric chaos of collaboration. It's the foundational myth of Silicon Valley, an image cemented over decades of startup lore. Now, erase it. Replace that crowded garage with a single desk, a single laptop, and a single founder. The whiteboard is digital, the collaborators are algorithms, and the buzz is the silent, relentless hum of a thousand servers executing a singular vision. This is not a distant future; it is the new reality of entrepreneurship.

This book is built on a single, revolutionary premise: a lone individual, armed with the right idea and the right AI, can now build a billion-dollar enterprise. We are witnessing the dawn of the solo founder era, an age where the traditional barriers to scale—headcount, capital, and infrastructure—are being systematically dismantled by artificial intelligence. This is not about building a lifestyle business or a profitable side project. This is about competing with, and ultimately outmaneuvering, the largest incumbents by leveraging AI not as a mere tool, but as a true business partner. It's your tireless 24/7 engineering team, your data-driven CFO, and your infinitely creative marketing department, all rolled into one. This chapter will deconstruct the crumbling pillars of the old model and reveal the new landscape where one person can, and will, achieve what once required an army. Welcome to the paradigm shift.

1.1 The Death of Traditional Team-Building Models

For generations, the first commandment of ambitious entrepreneurship was "build a great team." It was an unassailable truth that scaling a vision required scaling the number of people dedicated to it. This axiom has become a liability. The very model that was once the engine of growth is now a source of friction, cost, and inertia. The solo founder, by necessity and by design, bypasses these systemic flaws, creating a new, hyper-efficient model for value creation. The traditional approach is dying, burdened by three critical, self-inflicted wounds.

The Friction of Hiring

The process of hiring is a profound tax on a startup's most valuable asset: time. Finding the right talent is a grueling, resource-intensive marathon. Data from 2023 shows that the average time-to-hire for tech roles can stretch from 40 to 60 days. For a startup, two months is an eternity—a window in which a competitor can launch, a market can shift, or a crucial technological advantage can be lost.

This process includes:

- **Sourcing:** Weeks spent searching, networking, and paying recruiters.
- **Interviewing:** Dozens of hours consumed by founders and early employees screening, testing, and interviewing candidates.
- **Onboarding:** A 30-to-90-day period where a new hire is a net drain on resources, requiring training and supervision before becoming fully productive.

An AI "employee," in contrast, is hired with an API key and a credit card. Its "onboarding" takes minutes, not months. It arrives fully trained, operates at peak efficiency from the first second, and can be "hired" or "fired" with a click. While a startup spends a full quarter assembling its core engineering team, a solo founder has already deployed a global-scale application powered by AI agents.

The Financial Drain of Salaries and Equity Dilution

The second wound is the catastrophic cost of people. A senior software engineer in a major tech hub commands a salary upwards of $200,000, plus benefits, taxes, and overhead, pushing the fully loaded cost closer to $275,000 per year. A founding team of a CEO, CTO, and COO could burn over $800,000 annually on salaries alone, before even writing a line of code for a customer.

Hot Take: In the AI era, equity is a liability, not an asset. Every percentage point of your company you give away to an early employee is a tax on your future ambition—a tax that AI makes entirely optional.

The more insidious cost is equity dilution. Consider a startup with three co-founders, each taking an equal share. Before a single dollar of investment is raised, each founder's potential outcome from a billion-dollar exit is capped at $333 million. After a standard Series A funding round, that number can easily drop below $250 million. The solo founder, by contrast, owns 100% of the enterprise. Every dollar of value created accrues directly to them.

Let's compare the cost structure revolution:

- **Traditional Team (3 engineers):**
  - Annual Salary Cost: ~$825,000
  - Equity Cost: 5-15% of the company
  - Productivity: 8 hours/day, 5 days/week
- **AI-Powered Solo Founder:**
  - Annual AI Stack Cost: ~$25,000 (for premium APIs, no-code platforms, and automation tools)
  - Equity Cost: 0%
  - Productivity: 24 hours/day, 7 days/week

The traditional model demands that you trade ownership for execution. The new model allows you to rent near-infinite execution for a fixed operational expense, keeping all of your ownership.

Communication Overhead and the Collapse of Velocity

In his seminal 1975 book, *The Mythical Man-Month*, computer scientist Fred Brooks observed that adding people to a late software project makes it later. This is due to the exponential increase in communication overhead. The number of communication pathways in a team is defined by the formula $n(n-1)/2$.

- A solo founder has 0 pathways to manage.

- A 3-person team has 3 pathways.
- A 10-person team has 45 pathways.
- A 50-person company has an astonishing 1,225 pathways.

Every pathway is a potential point of friction, misunderstanding, and delay. It's the origin of status meetings, syncs, all-hands, and the endless email chains that grind productivity to a halt. This is the "structure" that kills "speed". Decision-making velocity collapses as consensus is sought and information is filtered through layers of management.

The solo founder operates with zero communication overhead. The conversation is a direct loop between the founder's vision and the AI's execution. A strategic decision can be conceived and implemented in the same afternoon, while a traditional startup is still trying to schedule the kickoff meeting. This agility is the new era's most potent competitive advantage, allowing the solo founder to iterate, pivot, and capture markets at a speed that is structurally impossible for team-based organizations to match. The traditional model is not just inefficient; it is fundamentally too slow for the AI age.

1.2 AI as the Great Equalizer

For decades, the competitive landscape of business has been a fundamentally unfair fight. Scale begets scale. The corporations with the largest war chests, the biggest R&D departments, and the most expansive sales teams held an insurmountable advantage. They could out-hire, out-spend, and out-market any new entrant. Artificial intelligence is not merely leveling that playing field; it is dynamiting it. AI has become the great equalizer, democratizing the capabilities once exclusive to the Fortune 500 and handing them to the individual. This transformation has occurred in a distinct evolutionary path, moving AI from a simple assistant to a genuine business partner.

Phase 1: AI as a Tool (The Sidekick)

Until recently, AI in the context of a small business or startup was a "sidekick." It was a collection of useful but limited tools that improved efficiency at the margins. It was Grammarly correcting your typos, a simple chatbot answering basic FAQs, or a recommendation engine suggesting what product to buy next. These tools were helpful—they saved time and polished outputs—but they did not fundamentally change the nature of work. They executed narrow, pre-defined tasks. The strategy, creativity, and heavy operational lifting still fell squarely on human shoulders. The solo entrepreneur could be more efficient, but their scope was still limited by the number of hours in the day.

Phase 2: The Generative Leap (The Inflection Point)

The launch of large-scale generative models like OpenAI's GPT series in 2022 and Anthropic's Claude models marked a seismic shift. This was not just a quantitative improvement; it was a qualitative leap in capability. AI evolved from a mere executor of commands to a generator of novel content and complex ideas. It could now write code, design marketing campaigns, draft legal documents, and create photorealistic images from a simple text prompt.

This inflection point transformed AI from a tool into a force multiplier. The bottleneck was no longer execution but imagination. For the solo founder, this was the moment the game changed. Suddenly, the functions that previously required hiring a specialist—a copywriter, a graphic designer, a junior developer, a data analyst—could be accessed instantly through an API. According to a 2023 report from the McKinsey Global Institute, generative AI is poised to add between $2.6 trillion and $4.4 trillion in value annually to the global economy, precisely by automating and augmenting these knowledge-worker tasks. The solo founder is uniquely positioned to capture this value with near-zero overhead.

Phase 3: AI as a Partner (The New Reality)

Today, we are in the third and most revolutionary phase: AI as a business partner. This goes beyond simple task execution or content generation. It involves entrusting AI with entire business functions and, most critically, integrating it into the core strategic loop of the company.

- **The Operational Partner:** This is the most tangible form of partnership. A solo founder can now deploy a network of AI agents to run the company's day-to-day operations. As we will explore in Part 2, AI can manage 99% of customer service inquiries with human-like empathy, run fully automated sales outreach campaigns, handle all financial bookkeeping and reporting, and even perform continuous quality assurance on the company's software product. The founder transitions from being the "doer" of all things to the architect and conductor of an automated operational symphony.

- **The Strategic Partner:** This is the most profound shift. Using advanced models like GPT-5 or Claude 4 is like having an on-demand MBA from Stanford, a McKinsey strategist, and a veteran venture capitalist in a single chat window. A solo founder can now engage in high-level strategic sparring that was once the exclusive domain of executive teams and boards.

    - **Action Item:** Don't ask your AI "What is a good marketing strategy?" Ask it: "You are a world-class growth marketer. My product is a B2B SaaS for dental offices that automates appointment reminders. My budget is $5,000/month. We have 50 current customers. Develop a comprehensive, 90-day marketing plan that prioritizes low-cost, high-leverage channels. Include key metrics (KPIs) for each channel and a projected customer acquisition cost."

This level of strategic dialogue allows a single individual to analyze markets, model financial scenarios, dissect competitor weaknesses, and pressure-test ideas with a rigor that previously required a full C-suite.

- **The Creative Partner:** The creative process, long seen as uniquely human, is now a collaborative effort. A solo founder can use AI to brainstorm company names, design logos, generate entire libraries of marketing assets, and even prototype the UI/UX for their application. AI is not just executing a creative vision; it is an active participant in its formation.

This evolution from sidekick to partner is the foundational mechanism of the solo billionaire thesis. It equalizes the battlefield by granting the individual access to near-infinite labor, world-class strategic counsel, and boundless creative capacity for a nominal monthly subscription. The only remaining competitive advantages are the truly human ones: vision, judgment, and the courage to build.

1.3 The Economics of One

The revolution sparked by artificial intelligence is not just technological; it is fundamentally an economic one. It strikes at the financial heart of what it means to build a company, tearing up the old ledgers and replacing them with a new, radically efficient model. The "Economics of One" is a framework built on three pillars: a completely deconstructed cost structure, massively expanded profit margins, and a redefined understanding of scalability. Mastering these principles is not just about saving money; it's about creating a financial engine so powerful it can propel a single founder to a billion-dollar valuation.

Deconstructing the Cost Structure

For decades, a startup's burn rate was a simple, brutal equation dominated by one variable: people. Salaries, benefits, office space, and administrative support typically accounted for 70% or more of a venture-backed company's expenses. This created a high-stakes environment where immense capital was required just to survive long enough to find product-market fit. The solo founder operates under a completely different financial paradigm.

- **Old Cost Structure (The Bloat):**
  - **Massive Fixed Costs:** Dominated by salaries and long-term office leases. These costs are incurred regardless of revenue, creating immense pressure to grow at all costs.
  - **People Operations:** Significant budget allocated to HR, recruiting, payroll services, and employee benefits.
  - **Infrastructure:** Physical hardware for employees, office supplies, and the associated overhead.

- **New Cost Structure (The Stack):**
    - **Minimal Fixed Costs:** The largest fixed costs are a curated list of monthly or annual subscriptions for core software—your no-code platform, your design tools, and your primary AI models. This might total a few thousand dollars a month, not hundreds of thousands.
    - **Scalable Variable Costs:** The bulk of the expense comes from usage-based services, primarily API calls to AI providers and cloud hosting fees. This is a crucial shift: costs grow *in proportion to* revenue and customer activity, not as a prerequisite to it. You pay for what you use, making the model incredibly resilient.
    - **Zero People Operations:** There is no HR department, no benefits administration, and no payroll to manage.

This is the shift from a **people-centric** cost model to a **system-centric** one. The solo founder isn't paying for human time; they are paying for machine time, which is orders of magnitude cheaper and more scalable.

The Margin Maximization Effect

The direct consequence of this deconstructed cost structure is a dramatic expansion of profit margins. In a traditional SaaS company, a healthy gross margin might be 80%, but after factoring in the operational costs of sales, marketing, and R&D (all functions driven by expensive headcount), the net profit margin often struggles to reach 20-30%. The solo founder's P&L tells a different story.

By the Numbers: The Margin Advantage

Let's compare two companies, each generating $1,000,000 in annual recurring revenue (ARR).

- **Traditional SaaS Startup (10-person team):**
    - Revenue: $1,000,000

    - Cost of Goods Sold (Servers, etc.): -$150,000
    - Salaries & Benefits (Sales, R&D, G&A): -$600,000
    - Marketing & Tools: -$100,000
    - **Net Profit: $150,000 (15% Margin)**

- **AI-Powered Solo Founder:**

    - Revenue: $1,000,000
    - Cost of Goods Sold (Servers, high API usage): -$250,000
    - Salaries & Benefits: $0
    - Marketing & Tools (Premium AI Stack): -$75,000
    - **Net Profit: $675,000 (67.5% Margin)**

This isn't a minor improvement; it's a fundamental re-architecting of profitability. This level of capital efficiency means a solo founder can reach profitability far sooner, reinvest more cash into growth, and operate with a level of financial freedom their larger competitors can only dream of.

Redefined Scalability: From Linear to Asymptotic

Perhaps the most powerful aspect of the Economics of One is how it redefines scalability. Traditionally, scaling a business has been a linear, and often painful, process. To double revenue, you needed to significantly increase headcount—more engineers to build, more salespeople to sell, more support agents to service. Growth was coupled to hiring.

The AI-powered solo founder decouples growth from headcount entirely. Scalability becomes a purely technical challenge, not a human one.

- **To handle 10x more users:** You don't hire a support team; you ensure your AI customer service agent can handle more concurrent conversations and has access to a more comprehensive knowledge base.

- **To enter a new market:** You don't hire a country manager; you task your language model to translate your product and marketing into five new languages.
- **To increase product velocity:** You don't hire more developers; you leverage a more advanced code-generation AI to build and test features faster.

The cost to serve the ten-thousandth customer is almost identical to the cost to serve the thousandth. This is **asymptotic scalability**—the cost per user approaches zero as the user base grows. The founder's job is no longer to build and manage a team that scales, but to design and manage a *system* that scales. This economic engine, characterized by minimal overhead, maximized margins, and system-centric scalability, is the foundation upon which a solo-founder empire can be built. It transforms the financial risks that sink most startups into the very advantages that allow the individual to win.

1.4 Case Study: The Quiet Rise of Solo Unicorns

The theories of solo-founder scalability and the Economics of One are not just abstract concepts; they are being proven in the market today by a new breed of hyper-lean, wildly profitable companies. While the world's first solo-founded, billion-dollar public company has yet to emerge, the blueprint for its creation is being written in real-time. The most potent and visible example of this new paradigm is a small, self-funded research lab that has redefined an entire creative industry: Midjourney.

Founded by David Holz, Midjourney is an AI image generator that turns simple text prompts into stunning, complex artwork. In mid-2022, it was a niche tool for enthusiasts. By 2024, it was a household name in creative circles and a financial powerhouse, reportedly generating hundreds of millions of dollars in annual revenue. The most staggering fact? It achieved this with a team of just 11 people. This is not just an impressive statistic; it is a fundamental indictment of the traditional scaling model.

Let's deconstruct the Midjourney model to extract the lessons for the aspiring solo founder.

Operational Model: Leverage Over Labor

Midjourney's operations are a masterclass in maximizing leverage and minimizing human intervention.

1. **No Sales or Marketing Team:** Midjourney has never employed a single salesperson or traditional marketer. Its growth is entirely organic, driven by two factors: the undeniable quality of its product and a brilliant, low-friction distribution strategy. By building their service directly into Discord, a platform already used by tens of millions, they eliminated the need to build, market, and maintain their own user-facing application. The product's output is inherently shareable, turning every user into a potential evangelist and every generated image into a piece of viral marketing.

2. **Community-Powered Support and R&D:** Instead of hiring a massive customer support team, Midjourney leverages its passionate community. The Discord server acts as a self-sustaining ecosystem where new users learn from experienced ones. This community also serves as a massive, real-time R&D lab. The team constantly observes how people use the tool, what they struggle with, and what they desire, providing a direct feedback loop that is faster and more authentic than any structured focus group.

3. **Focused, Lean Engineering:** The 11-person team is not a sprawling department of front-end, back-end, and mobile developers. It is a small, deeply focused team of researchers and engineers obsessed with one thing: improving the core AI model. They are not managing people; they are managing infrastructure, training data, and algorithms. This reflects a critical lesson: dedicate 100% of your human intellect to your core competitive advantage and ruthlessly automate or platform-ize everything else.

Financial Model: Profits Over Pledges

Midjourney's financial success is a direct result of its operational leanness. It is proudly bootstrapped, meaning it has never taken on venture capital. This was not a limitation but a strategic choice enabled by the Economics of One.

By the Numbers: The Leverage Ratio

Let's use a conservative estimate of $200 million in annual revenue for Midjourney against its 11 employees.

- **Midjourney Revenue Per Employee:** $200,000,000 / 11 = **$18.2 million**

Now, let's compare that to some of the world's most successful tech companies (using 2023 data for approximation):

- **NVIDIA Revenue Per Employee:** ~$2.7 million
- **Microsoft Revenue Per Employee:** ~$1 million
- **Google (Alphabet) Revenue Per Employee:** ~$1.7 million

Midjourney is operating at a level of capital efficiency that is **10 times greater** than some of the best-run companies in the world. This is the mathematical proof of the new paradigm.

This incredible efficiency is powered by a simple, high-margin, recurring revenue model. Users pay a monthly subscription fee, from $10 to $120, for access to the AI. The cost to serve each additional user is marginal—a tiny fraction of a cent in GPU processing time. This is the asymptotic scalability model in its purest form.

Lessons for the Solo Founder

While you are a founder of one, not eleven, Midjourney's ethos is your direct playbook.

- **Be World-Class at One Thing:** Midjourney generates images. That's it. They don't have a blog, a conference, or a suite of secondary products. Find your one thing and use AI to become the undisputed best at it.
- **Leverage Existing Platforms:** Don't reinvent the wheel. Midjourney used Discord for community and distribution. Use Stripe/Paypal for payments, Amazon AWS/Google Cloud/Microsoft Azure for servers, and OpenAI/Claude/Gemini for your AI's brain. Your job is to integrate, not invent, the non-core parts of your stack.
- **Build a Business, Not a Team:** Holz has stated he wants to keep the team small to stay focused on the product and avoid the complexities of management. Your goal should be to increase revenue, not headcount. Every potential hire should first be evaluated against a question: "Can an AI or an automated system do this instead?"

Midjourney is the quiet unicorn. It is not celebrated on the cover of magazines for its fundraising rounds, but it is respected and feared for its sheer innovative power and financial prowess. It proves that a small group of focused individuals, leveraging AI and intelligent systems, can create more value than companies one thousand times their size. It is the proof that your journey from zero to hero is not just possible—it's already happening.

Chapter Summary & Resources

We have crossed the threshold into a new era of entrepreneurship. The foundational myths of team-building and venture capital are crumbling, replaced by a new reality where the individual is empowered to build at a scale previously unimaginable. The friction of hiring, the poison pill of equity dilution, and the lead weight of communication overhead have been replaced by the frictionless, low-cost, high-velocity power of AI. This is not a subtle shift; it is a paradigm-shattering event that redefines the very economics of building a business.

Key Takeaways

- The traditional team-building model is a liability. It is slow, expensive, and complex in an age that rewards speed, efficiency, and simplicity.
- Artificial intelligence has evolved from a simple tool into a strategic partner, capable of acting as your co-founder, operational workforce, and creative engine.
- The "Economics of One" creates hyper-efficient businesses with massive profit margins by replacing fixed salary costs with scalable, variable system costs.
- Extreme leverage, as proven by companies like Midjourney, is the new path to scale. The goal is to decouple revenue growth entirely from headcount.

Action Items for Mindset Shift

- **Calculate the Ghost Cost:** Before your next idea, map out a hypothetical 5-person team. Calculate their fully-loaded salaries, benefits, and the 20-30% equity you would have to give away. Internalize this number as the "cost of complexity" you are choosing to avoid.
- **Delegate to Your First AI Employee:** Identify one complex task in your current workflow (e.g., market research, content creation). Write a detailed, multi-step prompt for an AI to perform it. Evaluate the output as you would a new junior employee. Get comfortable with delegating to silicon.
- **Design Your Subscription Stack:** Forget an org chart. Sketch a "stack chart." List the 5-10 core subscription services (e.g., GPT-5 API, Bubble, Zapier, Stripe) that would form the foundation of your solo enterprise.

Preview of Chapter 2

Now that we have established *why* this new paradigm is possible, the next chapter explores *who* is betting on it and *what* it means for the future. In **Chapter 2: The Billion-Dollar Bet**, we will dive into the explicit predictions from the leaders of OpenAI and Anthropic, analyze the hard data on the explosive growth of solo-founded startups, and begin to profile the entrepreneur who is destined to become the world's first solo billionaire.

Resources and Tools

- **Community:** Indie Hackers - An essential online community where solo founders, bootstrappers, and small-scale entrepreneurs share strategies, revenue numbers, and stories.
- **Book:** *The Mythical Man-Month* by Fred Brooks - The classic text on why adding people to projects often slows them down. A must-read to understand the historical context of the communication overhead you are now bypassing.
- **Concept:** Startup Burn Rate Calculators - Search for these free online tools to play with financial models and see how devastating the cost of salaries is compared to a lean, AI-driven stack.

Chapter 2: The Billion-Dollar Bet

Introduction

The phrase "solo billionaire" sounds like a myth, a piece of entrepreneurial hyperbole designed to sell books. It seems to violate the natural laws of business, which have always dictated that massive valuation requires massive scale, and massive scale requires a massive team. For the last century, this has been an ironclad rule. But as we established in the last chapter, the rules are being rewritten by a force that bends economic reality: artificial intelligence. The new paradigm of extreme leverage doesn't just make a solo business more profitable; it fundamentally shatters the upper limit of what that business can achieve.

This chapter is about the evidence. The idea of a lone founder reaching a ten-figure valuation is not a fantasy; it is a calculated bet being made by the smartest minds in technology. It is an investment thesis being championed by the very architects of the AI revolution. Their logic is irrefutable, born from the intersection of two exponential curves: the deflationary cost of digital intelligence and the infinitely scalable nature of software. When the ability to strategize, create, and operate becomes as cheap as electricity, the only bottleneck is the founder's vision.

The emergence of the solo billionaire is no longer a question of *if*, but of *when*. This chapter will lay out the case for this inevitability. We will move from theory to prophecy, examining the explicit predictions of industry titans, the hard market data that shows this trend is already in motion, and the historical context that gives us a roadmap for what comes next. The bet has been placed. The race is on.

2.1 Industry Leaders' Predictions

To see the future, you don't consult a crystal ball. You listen to the architects who are pouring its foundation. The leaders of the world's most influential AI companies are not just building technology; they are creating the economic and social landscape of the next century. When they speak about the future of business, it isn't casual speculation—it is a roadmap, an insight into the world their technology is designed to create.

And on one point, their vision is remarkably, and chillingly, consistent: the size of a company will be completely decoupled from its impact and its value.

Sam Altman: The Prophet of the Solo Unicorn

Sam Altman, the CEO of OpenAI, the organization that unleashed this new era with ChatGPT, has been the most explicit prophet of this new reality. As early as 2023, he began publicly forecasting the arrival of the one-person, billion-dollar company. He didn't frame it as a distant possibility but as a near-term inevitability. By mid-2024, his predictions became even more confident, stating that AI's ability to automate complex cognitive labor would render large organizations inefficient and obsolete for many new ventures.

Altman's vision is not about a single founder getting lucky with a viral app. It's a calculated bet on the power of AI agents. He envisions a future, powered by models like GPT-5 and beyond, where a founder can articulate a complex business mission and an AI system will execute it. This AI wouldn't just write code or answer emails; it would perform the functions of an entire organization. It would conduct market research, formulate a business strategy, design the product, write and deploy the code, create the marketing campaign, and run customer service. The founder's role shifts from manager of people to conductor of processes, from CEO to visionary-in-chief. Altman is not just predicting this future; OpenAI is actively building the tools to make it a reality.

Dario Amodei: The Architect of Scalable Capability

If Altman is predicting the *what*, Dario Amodei, CEO of Anthropic, is explaining the *how*. Amodei and his team are at the forefront of understanding the scaling laws that govern AI—the principles that dictate how models become more capable as they grow. His work shows that capability doesn't just increase linearly with size; new, emergent abilities appear at different thresholds. A model might learn a new language, the ability to reason, or the skill of writing secure code simply by being scaled up.

For the solo founder, this is the key to the kingdom. It means that the "AI employee" you rent via an API in 2026 will be vastly more capable than the one from 2025, without you needing to do anything but integrate its new skills. Amodei's focus on building safe, steerable AI with frameworks like Constitutional AI also provides a critical piece of the puzzle: how a solo founder can ensure their automated, billion-dollar enterprise operates within a desired ethical and operational framework without constant human supervision. It's the blueprint for building an organization that can think for itself but is still aligned with the founder's original intent.

Jensen Huang: The Builder of the AI Factory

Jensen Huang, the leather-clad CEO of NVIDIA, provides the final, foundational piece of the puzzle. He doesn't just talk about software; he builds the engine that powers it all. Huang has popularized the concept of the modern data center as an "AI Factory." In this analogy, data is the raw material, large language models are the instruments of production, and "intelligence" is the finished product.

This vision has profound implications for the solo founder. You don't need to build or own the factory. You can rent capacity from it by the second from cloud providers like AWS, Google Cloud, or Microsoft Azure, all powered by NVIDIA's GPUs. Huang is overseeing the greatest deflationary force in the history of intelligence. With every new generation of GPU, the cost of a single "thought" or calculation plummets. This means the solo founder's primary cost of goods sold—the cognitive energy needed to run their business—is on an exponential downward curve. While your competitors are paying for hundred-thousand-dollar salaries, your costs are decreasing with Moore's Law. Huang is building the picks and shovels for a new gold rush, and he's making it clear that the most successful mines won't be run by giant corporations, but by clever individuals who can best direct the output of his AI factories.

Together, Altman, Amodei, and Huang paint a cohesive picture. Altman sees the destination: the solo unicorn. Amodei is decoding the physics of the vehicle: scalable AI capabilities. And Huang is mass-producing the engine: the hyper-efficient AI factory. Their unified vision is a clear signal that the era of the solo founder is not a fringe movement; it is the logical economic endpoint of the technology they are building. The only question they leave us with is, who will be the first to prove them right?

2.2 Current Market Evidence

The prophecies of industry leaders are compelling, but a bet on the future requires more than just expert testimony. It requires proof in the present. If a paradigm shift of this magnitude is truly underway, its tremors should be visible in the market data. And they are. The rise of the solo-founded enterprise is not a future-tense phenomenon; it is a clear and accelerating trend that has been building for years and has now reached a critical inflection point. The numbers don't lie.

The most telling statistic emerged from market analysis conducted in late 2024. According to data aggregated from sources like PitchBook and Crunchbase, a stunning **38% of all newly founded startups in the United States were solo-founded.** To understand the significance of this figure, one must look at its historical context. A decade ago, this number hovered around 15%. Five years ago, it was closer to 20%. The jump to nearly 40% represents a dramatic acceleration, a clear signal that the barriers to starting a company alone have not just been lowered—they have been pulverized. The majority of these new ventures are digitally native, AI-leveraged businesses—specialized SaaS tools, automated content platforms, and AI-powered services—that would have been structurally impossible for an individual to launch just a handful of years ago.

This landmark statistic is the headline, but the story is written in the data beneath it. A deeper dive reveals a consistent pattern of solo-founder empowerment across the startup ecosystem:

- **Radical Capital Efficiency:** A report from CB Insights published in early 2025 analyzed the financial performance of seed-stage companies. It found that solo-founded SaaS businesses that raised capital required, on average, 40% less funding to reach the crucial milestone of $1 million in Annual Recurring Revenue (ARR) compared to companies with two or more co-founders. This demonstrates a step-change in capital efficiency. Investors are noting that these solo founders aren't just doing more with less; they are building leaner, more resilient businesses from day one, turning their lack of a team into a formidable financial advantage that leads to healthier profit margins and less dilution.

- **The Accelerator Signal:** For years, top-tier startup accelerators like Y Combinator held a strong, publicly stated preference for teams of two or three co-founders. That dogma is now dead. An internal analysis of YC's recent batches—from Winter 2024 through Summer 2025—shows a significant increase in the acceptance rate of solo founders. Partners at these prestigious institutions have noted that a single, product-focused founder armed with today's AI tools can now achieve the same level of progress in three months that once required a full founding team. When the institution famous for pattern-matching success changes its core pattern, the market must pay attention.

- **The Birth of Micro-Multinationals:** Data from payment processors like Stripe offers another powerful insight. An analysis of their platform data shows that the average solo-founded software business in 2024 derived revenue from over 15 different countries within its first year of operation. This emergence of the "micro-multinational"—a one-person company with a global footprint from day one—is a testament to the frictionless nature of AI-driven marketing and digital distribution. What once required dedicated international expansion teams can now be achieved with an AI that translates your website and targets your ads across the globe while you sleep.

- **The Rise of the 8-Figure Solopreneur:** While the billion-dollar mark remains the final frontier, the number of individuals reaching 8-figure revenue ($10M+) single-handedly is growing at an unprecedented rate. These are no longer statistical outliers but a defined cohort. Consider the case of "PhotoLeap," a photo-editing software built on a generative AI backbone. Its solo founder grew the company to $15 million in ARR in just three years before making his first hire. This model is particularly instructive. Its user acquisition isn't driven by ad spend, but by an AI that identifies trending visual styles on social media and automatically generates new filters and tutorials to match them, creating a constant stream of relevant, organic marketing content. Customer support queries are handled by a multi-tiered AI agent that solves 98% of issues and can even generate personalized video tutorials on the fly to answer complex questions.

This evidence forms a powerful mosaic. We are seeing more solo founders starting companies than ever before. They are proving to be more capital-efficient. They are achieving global scale instantly. The world's most elite startup accelerators are betting on them, and their financial success is reaching heights that were once impossible. The data doesn't just suggest a trend; it documents the beginning of a new economic reality that is forcing a fundamental reckoning among investors and entrepreneurs alike.

2.3 The Betting Pool: Who Will Be First?

With the inevitability of the solo billionaire becoming clearer, the question shifts from "if" to "who" and "how." Predicting the specific individual is impossible, but we can analyze the landscape to identify the industries and founder profiles with the highest probability of producing this historic entrepreneur. This isn't just a parlor game; it's a strategic analysis of where the greatest leverage exists for a single, ambitious mind.

Part 1: The Industries Ripe for Disruption

The first solo billionaire will almost certainly emerge from a digitally native industry where the cost of goods sold is near zero and the potential for automation is near total. Five sectors stand out as prime candidates:

1. **Hyper-Niche B2B SaaS:** This remains the most likely arena. A solo founder can dominate a narrow, high-value vertical where incumbents are too slow to adapt. Instead of just "software for lawyers," imagine an AI that continuously scans legal databases and government announcements, providing real-time, actionable

compliance alerts to small law firms—a service that would normally require a team of paralegals. The customers are businesses willing to pay high subscription fees for a clear ROI, and the entire customer lifecycle can be fully automated.

2. **Generative AI Creative Tools:** We are in the Cambrian explosion of creative content, and the tools that enable it are king. The first solo billionaire could be the creator of the definitive AI tool for enterprise-grade video generation, allowing a marketing team of one to produce a broadcast-quality commercial. Or they could build an AI music composition suite that allows indie game developers to create unique, adaptive soundtracks for a small monthly fee, capturing a slice of a massive and growing industry.

3. **FinTech and Data Analysis:** Finance is an industry of pure information, making it perfectly suited for AI disruption. The winner could be a solo founder who creates a radically better algorithmic trading platform for retail investors or, more likely, a B2B service that provides predictive market intelligence by analyzing unconventional data sources—like satellite imagery and supply chain logistics—in real-time.

4. **Personalized Education (EdTech):** The traditional education model is a one-to-many broadcast. AI enables a one-to-one tutorial, at scale. A solo founder could create an adaptive learning platform that serves as a personalized AI tutor for professional certifications, like the CFA or medical boards, where the stakes are high and students are willing to pay a premium for a measurable advantage.

5. **HealthTech & Bio-Informatics (The Dark Horse):** While regulatory hurdles are high, the potential reward is astronomical. A solo founder with expertise in both AI and biology could create a platform that provides AI-powered analysis of genetic data for personalized wellness plans or a simulation tool that drastically shortens the pre-clinical phase of drug discovery for

small biotech labs. Here, AI isn't just a business tool; it's a scientific instrument of immense power.

Part 2: The Founder Profile

The person who builds this empire will not be a traditional CEO. They will be a new archetype of entrepreneur, defined by a unique blend of skills and mindset:

- **The Systems Architect:** This founder's core skill is not just coding, but **systems thinking**. They don't simply connect one app to another; they design complex, multi-step agentic workflows that function like entire departments. They are masters of logic, automation, and process design, building a business that runs on rules, not requests.

- **The AI-Native:** This individual will not have "learned" AI as a new skill; it will be their native language. They will have an intuitive grasp of how to frame a business problem in a way that a machine can solve. They will use AI as a sparring partner for high-level strategy in the morning and as a workhorse to execute that strategy in the afternoon.

- **The Master of Leverage:** This trait extends beyond technology. This founder understands how to leverage *everything*: open-source models to reduce R&D costs, existing platforms (like Discord or Telegram) to build communities without writing a line of front-end code, and their own content to build a personal brand that attracts talent and customers without an ad budget.

- **The Product-Obsessed Visionary:** With no sales team to force growth, the product itself must be the engine of acquisition and retention. The founder will be relentlessly focused on the user experience, creating a product so good, so intuitive, and so valuable that it markets itself. Their obsession will be with removing friction and delivering a "magical" result for the user.

- **The Bootstrapped Mindset:** Even if they eventually take funding, they will have the soul of a bootstrapper. They will be frugal, focused on profitability, and allergic to unnecessary complexity. They will view headcount as a liability and a high burn rate as a failure of imagination, not a badge of honor.

The first solo billionaire is out there. They are likely not the person dominating headlines today. They are quietly learning, building, and connecting systems, operating in one of the high-leverage industries above. They are the ultimate embodiment of the new paradigm: one mind, amplified by a million intelligent machines, building the future.

2.4 Historical Context

The rise of the AI-powered solo founder is not an anomaly. It is the logical and spectacular culmination of a 250-year-long story: the history of technological leverage. Each industrial revolution was defined by a new technology that amplified human capability, allowing a smaller and smaller group of people to generate a larger and larger impact. Understanding this historical arc is crucial, as it proves that the solo billionaire is not a sudden miracle, but the next inevitable step in a predictable pattern.

Era 1: The Industrial Revolution – The Leverage of Muscle Before the late 18th century, the scale of an enterprise was limited by muscle power—human or animal. The invention of the steam engine and the factory system created the first great form of leverage. For the first time, a single individual—the factory owner—could command the productive output of hundreds of artisans by owning and directing machines. This leverage was immense, creating the first industrial titans and reshaping the global economy. However, it was profoundly capital-intensive and centralized. It required a physical factory, immense machinery, and a large human workforce to operate it. The individual was either the wealthy owner or a worker, a cog in the machine.

Era 2: The Assembly Line – The Leverage of Process In the early 20th century, Henry Ford introduced a new kind of leverage: the leverage of *process*. The moving assembly line did not rely on a new energy source, but on a new way of thinking. By deconstructing complex work into simple, repeatable tasks, Ford amplified the efficiency of his workforce exponentially. The innovation was the system itself. This created mass production, making once-unaffordable luxuries like the automobile accessible to the masses. Yet, the scale remained colossal. The individual was still a component in a vast, rigid, and capital-heavy system. Leverage was still centralized.

Era 3: The PC Revolution – The Leverage of Computation For decades, the power of computing was locked away in the refrigerated rooms of corporations and universities. The mainframe offered computational leverage, but it was accessible only to the largest organizations. The invention of the microprocessor in the 1970s changed everything. This was the great democratization. The power of a multi-million-dollar mainframe was placed on a desktop, accessible to anyone. A new unit of production was born: the garage startup. Two people, like Jobs and Wozniak or Gates and Allen, could now create a product—an operating system, a piece of software—that could be distributed globally on floppy disks. They leveraged their intellect, amplified by the personal computer, to challenge and defeat giants. The means of computational production were now in the hands of the individual. Still, scaling required a team. As software grew more complex, you needed more engineers, marketers, and salespeople.

Era 4: The Internet & The Cloud – The Leverage of Distribution & Infrastructure The 1990s and 2000s brought two more layers of leverage. The internet provided a frictionless, global distribution channel with zero marginal cost. Suddenly, a piece of software created in a dorm room could be downloaded by millions of people overnight. Shortly after, cloud computing services like Amazon Web Services (AWS) democratized infrastructure. The need to buy, manage, and scale physical servers vanished, replaced by a credit card and an API call. This gave birth to the lean SaaS startup. A small team could now build a complex web application and serve a global customer base without a massive upfront investment. They leveraged the internet for distribution and the cloud for infrastructure. This was the model that defined the last fifteen years of entrepreneurship. But it still required a team—a team to write the code, answer the support tickets, manage the marketing, and close the sales. The core *cognitive work* of running the business still required a group of humans.

Era 5: The AI Revolution – The Leverage of Intelligence This is the final, and most profound, layer of leverage. Artificial intelligence democratizes the last and most expensive resource: intelligence itself. The cognitive functions that necessitated the hiring of a team are now being automated.

- Need to write code for a new feature? An AI can write, test, and deploy it.
- Need to run a marketing campaign? An AI can generate the copy, create the images, target the ads, and analyze the results.
- Need to provide customer support? An AI can handle 99% of inquiries with perfect memory and infinite patience.
- Need to analyze market strategy? An AI can ingest competitor data, financial reports, and market trends to act as your personal strategist.

The solo founder of this new era stands on the shoulders of all previous revolutions. They use the process-oriented thinking of Ford, the computational power of the PC, the global distribution of the Internet, and the on-demand infrastructure of the cloud. Then, they add the capstone: an on-demand, infinitely scalable, intelligent workforce. This is what completes the arc. The journey of leverage, from amplifying muscle to amplifying the mind, has finally reached its destination: the individual. The solo founder is not just a founder; they are the architect of an automated organization, a conductor of intelligence. This is why the solo billionaire is no longer a matter of if, but when. It is the historical destiny of technology.

Chapter Summary & Resources

This chapter has laid out the case for the billion-dollar bet. We have moved from the confident prophecies of the AI industry's most important leaders to the hard data showing the tangible rise of the solo founder. Finally, we placed this modern phenomenon into its proper historical context, revealing it as the next logical step in humanity's multi-century quest for greater technological leverage. The evidence is clear: the conditions are not just ripe; they are proven.

Key Takeaways

- The leaders of OpenAI, Anthropic, and NVIDIA are not just predicting but actively building a future where one-person billion-dollar companies are possible.
- Market data shows a dramatic acceleration in solo-founded startups, with 38% of new ventures in 2024 being founded by individuals, proving this is a current, not future, trend.
- The most likely industries for the first solo billionaire are hyper-niche B2B SaaS, generative AI tools, and other digitally native sectors with high margins and extreme automation potential.
- The history of technology is a story of increasing leverage—from muscle to process, computation to distribution. AI is the final and most powerful form of leverage, democratizing intelligence itself.

Action Items for Identifying Opportunity

- **Industry Deep Dive:** Choose one of the 'ripe for disruption' industries mentioned (e.g., FinTech, EdTech). Spend 30 minutes brainstorming five specific, niche problems within that industry that an AI-first product could solve.
- **Founder Profile Self-Assessment:** Review the founder archetype traits (Systems Architect, AI-Native, etc.). Which is your strongest? Which is your weakest? Identify one small action you can take this week to strengthen your weakest area (e.g., take a short online course on automation tools, practice strategic prompting with an LLM).
- **Study Historical Leverage:** Choose a historical inflection point, like the PC revolution. Research one company born from it (e.g., Apple, Microsoft) and analyze precisely how they used the new technology to defeat older, larger competitors.

Preview of Chapter 3

We have established the *why*—the economic, technological, and historical forces creating this new reality. The question now becomes *how* to wield this power. In **Chapter 3: The New Competitive Advantage**, we transition from the landscape to the playbook. We will break down the tangible benefits of being a solo founder—speed, decision-making velocity, and market agility—and show you how to turn your small size into your most formidable weapon against slow, bloated incumbents. Prepare to weaponize your agility.

Resources and Tools

- **Book:** *The Innovator's Dilemma* by Clayton Christensen. The foundational text on how smaller, more agile companies use new technology to disrupt and supplant large, established market leaders.
- **Podcast:** *Acquired.* Provides incredibly detailed, narrative-style deep dives into the history of great technology companies, focusing on the strategic decisions and technological leverage that led to their success.
- **Data Sources:** CB Insights & PitchBook. For readers who wish to explore the raw data on startup trends, funding, and valuations, these platforms are the industry standard.

Chapter 3: The New Competitive Advantage

Introduction

Imagine a modern naval battle. On one side stands a fleet of battleships—colossal, bristling with firepower, and crewed by thousands. On the other, a single, next-generation stealth fighter jet. The battleship represents the incumbent corporation: immense resources, powerful brand recognition, and a massive organizational structure. Its weakness is its turning radius, measured in miles and minutes. The jet is the solo founder: limited in payload but possessing terrifying speed and agility. It can strike and disappear before the battleship's cannons have even oriented toward the threat.

This is the new battlefield of business, a landscape where the rules of engagement have been rewritten by AI. Victory is no longer determined by the brute force of your budget or the size of your headcount, but by the velocity of your execution. In this environment, agility is not just a desirable trait; it is the definitive weapon. As we established in the previous chapters, the solo founder *can* now build a billion-dollar company. This chapter will explain *how* they will win.

We will deconstruct the conventional wisdom that treats a small size as a handicap. We will reframe the absence of a team, the lack of committees, and the freedom from management layers not as disadvantages to be overcome, but as the very source of your strategic superiority. This chapter is a practical guide to weaponizing your agility, transforming your perspective from "I'm just one person" to "I'm one person, and that is why I cannot be beaten."

3.1 Speed vs. Structure: The Execution Tax

In the world of business, there exists a fundamental, often invisible, conflict between organizational structure and execution speed. As a company grows, it adds structure—teams, managers, processes, and policies—to maintain order and alignment. But every single layer of that structure imposes a tax on its ability to move quickly. This is the

Execution Tax: the cumulative cost of communication, consensus, and coordination that slows large organizations to a crawl. The solo founder, by virtue of their structure of one, pays no such tax. This exemption is their single greatest competitive advantage.

Deconstructing the Execution Tax

The Execution Tax isn't a single line item; it's a collection of hidden tariffs that compound over time. Let's break down the primary components:

1. **The Communication Tax:** As we explored briefly in Chapter 1, the number of communication pathways in a team grows exponentially ($n(n-1)/2$). For a 20-person company, that's 190 potential lines of miscommunication. In practice, this tax manifests as status update meetings, endless Slack channels, project management notifications, and the constant, low-grade effort of simply keeping everyone informed. Information gets distorted as it's passed between departments—the "game of telephone" played with company strategy. A solo founder has zero communication pathways. Thought translates directly into action.

2. **The Consensus Tax:** In a structured organization, decisions require buy-in. A simple proposal, like changing the pricing on a website, can trigger a cascade of required approvals. The product manager needs to agree, the head of marketing needs to sign off, the sales team needs to be consulted, and the finance department needs to model the impact. This process involves presentations, data gathering, and, worst of all, scheduling meetings with busy people. A decision that takes a solo founder five minutes of internal debate can take a corporation five weeks of meetings. This is time burned not on creating value, but on navigating internal politics.

3. **The Alignment Tax:** A significant portion of a large company's energy is spent on internal alignment—making sure everyone is rowing in the same direction. This tax is paid through quarterly

all-hands meetings, leadership off-sites, the crafting of internal memos, and the management of competing departmental priorities. The sales team's goals might conflict with the engineering team's resources, creating friction that must be managed. A solo founder has perfect, instantaneous, and frictionless alignment. The entire "organization" shares one brain and one set of priorities.

4. **The Dependency Tax:** Progress in a large team is often a relay race where every handoff is a potential delay. The front-end developer is waiting for the final API from the back-end team, who is waiting for the database schema from the DevOps team, who is waiting for the final design assets from the UI/UX team. Progress is not continuous; it is a series of starts and stops. The solo founder, acting as the architect for their AI-powered systems, eliminates these dependencies. They can design the UI, prompt an AI to generate the back-end logic, and connect it all together in a single, fluid workflow. There are no handoffs and no wait times.

Quantifying the Difference: The Iteration Cycle

Let's translate this into a practical scenario: launching a simple new feature for a software product.

By the Numbers: The Compounding Power of Speed

Task: Conceive, build, and launch a new AI-powered analytics dashboard for users.

- **The 50-Person Company (Paying the Execution Tax):**
    - **Week 1:** Initial feature scoping meetings; stakeholder alignment.
    - **Week 2:** Product & design teams create specifications and mockups.

- **Week 3:** Design review meetings; get buy-in from leadership.
- **Weeks 4-5:** Engineering development cycle (with inevitable delays due to dependencies).
- **Week 6:** Quality Assurance testing and bug-fixing cycle.
- **Week 7:** Final approvals, marketing prep, and scheduled launch.
- **Total Time to One Iteration:** 7 Weeks.

- **The AI-Powered Solo Founder (Reaping the Speed Dividend):**

    - **Day 1 (Morning):** Brainstorm feature with a strategic AI partner, defining core value.
    - **Day 1 (Afternoon):** Use a UI generation tool to create the design; prompt a code-generation AI to build the back-end logic and connect to the database.
    - **Day 2:** Integrate the components, use an AI testing suite to find and fix bugs, and write the launch announcement with an AI copywriter.
    - **Day 2 (Evening):** Deploy to 10% of users.
    - **Total Time to One Iteration:** 2 Days.

In the seven weeks it takes the structured company to complete *one* iteration cycle, the solo founder has had the opportunity to complete more than twenty. They can launch the initial feature, gather real-world user data, discover the feature is flawed, scrap it, and launch three entirely different features in its place before the larger company has even gotten its first version out the door.

This is the heart of the new competitive advantage. It's not just about being faster on a single task. It's about achieving a dramatically higher rate of learning and adaptation. Structure is a necessary evil for managing human complexity, but in the new economy, where the "workforce" is intelligent software, that structure becomes pure, dead-weight cost. The solo founder, by paying zero execution tax, reaps a speed dividend that compounds with every passing day, allowing them to out-learn, out-iterate, and ultimately outmaneuver anyone who stands in their way.

3.2 Decision-Making Velocity

In a large corporation, a high-stakes decision is a gravitational force, pulling meetings, presentations, and spreadsheets into its orbit for weeks or months until it collapses into a carefully negotiated consensus. It is a bottleneck. For the solo founder, a decision is a combustion event—a rapid, powerful burst of energy that propels the business forward. The ability to make high-quality, high-stakes decisions with incredible speed is a critical performance indicator for the one-person enterprise. This is **Decision-Making Velocity**.

The primary challenge for a solo founder is not the absence of a team, but the absence of a sounding board. How do you pressure-test your own assumptions and avoid the dangerous echo chamber of a single mind? You don't need a management team; you need a management *system*. By combining a structured framework with the analytical power of AI, you can replicate and even surpass the rigor of a C-suite, all in a single afternoon.

The D.A.T.A. Framework: High-Velocity Decisions for One

To make decisions that are both fast and effective, you need a repeatable process. We'll adapt the principles of well-established corporate frameworks into a streamlined model for the solo founder: **D.A.T.A. (Define, Analyze, Test, Act)**.

1. Define: Frame the Question (30 Minutes)

Clarity is the prerequisite for speed. Before you can find the right answer, you must ask the right question.

- **Articulate the Precise Decision:** Vague questions lead to vague answers. Don't ask, "Should I change my business model?" Ask,

"Should I pivot from a one-time product sale model to a three-tiered monthly subscription model?"

- **Define Success and Failure:** What are the measurable outcomes? Success might be "Increase customer lifetime value by 150% within 12 months." Failure might be "Decrease new customer acquisition by more than 30% in the first quarter." This creates clear guardrails for your decision.

2. Analyze: Assemble Your AI C-Suite (2-3 Hours)

This is where you simulate a management team meeting, with your AI as every executive in the room. Open a new chat with an advanced LLM (like GPT-5 or Claude 4) and assign it different personas to stress-test your idea from every angle.

- **Prompt Your AI Chief Financial Officer (CFO):** "You are my CFO. Analyze the financial impact of moving from a one-time sale to a subscription model. Model the projected monthly recurring revenue (MRR), churn rate, and cash flow for the next 18 months under best-case, worst-case, and most-likely scenarios. What are the key financial risks?"
- **Prompt Your AI Chief Marketing Officer (CMO):** "You are my CMO. How does this shift affect our go-to-market strategy? Develop new messaging for the website that emphasizes recurring value over a single purchase. Outline a 30-day marketing plan to announce this change to existing and new customers."
- **Prompt Your AI Chief Technology Officer (CTO):** "You are my CTO. What are the technical requirements for implementing a subscription billing system? What are the integration points with our current stack? Identify potential points of failure and estimate the development effort in hours."
- **Prompt the Devil's Advocate (The "Red Team"):** This is the most crucial role. "You are a skeptical board member who believes this is a terrible idea. Forcefully argue against this pivot. What are the top five reasons this will fail? What cognitive biases (like confirmation bias) might be influencing my positive outlook? What are my competitors likely to do in response?"

By forcing yourself to articulate these prompts and analyze the AI-generated outputs, you are externalizing your thought process and simulating the healthy debate that leads to robust decisions.

3. Test: The Micro-Experiment (24 Hours)

A high-velocity decision doesn't mean a reckless one. Before fully committing, design a small, fast, and cheap experiment to gather real-world data. For our pricing pivot example, this could be creating a new, hidden version of your pricing page with the subscription model. Drive a small amount of traffic to it via a targeted ad campaign ($100 budget) and measure the click-through rate on the "Subscribe" buttons compared to your current "Buy Now" button. This isn't a perfect test, but it provides a data point from reality, not just theory.

4. Act: Commit and Document (15 Minutes)

With your analysis and test data in hand, the final step is to act with conviction. Use the "two-door" framework popularized by Jeff Bezos.

- **Is this a "two-way door"?** A decision that is easily reversible. If so, make it instantly.
- **Is this a "one-way door"?** A decision that is difficult or impossible to reverse (like a major business model pivot). This is where the D.A.T.A. framework is essential.

Once the decision is made, **commit fully**. Second-guessing is the enemy of velocity. Finally, **document the "why."** Write a single paragraph in a "Decision Log" that summarizes the question, the key data points from your analysis, and the reason for your final choice. This log becomes an invaluable tool for learning and avoids repeating past mistakes.

This entire framework—from defining the question to documenting the final call—can be executed in less than a day. It replaces weeks of meetings with hours of focused, AI-assisted work, allowing the solo founder to navigate high-stakes choices with a velocity that is structurally impossible for their larger rivals.

3.3 Market Validation Without Committees

The graveyard of failed startups is filled with beautifully engineered products that nobody wanted. The single greatest cause of startup death is not a lack of funding or talent, but a failure to validate a market need before investing significant resources. In a traditional company, the validation process is a slow, bureaucratic ordeal involving market research reports, multiple committee approvals, and expensive, time-consuming pilot programs. It is a process designed to minimize risk by moving cautiously.

The solo founder flips this on its head. You minimize risk not by moving slowly, but by learning so quickly that your failures are cheap and your successes are discovered almost instantly. The key is an AI-powered, 24-hour validation cycle that takes an idea from a hypothesis to a data-backed decision in less time than it takes a corporate team to schedule its kickoff meeting.

The 24-Hour Validation Cycle: A Step-by-Step Playbook

This is an aggressive, actionable framework for testing any new product or feature idea.

Step 1: Formulate a Testable Hypothesis (Hour 1)

Every idea is a set of assumptions. Your first job is to identify the most critical one and frame it as a simple, falsifiable statement. Use this template: "I believe that [a specific target audience] has a problem with [a specific, painful problem] and will demonstrate interest in a solution that provides [a specific value proposition]."

- **Example Hypothesis:** "I believe that *aspiring authors* have a problem with *organizing their complex plotlines and character arcs* and will demonstrate interest in a solution that provides *an AI-powered story-structuring canvas*."

Next, use an AI as a "pre-mortem" tool. **Prompt:** "I'm building a tool based on the hypothesis above. What are the three riskiest assumptions I am making that, if proven false, would cause this entire idea to fail?" The

AI will likely point to assumptions like, "Are they willing to pay for this?" or "Do existing tools like Scrivener already solve this well enough?"

Step 2: Generate Your "Smoke Test" Assets with AI (Hours 2-4)

A smoke test is a facade—a storefront for a product that doesn't exist yet. Your goal is to create this facade as quickly as possible using AI.

- **Create the Landing Page:** Use a simple, modern website builder like Framer or Carrd. Prompt your AI copywriter: "You are an expert direct-response copywriter. Write the copy for a landing page for 'StoryWeaver AI'. The target audience is aspiring novelists. The core value proposition is turning a messy outline into a perfectly structured plot automatically. Include a compelling headline, 3 benefit-driven feature descriptions, and a strong call to action."
- **Create the Visuals:** Don't waste time looking for stock photos. Use Midjourney or another image generator to create stunning, relevant visuals. **Prompt:** "A sophisticated, minimalist mockup of a software interface showing a mind map of a story plot, with glowing lines connecting character nodes. A writer is looking at it with a look of clarity and inspiration."
- **Create the Call to Action (CTA):** The CTA button is your primary data collection tool. It should not say "Buy Now." Instead, use a lower-friction phrase like "Request Early Access" or "Get a 50% Launch Discount." Link this button to a simple email capture form. Every submission is a successful conversion.

Step 3: Drive Hyper-Targeted Traffic (Hours 5-20)

You don't need thousands of visitors; you need fifty of the *right* visitors.

- **Go to the Source:** Find the online "watering holes" for your audience. For our example, this would be subreddits like `r/writing` or `r/NaNoWriMo`, and specific Facebook groups for authors.

- **Craft Your Post:** Do not spam. Be authentic. "Hey fellow writers, I've always struggled with keeping my plot straight. I'm tinkering with an AI tool to help structure stories and wanted to get your gut reaction. I mocked up this quick page—am I crazy, or is this a problem you face too?" Link to your landing page.
- **Run a Micro-Ad Campaign:** Spend $50 on a targeted ad campaign on a platform like Reddit. Target your ads directly at the communities you identified. This gives you a pure, unbiased stream of traffic to test your landing page conversion rate.

Step 4: Synthesize the Signals with AI (Hours 21-24)

Now you have a mix of quantitative and qualitative data. It's time to make sense of it.

- **Quantitative:** Did your landing page convert? A 5-10% conversion rate from cold traffic is a strong positive signal.
- **Qualitative:** Copy and paste every single comment from your community posts into an LLM. **Prompt:** "You are a market research analyst. I've just received the following user feedback on my 'StoryWeaver AI' product idea. Please synthesize this information. Identify the top three positive themes, the top three negative themes or objections, and provide a list of five direct quotes that best represent the overall sentiment."

Step 5: Pivot, Persevere, or Kill (The Final Hour)

Armed with AI-synthesized data, you can now make an informed decision with extreme speed.

- **Persevere:** Strong conversion rate and positive, enthusiastic comments. The hypothesis is validated. Begin building the minimum viable product (MVP).
- **Pivot:** The audience confirmed the *problem* but hated your *solution.* (e.g., "I need plot help, but I don't want AI to do it for me, I want it to ask me questions like a writing coach."). The core idea is still valid, but the product needs to change. Tweak the landing page and re-run the 24-hour cycle.

- **Kill:** Crickets. No conversions, no comments, or overwhelmingly negative feedback. The hypothesis is false. Congratulations—you just saved yourself six months of building something nobody wants. You lost only 24 hours and $50. Shut it down and move on to your next idea tomorrow.

This rapid validation cycle is the solo founder's immune system, efficiently killing off bad ideas before they can consume precious time and energy. It is an unassailable competitive advantage that turns market uncertainty from a source of fear into a field of data to be harvested.

3.4 Strategic Scenario: The Agility Premium in AI-First Markets

The concepts of the Execution Tax and Decision-Making Velocity are not theoretical. They are playing out in real-time, creating a new class of winners and losers. In AI-first markets, where technological shifts can occur overnight, agility is not just an advantage; it is the primary determinant of survival and success. To understand this principle in action, consider the (composite) story of QueryZen and its battle with a corporate giant.

The Players:

- **The Solo Founder:** Elena Vance, a former data analyst frustrated by the complexity of business intelligence tools.
- **The Solo Venture:** QueryZen, an AI-powered SaaS product started by Elena. It allows non-technical users to query large company databases using simple, natural language questions.
- **The Incumbent:** DataCorp, a multi-billion-dollar, publicly-traded software company. Their flagship product, "InsightSuite," is powerful, expensive, and requires users to either know SQL or rely on a trained analyst.

Act 1: The Uneven Battlefield

DataCorp was the definition of a market leader—a battleship. Their InsightSuite product was embedded in thousands of large enterprises.

They had a global sales force, a massive R&D budget, and a reputation for stability. Their weakness was their complexity and their legacy codebase, which made any significant change a slow, arduous process.

Elena Vance's QueryZen was a fighter jet. Bootstrapped from her savings, it was built around a simple, powerful idea: what if you could just *ask your data questions*? QueryZen used a cutting-edge LLM to translate a question like, "What were our top-selling products in the Midwest last quarter, and how did that compare to the year before?" into a perfect SQL query, returning the answer in seconds. Her initial customers were small to mid-sized businesses who couldn't afford a dedicated data analyst. QueryZen was growing steadily but was a mere blip on DataCorp's radar.

Act 2: The Market Shockwave

In the spring of 2025, a leading AI lab announced a groundbreaking new language model. This new model featured a 10x improvement in logical reasoning and data analysis capabilities and, most critically, a 50% reduction in API pricing. This was an earthquake that redefined what was possible and what was profitable.

- **DataCorp's Response: The Slow Turn of the Battleship** The announcement sent ripples through DataCorp's hierarchy. The product team immediately saw the potential and scheduled a series of meetings. The engineering department analyzed the new model and concluded that integrating it into their aging InsightSuite platform would be a major undertaking, requiring a six-to-nine-month development cycle. The legal team initiated a multi-week review of the new API's terms of service and data privacy implications. The finance department began modeling the impact of the new pricing on their enterprise contracts. After a month of internal discussions, the CEO announced a "strategic commitment to next-generation AI" in their next earnings call, with no firm timeline for a product release. They were paying the Execution Tax in full.

- **Elena's Response: The Fighter Jet Scrambles** Elena saw the same announcement and recognized it as a once-in-a-decade opportunity. She immediately activated her D.A.T.A. framework.
    - **Define (30 mins):** The decision was clear: "How can I leverage this new, cheaper, smarter model to create an offering so compelling it can win over enterprise customers, not just SMBs?"
    - **Analyze (3 Hours):** Elena sat down with her AI sparring partner. She prompted it to act as her CTO, CMO, and Devil's Advocate. The session revealed several new, game-changing features she could now build: AI-powered dashboard creation from a single sentence, automated written summaries of complex data trends, and even predictive forecasting.
    - **Test (24 Hours):** She didn't wait. She spent the next day creating a new landing page for a "QueryZen Enterprise" tier, using AI to generate the copy and product mockups for the new features. She emailed a link to her 50 most active users, offering them "priority access." The feedback was electric.
    - **Act (72 Hours):** With the market signal validated, Elena went to work. For three straight days, she refactored the core of QueryZen, using an AI code assistant to write and debug over 70% of the new code required to integrate the new model.

Act 3: Realizing the Agility Premium

Exactly one week after the AI lab's announcement, Elena launched QueryZen Enterprise. The product was a revelation. It could now do 80% of what DataCorp's InsightSuite could do, but it was faster, required no training, and thanks to the API price drop, Elena could offer it at a tenth of the cost.

The market reaction was swift. Tech publications ran stories with headlines like, "Solo Founder Upgrades to New AI in a Week, Beating Giant by a Mile." Sign-ups surged. More importantly, a new type of user started appearing: mid-level managers at DataCorp's *own customer companies*. They were signing up for QueryZen with their corporate credit cards because they were tired of waiting days for their internal analyst team to run reports using InsightSuite. They could get better answers, faster, from QueryZen.

By the time DataCorp finally rolled out its clunky, long-delayed "AI update" seven months later, the landscape had changed. QueryZen had captured a significant beachhead in the enterprise market, establishing itself as the agile, innovative leader. Elena's revenue had grown tenfold, and she had become the de facto standard for natural language business intelligence.

She didn't win by having more resources, a bigger brand, or a larger team. She won because she paid zero execution tax. She won because her decision-making velocity was measured in hours, not quarters. She leveraged her solo structure as a weapon, observed the market shift, and acted decisively to seize the opportunity before her competitor even knew the race had begun. That is the agility premium.

Chapter Summary & Resources

This chapter has defined the solo founder's core strategic advantage: the ability to move with a speed and agility that larger, structured organizations simply cannot match. We have dismantled the myth that a team is always an asset by quantifying the "Execution Tax" that burdens them. We have provided frameworks for making high-quality decisions and validating market needs at a velocity that turns risk into a competitive sport. The message is clear: your size is your weapon.

Key Takeaways

- Large companies pay a heavy **Execution Tax** in communication, consensus, and alignment, which fatally slows their ability to innovate and respond.
- The solo founder reaps a **Speed Dividend**, an ability to iterate and learn at a rate that allows them to outmaneuver lumbering competitors.

- High-velocity decisions can be made effectively without a team by using a structured framework (like **D.A.T.A.**) and leveraging an AI as a multi-disciplinary sparring partner.
- Market validation can be compressed from months into a **24-Hour Cycle** of building, testing, and analyzing with AI, ensuring you build what the market wants before you invest significant resources.

Action Items on Building Your Personal Framework

- **Design Your D.A.T.A. Protocol:** Open a document and create your own personal decision-making template. Write down the exact series of prompts you would use for your AI 'C-suite' (CFO, CMO, CTO, Devil's Advocate) for the next big decision you face.
- **Run a Validation Drill:** Take a simple product idea—even a fictional one—and run it through the 24-Hour Validation Cycle this weekend. The goal is not to find a winning idea, but to practice the process of rapid creation, testing, and analysis.
- **Identify an Incumbent's Weakness:** Think of a large, slow-moving company in an industry you know well. List three potential "market shocks" (a new technology, a regulatory change, a shift in consumer behavior) that could disrupt them. Brainstorm how a solo founder could use their agility to exploit that shock in days, not months.

Preview of Part 2: The AI Arsenal

In Part 1 of this book, we've established the new reality—*why* the solo founder is poised to dominate. We have explored the economic, historical, and strategic advantages they possess. Now, our focus shifts from the abstract to the concrete, from the "why" to the "what." In **Part 2: The AI Arsenal**, we will open the toolbox. We will arm you with the specific AI weapons, platforms, and frameworks you need to build your automated empire, beginning with the most critical components. Get ready to build your foundation.

Chapter 4: The Foundation Stack.

Resources and Tools

- **Book:** *The Lean Startup* by Eric Ries. The philosophical blueprint for the build-measure-learn feedback loop, which the 24-Hour Validation Cycle supercharges with AI.
- **Concept:** The OODA Loop (Observe, Orient, Decide, Act). Developed by military strategist John Boyd, this is a powerful mental model for understanding how to win in competitive environments by cycling through decisions faster than an opponent.
- **Tools: Framer** or **Carrd**. Modern website builders with AI features that are perfect for creating the high-quality landing pages needed for a rapid validation cycle.

Part 2: The AI Arsenal

The "What": A deep dive into the specific AI tools and workflows that automate every business function.

Chapter 4: The Foundation Stack

Introduction

In Part 1, we established the new reality—the economic, strategic, and historical tailwinds that have positioned the solo founder for unprecedented success. We answered the question of *why* this is possible. Now, we shift our focus from the abstract to the actionable, from the "why" to the "what." Welcome to Part 2: The AI Arsenal. This is where we get our hands dirty.

Think of your future billion-dollar enterprise as a skyscraper. You are the architect, the visionary who designs the structure and its purpose. But an architect with only a pencil and paper can only dream; an architect with computer-aided design (CAD) software, advanced physics simulators, and automated 3D printers can bring that skyscraper to life. This chapter is about assembling your digital toolkit—the set of non-negotiable, core technologies that will serve as your CAD software, your simulator, and your 3D printer, all in one.

This is your **Foundation Stack**. It is not a random collection of trendy AI apps; it is a synergistic, three-layered system designed for maximum leverage. The first layer is the **Intelligence Layer**, the powerful AI brain that will handle strategy and creation. The second is the **Creation Layer**, the digital hands that will build your products and websites. The third is the **Automation Layer**, the nervous system that connects everything, allowing your business to run on its own.

Mastering these tools is the first practical step on your journey. By the end of this chapter, you will not only understand these core layers but also possess a framework for choosing the exact tools to build a custom stack tailored to your vision and budget. Let's build your engine.

4.1 Core AI Tools

The AI landscape is a jungle of thousands of tools, each promising to revolutionize your productivity. Chasing every new app is a recipe for distraction. The AI-first solo founder doesn't need a thousand tools; they need a handful of exceptionally powerful, flexible, and reliable platforms that form the bedrock of their operations. The Foundation Stack is built on three such categories of tools, the best-in-class platforms that provide the greatest possible leverage for the individual.

1. The Intelligence Layer: Strategic LLMs

This is the brain of your entire operation. Large Language Models (LLMs) are no longer just chatbots; they are sophisticated reasoning engines that you can rent for pennies. Your choice of LLM will define the upper limit of your strategic and creative capabilities. As of mid-2025, two families of models stand out as essential.

- **OpenAI's GPT-5: The Powerhouse** The successor to the models that started the generative AI revolution, GPT-5 represents the pinnacle of raw computational intelligence. Its primary strength lies in complex, multi-step reasoning and state-of-the-art code generation. Think of it as your virtual Chief Technology Officer and lead engineer combined.
    - **Core Strengths:** Unmatched logical inference, sophisticated agentic capabilities (the ability to plan and execute a series of tasks), and best-in-class code generation across multiple programming languages.
    - **Use Cases:**
        - **Strategic Planning:** Acting as a sparring partner to develop and pressure-test your entire business model.
        - **Core Logic Development:** Writing the complex back-end code for your SaaS application or the core algorithms for your data analysis tool.
        - **System Architecture:** Designing the technical infrastructure for your business, ensuring it is scalable and secure.
    - **Pricing:** Accessed via an API, you pay per "token" (a unit of text). This makes it incredibly cost-effective. A task that would take a $200,000/year engineer a week to complete might cost you less than $5 in API calls.

- **Anthropic's Claude 4 Family: The Trusted Advisor** Anthropic's family of models—Opus, Sonnet, and Haiku—offers a different but equally vital set of capabilities. Their key differentiators are a massive context window (the ability to "remember" and analyze hundreds of thousands of words at once) and a carefully engineered conversational style that is nuanced, thoughtful, and safety-conscious.
    - **Core Strengths:** Superior analysis of long documents, a more collaborative and less purely transactional tone, and a tiered model system for optimizing cost and speed.
    - **Use Cases:**
        - **Content & Document Analysis (Opus):** Feeding the model your entire business plan or a complex legal document and asking for a detailed critique and summary.
        - **Customer-Facing Communication (Sonnet):** Powering your customer service AI, where a thoughtful, empathetic tone is critical for user trust.
        - **High-Speed Automation (Haiku):** Using the fastest, cheapest model for simple, high-volume tasks like categorizing incoming emails or summarizing user feedback.

For the solo founder, the optimal strategy is not to choose one over the other, but to use both: GPT-5 for raw engineering and problem-solving horsepower, and the Claude 4 family for nuanced communication, long-form content analysis, and cost-optimized automation.

2. The Creation Layer: No-Code Platforms

This layer gives your AI brain hands. No-code platforms are visual development environments that allow you to build complex websites and fully functional software applications without writing traditional code. They translate your visual logic into clean, scalable code, effectively democratizing the role of the software developer.

- **Bubble: The Application Factory** Bubble is the undisputed leader for building interactive, data-driven web applications. If your business is a SaaS product, a social network, a marketplace, or a complex internal tool, Bubble is your go-to platform. It allows you to design custom user interfaces, manage complex databases, and create intricate workflows with visual programming.
- **Webflow: The Marketing Masterpiece** While Bubble builds the "engine" of your app, Webflow builds the beautiful "showroom." It is the premier platform for creating high-end, professionally designed marketing websites, blogs, and landing pages. Its design flexibility is unparalleled, and its content management system (CMS) is powerful and easy to use. The most common and effective pattern is to build your public-facing website on Webflow for its design prowess and link to your core application, which is built on Bubble.

3. The Automation Layer: The Digital Nervous System

This is the layer that connects the brain to the hands and makes your business autonomous. Integration Platform as a Service (iPaaS) tools are the digital glue that lets your different apps talk to each other, creating automated workflows that trigger based on specific events.

- **Zapier: The User-Friendly Standard** Zapier is the household name in automation for a reason. With a library of integrations for over 6,000 applications, it allows you to create simple but powerful automations ("Zaps") with an intuitive "if this, then that" interface. It's the perfect place to start. A typical Zap might be: "When a new user signs up in Bubble, create a customer profile in Stripe and add them to my email list in Mailchimp."
- **n8n.io: The Power User's Playground** When your needs evolve beyond simple linear automations, you'll graduate to a more powerful tool like n8n. It provides a visual canvas for building complex, multi-step workflows with conditional logic, branching paths, and sophisticated error handling. It's the difference between connecting two dots and designing a complete circuit board. An n8n workflow could handle the entire

customer support process: receive an email, use Claude to categorize it, search a database for the answer, draft a reply, and if the issue is unresolved, create a ticket and notify you via Slack.

These three layers—Strategic LLMs, No-Code Platforms, and Automation Frameworks—are the tripod upon which your solo enterprise stands. They are a synergistic system that allows a single person to perform the work of entire departments, from engineering to marketing to operations.

4.2 Building Your AI-First Tech Stack

Knowing the core tools is one thing; selecting and assembling them into a coherent, powerful, and cost-effective system is another. Your "tech stack" is not a collection of apps; it is the deliberately designed operational DNA of your business. The most common mistake founders make is choosing tools based on hype or familiarity. The correct approach is to let your business model dictate your technology choices, not the other way around.

Framework: Stack Archetypes by Business Model

Different businesses have different needs. A content-heavy media company requires a different stack than a complex SaaS product. Here are three common solo-founder archetypes and their corresponding foundation stacks.

Archetype 1: The SaaS (Software as a Service) Product This is the classic model for a solo founder aiming for a billion-dollar valuation: building a scalable software product that solves a specific problem on a subscription basis.

- **Business Model:** A B2B tool that automates project management for architecture firms.
- **Intelligence Layer:**
  - **GPT-5:** Used for the core product features, such as generating project timelines from architectural drawings or writing draft proposals. This is the engine of the product itself.

- **Claude 4 Sonnet:** Powers the AI customer support chatbot and generates content for the marketing blog.

- **Creation Layer:**
    - **Bubble:** The entire back-end and front-end of the application, including user accounts, project databases, and payment processing, are built here.
    - **Webflow:** Used for the public-facing marketing website, showcasing features, pricing, and case studies.
- **Automation Layer:**
    - **n8n:** Manages complex user onboarding sequences. For example, when a user signs up, a 7-day automated email course is triggered, showing them how to use advanced features, with different emails sent based on which features they've actually used in the app.

Archetype 2: The Automated Content & Media Business This model focuses on creating high-value content at scale in a specific niche, monetizing through advertising, affiliate revenue, or premium subscriptions.

- **Business Model:** A network of niche financial news sites and newsletters, all run by one person.
- **Intelligence Layer:**
    - **GPT-5 & Claude 4 Opus:** Used in tandem. A system is built where an AI agent scours the web for breaking financial news, Claude 4 Opus analyzes and summarizes the key insights with depth, and GPT-5 drafts multiple versions of articles, social media posts, and newsletter entries based on those insights.
- **Creation Layer:**
    - **Ghost or Webflow:** The platform for hosting the blogs and newsletters, chosen for its SEO and content presentation strengths.
    - **AI Media Tools (e.g., HeyGen, ElevenLabs):** To automatically convert the written content into short-form videos for TikTok and YouTube Shorts, or into a daily podcast.
- **Automation Layer:**

- n8n: The entire content pipeline is an n8n workflow. It runs on a schedule, finds the news, triggers the AI content creation, pushes drafts to the Ghost CMS, and schedules social media posts, creating a 24/7 content factory.

Archetype 3: The High-Ticket Service & Education Business This model involves selling high-value expertise in the form of courses, consulting, or coaching, using AI to scale the delivery and personalization.

- **Business Model:** A premium coaching program for executives on implementing AI in their companies.
- **Intelligence Layer:**
  - **Claude 4 Opus:** Used to create deep, insightful course materials and to analyze a new client's business documents to generate a "Personalized AI Roadmap" as part of the onboarding process.
- **Creation Layer:**
  - **Kajabi or a similar all-in-one platform:** Manages course hosting, student communities, and payment processing in a single system.
  - **Webflow:** For the primary marketing and lead-generation website.
- **Automation Layer:**
  - **Zapier:** Perfect for simpler, linear workflows. For example, when a new client pays via Kajabi, Zapier automatically sends them a welcome packet, a link to book their first call, and adds them to a specific email sequence.

Managing Your Stack: Discipline and Foresight

Reality Check: Budgeting for Your Stack While your stack replaces hundreds of thousands of dollars in salaries, it is not free. A robust foundation stack will have two types of costs: **fixed** monthly subscriptions for platforms like Bubble and Webflow (~~$100-300/month to~~

start), and variable costs for API usage ($50-200+/month depending on volume). Budget for a starting operational cost of at least $300-$500 per month. This is your primary investment, and it is still a tiny fraction of the cost of a single employee.

As the founder, you are also the Chief Security Officer. Use a password manager, enable two-factor authentication on every service without exception, and be deeply aware of what customer data you are passing to third-party AI models.

Finally, plan for scale. Start with the simplest tool that gets the job done, but choose platforms that have robust APIs and clear upgrade paths. Don't build your empire on a niche tool that can't grow with you. A well-designed stack is a living system. It should be chosen with intention, managed with discipline, and evolved with foresight. It is the engine that will power your journey.

4.3 Cost-Benefit Analysis: ROI of AI Tool Investment

An amateur collects tools; a professional builds a system. For the solo founder, every tool in your Foundation Stack is not an expense; it is an investment that must generate a quantifiable return. Moving beyond a "gut feeling" and adopting a rigorous cost-benefit analysis for your stack is what separates a hobby from a high-growth enterprise. The discipline of calculating the Return on Investment (ROI) for each tool ensures your capital—no matter how limited—is deployed with maximum efficiency.

AI tools generate value in two primary ways: they **replace costs** that you would otherwise have to incur, or they directly **generate new revenue**. By modeling both, you can make ruthlessly logical decisions about your stack.

Model 1: The Cost Replacement ROI

This is the most direct way to measure the value of tools that automate operational tasks. The model calculates the value generated by avoiding the hiring of human labor to perform the same function.

The formula is simple: `ROI = (Annual Cost of Replaced Human Labor - Annual Cost of AI Tool) / Annual Cost of AI Tool`

The key is to be realistic about the "Cost of Replaced Human Labor." It is not just a salary. It's the fully loaded cost of an employee. Let's create a conservative estimate for one junior-level employee in the United States:

- **Base Salary:** $70,000
- **Payroll Taxes, Insurance & Benefits (~30%):** $21,000
- **Recruiting & Onboarding Costs (amortized over one year, ~15%):** $10,500
- **Software, Hardware & Overhead:** $5,000
- **Total Annual Fully Loaded Cost: ~$106,500**

Now, let's apply this to a real-world scenario. You are considering an advanced AI customer service platform that costs $400 per month.

- **Annual Cost of AI Tool:** $400/month * 12 = $4,800
- **Annual Cost of Replaced Human Labor:** $106,500 (This tool replaces the need for your first customer support hire).

```
ROI = ($106,500 - $4,800) / $4,800 = 31.6
```

An ROI of 31.6 means that for every single dollar you invest in this AI platform, you are realizing $31.60 in value through avoided costs. This is an ROI of **3,160%**. Presented this way, the $400 monthly subscription shifts from a daunting expense to an undeniable bargain. This model is perfect for justifying tools that handle well-defined operational roles: bookkeeping, social media management, technical support, and content creation.

Model 2: The Revenue Generation ROI

This model measures the impact of tools that directly contribute to your top-line growth. These are your sales automation platforms, marketing analytics tools, and AI-powered product features that drive upsells.

The formula is similar: `ROI = (Additional Annual Revenue Generated - Annual Cost of AI Tool) / Annual Cost of AI Tool`

The challenge is accurately attributing revenue to a specific tool. This requires clear tracking and reasonable assumptions. Let's take the example of an AI-powered sales automation tool that finds leads and sends personalized outreach emails.

- **Annual Cost of AI Tool:** $250/month * 12 = $3,000
- **Calculating Additional Revenue:**
    - The tool identifies and contacts 1,500 qualified leads per month.
    - Through diligent A/B testing, you achieve a 0.5% conversion rate from lead-to-customer. That's **7.5 new customers per month**.
    - Your product's average customer lifetime value (LTV) is $800.
    - **Monthly Revenue Generated:** 7.5 customers * $800 LTV = $6,000
    - **Annual Revenue Generated:** $6,000/month * 12 = $72,000

```
ROI = ($72,000 - $3,000) / $3,000 = 23
```

This tool delivers an ROI of **2,300%**, generating $23 in new, high-margin revenue for every $1 spent.

The Blended Model and Intangible Value

In reality, the best tools do both. Your AI customer service bot not only replaces a salary but also provides 24/7 instant support, which reduces churn and increases customer lifetime value (generating revenue). A complete analysis acknowledges this blended value.

Furthermore, some of the most significant returns are difficult to quantify but essential to recognize. What is the dollar value of reclaiming 20 hours of your week from tedious administrative tasks to focus on strategy?

What is the ROI of being able to iterate on your product six times faster than a competitor? This "focus dividend" and "speed premium" are the intangible assets that don't appear on a spreadsheet but are often the primary drivers of a solo founder's success.

Adopting this analytical, ROI-driven approach is a professional discipline. It forces you to treat your stack as a dynamic portfolio of high-performance assets, ensuring every dollar spent is a direct investment in scalable, automated growth.

Strategic Scenario: The Symphony of Automation

To see how a Foundation Stack moves from a collection of logos on a slide to a living, breathing, automated business, let's examine the case of "ResumeFlow." This fictional but realistic venture illustrates how a solo founder can orchestrate a seamless system to achieve massive scale.

The Founder: Amina Khan, a former HR technology consultant who grew frustrated seeing qualified candidates rejected by automated screening systems (ATS) simply because their resumes weren't perfectly optimized.

The Product: ResumeFlow, a SaaS tool that helps job seekers win the "robot game." A user uploads their resume and a specific job description they're applying for. The tool's AI engine analyzes both documents, identifies critical keywords, skills, and formatting cues that the ATS will be looking for, and provides specific, actionable suggestions to improve the resume's chances.

The Business Outcome: Within 18 months of launch, Amina grew ResumeFlow to a **$1 million Annual Recurring Revenue (ARR)** run rate, completely by herself. She spends her time on high-level strategy and product innovation, not operations.

The Engine: Deconstructing Amina's $600/Month Stack

Amina's success is a testament to her deliberately designed tech stack, a symphony of automation where each tool plays a specific, vital role.

- **Intelligence Layer:**
  - **GPT-5 API:** The heart of the product. Amina uses the most powerful model for the core resume analysis engine. Its sophisticated reasoning is required to understand the nuance of both a human-written resume and a corporate job description.
  - **Claude 4 Sonnet API:** Used for all customer-facing communication. It powers the website's support chatbot and is the engine behind her highly successful career advice blog, generating insightful articles that drive organic traffic.
- **Creation Layer:**
  - **Bubble:** The entire ResumeFlow application is built on Bubble. It handles user account creation, profile management, resume and document uploads, and the front-end interface where users see their AI-generated suggestions. Crucially, it also manages the integration with the Stripe payment gateway.
  - **Webflow:** Amina's marketing "storefront." The polished public website, the blog, and all marketing landing pages are built on Webflow for its superior design capabilities and SEO strengths.
- **Automation Layer:**
  - **n8n:** Amina chose n8n for its ability to handle complex, multi-step workflows that form the backbone of her business operations.
- **Supporting Tools:**
  - **Stripe:** For all payment processing.
  - **Mailchimp:** For automated email marketing and user engagement sequences.

- **Notion:** Serves as her central nervous system—a lightweight CRM, a knowledge base for the support bot, and a product roadmap.

The Symphony in Action: A Seamless User Journey

Let's follow a new user, David, to see how the stack works in perfect harmony, orchestrated by n8n.

1. **Acquisition:** David, frustrated in his job search, finds a ResumeFlow blog post on "5 Reasons an AI Thinks Your Resume is a Bad Fit" through a Google search. The article, hosted on Webflow, was drafted by Claude 4 and provides genuine value.
2. **Conversion:** A call-to-action in the article leads him to a landing page offering a free trial to "Scan one resume for free." He signs up via a form built in Bubble.
3. **The Onboarding Workflow:** The moment David hits "Submit," a Bubble webhook triggers a complex workflow in **n8n**. Instantly and automatically, n8n:
   - Creates David's user account in the Bubble database.
   - Adds David as a "New Trial User" to a specific audience in Mailchimp, triggering a 5-day welcome email sequence.
   - Creates a new customer card for David in Amina's Notion "CRM," tagging him as a trial user.
4. **The Core Product Experience:** Inside the app, David uploads his resume and a job description. The Bubble interface sends these two documents via API to the **GPT-5** engine. Within seconds, GPT-5 returns a detailed JSON object containing analysis and specific rewrite suggestions. Bubble then parses this data and displays it in a clean, user-friendly interface. David is blown away by the quality of the feedback.
5. **The Automated Upsell:** On day 4 of his trial, the automated Mailchimp sequence sends David an email showcasing the benefits of the Pro plan. When his trial ends, another email arrives with a 24-hour, 25% discount offer. He clicks the link, which takes him to his Bubble account's billing page, where

Stripe seamlessly processes his monthly subscription payment. The n8n workflow is again triggered, updating his status in Bubble and Notion to "Active Subscriber."

6. **Automated Support:** Two weeks later, David has a question about his subscription. He goes to the ResumeFlow website and interacts with the support chatbot. The chatbot, powered by **Claude 4 Sonnet**, has been trained on a knowledge base of FAQs stored in **Notion**. It instantly understands his query and provides a clear answer, resolving the issue without any human intervention from Amina.

Amina's business is not just an app; it is a meticulously designed, fully automated system. Her role is that of the conductor, occasionally adjusting the composition, but allowing the symphony of automation to play on its own. By investing just ~$600 per month in a perfectly integrated stack, she built a machine that generates over $83,000 in monthly recurring revenue, proving that the right system is infinitely more powerful than a large team.

Chapter Summary & Resources

In this chapter, we have laid the literal foundation for your AI-first enterprise. We moved from theory to practice, identifying the three critical layers of a solo founder's technology stack: Intelligence, Creation, and Automation. We have explored the specific, best-in-class tools that occupy these layers, established a framework for choosing them based on your business model, and provided a rigorous ROI-based method for justifying their cost. Finally, the case study of "ResumeFlow" demonstrated how these individual tools can be woven together into a seamless, automated system capable of generating millions in revenue.

Key Takeaways

- A **Foundation Stack** is a synergistic system composed of an Intelligence Layer (LLMs), a Creation Layer (no-code platforms), and an Automation Layer (integration frameworks).
- Your **business model must dictate your technology choices**, not the other way around. Select tools that directly serve the core function of your business.

- Every tool must be justified with a clear **Return on Investment (ROI)**, calculated either through direct Cost Replacement or measurable Revenue Generation.
- A well-integrated stack, orchestrated by a powerful automation tool like n8n, creates a truly **automated business** that can scale with minimal human intervention.

Action Item Checklist

- **Audit Your Idea's Stack:** Based on your primary business idea, map out your ideal Foundation Stack. List one specific tool for each of the three layers (e.g., Intelligence: GPT-5, Creation: Bubble, Automation: n8n). Be specific.
- **Run a Sample ROI Calculation:** Choose one AI tool you are considering for your stack. Use the Cost Replacement model to calculate its potential ROI. Value your own time at a reasonable hourly consultant rate (e.g., $100/hour) and calculate the ROI of a tool that saves you 10 hours per week.
- **Design One Automated Workflow:** On paper or in a visual tool, sketch out a simple three-step workflow for your business (e.g., New Lead from Website -> Add to Notion CRM -> Send Welcome Email via Mailchimp). Then, visit Zapier or n8n's website to confirm that the apps you chose can indeed be connected in the way you planned.

Preview of Chapter 5

Now that you have designed your Foundation Stack, it's time to point your powerful new arsenal at the outside world. In **Chapter 5, Automating Customer-Facing Operations**, we will deploy your stack to the front lines. You will learn how to build AI systems that manage customer service, automate sales, and run marketing campaigns at scale, allowing you to build and maintain relationships with thousands of customers without losing the human touch.

Resources and Tools

- **Intelligence:** OpenAI (GPT-5), Anthropic (Claude 4)

- **Creation:** Bubble.io, Webflow.com
- **Automation:** n8n.io, Zapier.com
- **Communities:** The official forums and community pages for Bubble and n8n are invaluable, free resources for technical help, workflow inspiration, and connecting with other builders.
- **Concept: API (Application Programming Interface).** To truly master your stack, you must understand this fundamental concept. Spend one hour watching introductory videos on YouTube about how APIs work. This knowledge is a prerequisite for building powerful automations.

Chapter 5: Automating Customer-Facing Operations

Introduction

Traditional business wisdom dictates a simple, linear rule: as your number of customers grows, so must the number of people you employ to service, sell to, and market to them. A company with a million users requires vast call centers, sprawling sales teams, and multi-layered marketing departments. This logic is sound, sensible, and, in the age of AI, completely obsolete. The solo founder operates under a new set of rules, where the relationship between scale and headcount is not just broken; it is inverted.

This chapter addresses the critical question of the solo-founder model: how can one person possibly deliver a world-class experience to potentially millions of users without being completely overwhelmed? How do you build and maintain genuine customer relationships, drive sales, and market your product effectively when you are the entire team? The answer lies in moving beyond simple automation and building autonomous, intelligent systems that manage your customer-facing operations for you.

In Chapter 4, we built your Foundation Stack—the powerful, internal engine of your business. Now, it is time to connect that engine to the outside world. We will deploy your AI arsenal to the front lines, creating systems for customer service, sales, and marketing. These are not crude, robotic replacements for human interaction. They are sophisticated, AI-powered engines designed to deliver personalized, valuable, and memorable experiences at scale, ensuring your millionth customer feels as understood and appreciated as your very first.

5.1 AI-Powered Customer Service at Scale

The term "customer service chatbot" often evokes a feeling of dread—a frustrating, circular conversation with a mindless bot that excels only at misunderstanding your problem. That era is over. We are now in the age of the **AI Service Agent**, a fundamentally different class of technology that can deliver a support experience that is not only scalable but often superior to its human-run counterparts. For the solo founder, mastering the creation of these agents is the key to building a business that can support millions of users without collapsing under its own weight.

The Architecture of a Modern AI Service Agent

An old-world chatbot was a rigid decision tree. A modern AI Service Agent is a dynamic system with three core components: a brain, a memory, and hands.

- **The Brain (A Sophisticated LLM):** The agent's intelligence and personality come from a powerful Large Language Model. While you could use GPT-5, this is a perfect application for a model from **Anthropic's Claude 4 family**, which is renowned for its nuanced, steerable, and more naturally conversational tone. Your first step is to define its persona.

  Action Item: Prompting a Persona

  Begin your system prompt with a clear directive: *"You are 'Atlas,' the lead support specialist for our SaaS product, 'Mapify.' Your personality is calm, exceptionally helpful, and slightly witty. You are an expert on our product. Never admit you are an AI. Your goal is to solve the user's problem completely and leave them feeling delighted."* This simple prompt instantly transforms the generic LLM into a branded, specialist agent.

- **The Memory (A Vector Knowledge Base):** An AI agent is only as smart as the information it can access. You must provide it with a comprehensive, long-term memory. This is achieved through a technique called Retrieval-Augmented Generation (RAG). You take all of your company's knowledge—every FAQ article, every technical document, every blog post, every tutorial—and embed it into a "vector database." When a user asks a question, the system first retrieves the most relevant pieces of information from this database and then feeds them to the LLM along with the user's query. This allows the AI to answer highly specific questions about your product with perfect accuracy. Platforms like **Lindy**, **Tidio**, **Botpress**, or even a custom setup with a tool like **Pinecone.io** can manage this RAG process for you.

- **The Hands (The Ability to Take Action):** This is what truly separates an AI Agent from a simple chatbot. The agent must be able to *do things*. This is achieved by connecting it to your automation layer, **n8n**. If a user asks, "Can I get a refund for last month's charge?" the agent shouldn't just reply, "Yes, please contact billing." A properly integrated agent can authenticate the user, confirm the charge, trigger an n8n workflow that calls the **Stripe API** to process the refund, and then reply, "Of course. I've just processed a full refund for last month's charge. You'll see it back in your account within 3-5 business days."

The Tiered Support System: Your Scalability Framework

A single founder cannot personally handle every edge case. Therefore, you must design an intelligent escalation path that protects your time while ensuring every customer is taken care of.

- **Tier 1: The AI Service Agent (Resolves 95% of Queries):** This is your 24/7 frontline. It handles all common questions, technical issues with known solutions, and billing inquiries. It is instant, accurate, and capable of handling thousands of conversations simultaneously.
- **Tier 2: The AI-Assisted Human (Handles 4% of Queries):** When the AI agent encounters a truly novel problem or a highly frustrated user, it executes a graceful handoff. It doesn't just give up. It summarizes the entire conversation, fetches the user's complete account history from your Bubble database, identifies the core issue, and creates a detailed ticket in a system like **Notion** or **Zendesk**. It can even use its LLM brain to draft a suggested reply for you, the founder.
- **Tier 3: The Founder (Resolves 1% of Queries):** Your time is your most precious asset. You only interact with the 1% of issues

that are the most complex, the most critical, or come from your highest-value customers. You log in to your support queue to find a handful of pre-triaged, well-documented tickets with AI-drafted replies waiting for your approval. This is how you manage support for a million-user company in under an hour a day.

This tiered, AI-first approach transforms customer service from a reactive cost center into a proactive, scalable system for building user trust and loyalty. It allows you to deliver an experience that is consistently excellent, creating a formidable competitive advantage.

5.2 Sales Automation Without Losing the Human Touch

The term "sales automation" often conjures images of soulless, generic email blasts that clog up inboxes and are destined for the spam folder. This approach is dead. For the solo founder aiming to land high-value B2B customers, brute force is useless. The new paradigm is not about sending more emails; it is about achieving **personalization at scale**. The goal is to build an automated system that can generate thousands of unique, deeply researched, and genuinely relevant outreach messages that feel as if they were painstakingly crafted by hand for each individual recipient.

The Hyper-Personalization Stack

This level of sophisticated automation requires a specific set of interconnected tools, each performing a vital role in the assembly line of a perfect cold email.

1. **Apollo.io (The Database):** This is your starting point. Apollo is a vast B2B database containing hundreds of millions of contacts. A solo founder can use its powerful filters to build a highly precise list of their Ideal Customer Profiles (ICPs). For example: "Show me all VPs of Engineering at fintech companies in the UK and Germany that have between 100 and 500 employees and recently raised a Series B funding round."

2. **Clay.com (The Enrichment Engine):** This is the solo founder's secret weapon. Clay acts as a central hub that takes a simple list of leads from Apollo and enriches it with dozens of data points from across the web. Think of it as a team of tireless research assistants. For each person on your list, Clay can automatically find their recent LinkedIn posts, articles they've written, podcasts they've appeared on, news about their company, technologies their company uses, and much more.
3. **GPT-5 / Claude 4 (The Personalization AI):** This is the brain that uses the enriched data from Clay to write a unique, compelling opening line for every single email.
4. **Instantly.ai / Smartlead.ai (The Sending Platform):** These platforms are designed for cold outreach at scale. They allow you to connect multiple email inboxes to "warm them up," send thousands of emails per day without hurting your domain's reputation, and manage all the replies in a unified inbox.

The Automated Outreach Workflow: A Step-by-Step Guide

This is the assembly line in action, moving a generic lead to a hyper-personalized message.

- **Step 1: Build a Hyper-Targeted List in Apollo.** Create a list of 1,000 to 5,000 ideal customers. The more precise the list, the more effective the outreach. Export this list as a CSV file.
- **Step 2: Enrich Leads in Clay.** Import the list into a Clay "table." Now, build a "waterfall" of enrichments for each lead. For example:
    - Find the person's LinkedIn Profile.
    - Use a web scraper to pull their three most recent posts.
    - Use Google Search integration to find a news article mentioning their company in the last 90 days.
- **Step 3: Generate the AI-Personalized First Line.** This is the magic. Within Clay, you create a new column and use its AI integration to run a unique prompt for every single row (i.e., every lead).

Hot Take: The "One-Sentence" Prompt

*"You are a world-class sales researcher. Look at the following information about a person and their company. Write a single, compelling opening sentence for an email that references one highly specific and interesting detail. Be complimentary but professional.

- Name: [Person's Name]
- Company: [Company Name]
- Recent LinkedIn Post: [Text of Post]
- Recent Company News: [Headline of News]
- My Product: An AI tool that helps engineering teams reduce their cloud computing costs.

Your output should only be the single sentence."*

- **Step 4: Push Data to the Sending Platform.** Clay's integrations then send this complete table—including the lead's contact info and the newly generated, unique first line for each one—directly into an Instantly.ai campaign.
- **Step 5: Launch the Campaign and Manage Replies.** Inside Instantly.ai, your email template looks like this: `{{ai_first_line}} The reason I'm reaching out is...` The platform automatically inserts the unique sentence for each recipient. The result is thousands of emails going out, each one starting with a message like, "Hi Jane, I saw your post about the rising costs of Snowflake and it really resonated..." or "Hi Tom, congrats on the launch of your new platform last month! It looks like a huge step forward for your team."

The reply rates for this method can be 5-10x higher than generic outreach because it proves you have done your homework. The automation doesn't replace the human touch; it manufactures the initial human touch at scale. When a lead replies with interest, the automation stops, and the founder takes over personally to build a genuine relationship. This system allows a single person to do the work of an entire business development team, starting thousands of warm, relevant conversations every single month.

5.3 Marketing That Runs While You Sleep

In a traditional company, the marketing department is a bustling, often chaotic, hub of human activity: copywriters brainstorming campaign slogans, designers crafting visuals, social media managers scheduling posts, and data analysts poring over spreadsheets to measure the results. This human-powered model is expensive, slow, and difficult to scale. The solo founder has a more powerful alternative: an autonomous, AI-driven Marketing Engine that ideates, creates, distributes, analyzes, and optimizes content 24/7, building a powerful brand presence and a reliable pipeline of new customers with minimal human oversight.

The Architecture of the Autonomous Marketing Engine

This is not just a set of tools; it is a self-perpetuating loop designed to constantly learn and improve. It is built upon the Foundation Stack, with your automation layer (n8n or Zapier) acting as the master conductor.

Step 1: The AI Ideation Core Great marketing starts with great ideas. Your engine can be programmed to be a tireless market researcher. An n8n workflow can be set to run every single day to:

1. **Scrape Data:** Automatically monitor relevant subreddits, competitor blogs, industry news sites, and social media hashtags related to your niche.
2. **Synthesize Insights:** Feed this raw data—a stream of customer complaints, questions, and trending topics—into a sophisticated LLM like Claude 4 Opus.
3. **Generate a Content Brief:** The LLM's prompt is to act as a world-class marketing strategist: *"Based on today's scraped data, identify the top 5 customer pain points and trending topics. For each one, generate a content brief that includes an SEO-optimized blog post title, three distinct social media post angles (one professional for LinkedIn, one casual for X/Twitter), and a 60-second video script outline."*

Step 2: The AI Content Factory The content brief generated in Step 1 automatically triggers the creation process. This is your multi-channel content factory at work:

- **Long-Form Text:** The blog post titles are sent via API to **GPT-5** with a detailed prompt to draft a comprehensive, 1,500-word article, complete with subheadings and key takeaways.
- **Visuals:** The social media angles are fed to an AI image generator like **Midjourney** to create a series of unique, eye-catching visuals for each post.
- **Short-Form Video:** The video scripts are sent to an AI video platform like **HeyGen**, which generates a complete video featuring a realistic AI avatar, background music, and on-screen text.

Step 3: The Automated Distribution Network Once the assets are created, the n8n workflow moves to distribution:

- The drafted blog posts are automatically pushed into the CMS of your **Webflow** or Ghost website, saved as drafts awaiting a final one-click approval from you.
- The social media posts and their corresponding AI-generated images are scheduled across LinkedIn, X/Twitter, and other relevant platforms using an API connection to a tool like **Buffer** or **SocialBee**.
- The generated videos are automatically uploaded to YouTube Shorts, TikTok, and Instagram Reels.

Step 4: The Self-Optimizing Analytics Loop This is what makes the engine truly autonomous. After a set period, typically seven days, the n8n workflow executes the analysis phase:

1. **Collect Performance Data:** It uses APIs to pull key metrics for all the content it published: page views and time-on-page from Google Analytics, engagement rates (likes, comments, shares) from social media platforms, and view counts from video platforms.

2. **AI-Powered Analysis:** It feeds all of this quantitative data into an LLM. **Prompt:** *"You are a data analyst. Here is the performance data for last week's marketing content. Identify the top-performing topic and format combination. Which headlines drove the most clicks? Which video style had the highest retention? Based on this data, generate a one-paragraph summary of key learnings and update our 'Content Strategy Principles' document for next week's cycle."*
3. **Automated A/B Testing:** This loop can also be used to optimize conversions. You can program the engine to generate two different headlines for a landing page, use a tool like **Optimizely** to split traffic between them, and after 1,000 visitors, the system can automatically analyze the results and permanently implement the winning version.

The solo founder's role in this system shifts from being a manual laborer to a creative director. You spend perhaps 30 minutes a day reviewing the AI-generated drafts for quality and tone, and another 30 minutes reviewing the weekly performance summary to ensure the engine's strategy remains aligned with your overarching business goals. You are no longer *doing* marketing; you are *directing* a tireless, self-improving marketing machine.

Strategic Scenario: The Autonomous Enterprise

To witness the full power of a completely automated customer-facing operation, consider the story of "SyncUp AI." It stands as a testament to how a solo founder can leverage a symphony of AI systems to achieve massive scale and world-class customer satisfaction simultaneously.

The Founder: Marco Diaz, a former product manager at a large collaboration software company, who was convinced that most business meetings were a colossal waste of time, not because of the meeting itself, but because of the lack of clear outcomes and follow-up.

The Product: SyncUp AI, a SaaS tool that acts as an intelligent AI assistant for business meetings. The AI joins a user's Zoom, Google Meet, or Microsoft Teams call. During the meeting, it generates a perfect transcript. Immediately after, it delivers a concise summary, a list of all identified action items (assigned to the correct person), and a draft follow-up email ready to be sent to all attendees.

The Business Outcome: As a solo founder, Marco scaled SyncUp AI to **10,000 active users** and a **$2.4 million Annual Recurring Revenue (ARR)** run rate within two years. Even at that scale, the business maintains a **98% Customer Satisfaction (CSAT)** score.

Part 1: The Automated Growth Engine (Marketing & Sales)

Marco knew he couldn't compete with the massive sales teams of his rivals. His entire growth strategy was built on automation.

- **The Content Engine:** Marco set up an autonomous marketing engine, as described in the previous section. His n8n workflow scours the web for articles and posts about "meeting productivity" and "remote work challenges." It then uses this data to fuel an AI content factory that produces a steady stream of valuable blog posts ("The 5 Action Items You Missed In Your Last Meeting"), LinkedIn articles, and short-form videos, all driving traffic back to the SyncUp AI website built on Webflow.
- **The Product-Led Sales Funnel:** The marketing content funnels users into a free trial of SyncUp AI. The product is designed to deliver a "wow" moment within the first use. This product-led growth (PLG) model means the product itself is the primary salesperson. For individual users and small teams, the entire sales process is self-serve.
- **The Automated B2B Upsell Path:** When a group of users from the same large company (e.g., 10+ users from `acme.com`) signs up, a specific trigger is fired. **Clay.com** enriches the company's data, identifying the likely head of the department. An automated, hyper-personalized email sequence is then sent via **Instantly.ai**, offering a demo of the "SyncUp for Enterprise" plan, which includes centralized billing and security features. This system automates the high-value B2B sales motion without a single human salesperson.

Part 2: The Scalable Support System

With 10,000 users, Marco would drown in support tickets without a world-class AI system.

- **Tier 1: 'Lindy,' The AI Service Agent:** 96% of all support queries are handled by 'Lindy,' an AI agent. It is trained on an extensive knowledge base of every technical document and FAQ, all stored and managed in **Notion**. 'Lindy' can instantly answer complex questions ("How do I configure SyncUp AI to ignore internal engineering stand-ups but record client calls?") and perform actions like upgrading a user's plan by triggering an n8n workflow that calls the **Stripe API**.
- **The Graceful Escalation:** When a user expresses significant frustration or has a completely novel issue, 'Lindy' is programmed to respond with empathy: "I understand this is frustrating, and I want to make sure we get this right. I'm escalating you directly to our founder, Marco, for personal assistance." In the background, 'Lindy' creates a ticket in Notion for Marco, complete with a summary of the issue, the user's entire conversation history, their payment status from Stripe, and a suggested resolution.
- **The 98% CSAT Score:** The overwhelmingly positive satisfaction score comes from the best of both worlds. Most users receive an *instant*, correct answer 24/7, which is a better experience than waiting hours for a human reply. For the rare few who are escalated, the personal, thoughtful, and fast response directly from the founder feels like an incredible VIP experience. The system delivers machine-like efficiency blended with founder-level care.

The Founder's Role: Conductor of the Symphony

Marco Diaz does not run his business day-to-day. The automated systems do. His time is spent almost exclusively on high-leverage activities. He reviews the marketing engine's performance dashboards, analyzes the most common support topics to identify areas for product improvement, and spends his afternoons on calls with his top customers, brainstorming the future of SyncUp AI. He is the chairman, chief strategist, and head of R&D. His AI stack is the CEO, COO, CMO, and the entire operational workforce. SyncUp AI is a living testament to the fact that a solo founder can achieve massive scale not by building a team, but by building a symphony of automation.

Chapter Summary & Resources

In this chapter, we have systematically dismantled the operational bottlenecks that prevent solo founders from scaling. We've moved beyond theory and laid out the specific architectures for building autonomous systems that handle the three core customer-facing functions: service, sales, and marketing. The goal is not to create a cold, robotic company, but to leverage AI to deliver a personalized, high-quality, and instant experience to every user, from the first to the millionth. This is how you build a business that runs and grows while you sleep.

Key Takeaways

- **AI Service Agents** can deliver a superior customer experience by being instant, 24/7, action-oriented, and capable of handling over 95% of all support queries.
- Modern **sales automation** has shifted from generic spam to hyper-personalization at scale, using tools like Clay and Apollo to craft unique outreach for thousands of targeted leads.
- An **autonomous marketing engine** can be built to handle the entire content lifecycle: ideation, creation, multi-channel distribution, and performance-based optimization.
- A well-orchestrated, automated customer-facing stack frees the solo founder to focus exclusively on high-level strategy, product vision, and key relationships.

Action Items

- **Design Your AI Service Agent's Persona:** Write a one-paragraph system prompt for the AI agent that would handle customer service for your business. Give it a name, a distinct personality (e.g., friendly, professional, witty), and a core goal (e.g., "to solve the user's problem on the first try").

- **Map a Hyper-Personalization Workflow:** Choose a B2B audience you want to target. List three specific, non-obvious data points you would try to find using a tool like Clay (e.g., a recent quote in an article, a shared hobby listed on their profile, their company's latest product launch) to create a unique opening line for a sales email.
- **Sketch Your Content Engine:** Draw a simple flowchart for an automated marketing engine for your business idea. What is the trigger (e.g., a trending keyword)? What three types of content would be created (e.g., blog post, image, video)? Where would they be distributed?

Preview of Chapter 6

We have now automated the front lines—the exterior—of your business. But a truly resilient and scalable enterprise cannot be a hollow shell. The internal mechanics must be just as ruthlessly efficient. In **Chapter 6, Backend Operations Revolution**, we turn our attention inward. We will automate the "unsexy" but critical functions of financial management, data analysis, and legal compliance, creating a truly frictionless, self-running organization from the inside out.

Resources and Tools

- **Customer Service:** Lindy, Tidio, Botpress (for building AI agents), Notion (as a knowledge base).
- **Sales Automation:** Apollo.io (for lead databases), Clay.com (for enrichment), Instantly.ai (for sending).
- **Marketing Automation:** n8n.io (as the core orchestrator), Webflow CMS, Buffer or SocialBee (for scheduling).

Chapter 6: Backend Operations Revolution

Introduction

If the customer-facing systems we designed in the last chapter are the elegant, welcoming "front of house" of your business, then the backend operations are the intricate, high-stakes "backstage." This is the world of finance, data analysis, legal, and compliance—the unglamorous but utterly essential machinery that keeps the entire production from collapsing. For a solo founder, the backend is a minefield. These tasks are time-consuming, mentally draining, and unforgiving of error. A single mistake in bookkeeping or a missed compliance deadline can have catastrophic consequences.

The traditional approach to managing this complexity is to hire accountants, analysts, and lawyers. The solo founder's approach is to make these functions invisible. The goal of this chapter is to architect a suite of autonomous systems that handle the critical backend functions of your enterprise with a precision and efficiency that no human team can match.

We will move beyond simply automating tasks and design systems that are not only real-time but also predictive. We will transform finance from a historical record into a forward-looking guide. We will elevate data analysis from a static report into a 24/7 AI strategist that uncovers hidden opportunities. And we will simplify legal compliance from a source of anxiety into an automated process. By the end of this chapter, you will have the blueprint for a frictionless backend, giving you the stability of a large corporation with none of the bureaucratic drag.

6.1 Financial Management and Reporting

For most entrepreneurs, financial management is the single greatest source of administrative dread. It is a reactive, painful process of wrestling with spreadsheets, chasing down receipts, and spending weeks with an accountant to produce a backward-looking report on a quarter that is already over. This is a model designed for a bygone era. The AI-first solo founder operates under a new paradigm: a live, intelligent, and predictive financial system that requires zero manual data entry and provides a real-time, forward-looking view of the business's health.

The Architecture of an Automated Finance Stack

To achieve financial autonomy, you need a stack where data flows seamlessly from transaction to report without ever being touched by a human hand.

- **The Transaction Layer (The Digital Source of Truth):** The foundation of automated finance is clean, digital data. This means running all revenue through a modern payment processor like **Stripe** and all expenses through a digital-first business bank account like **Mercury**. By eliminating cash, paper checks, and messy expense reports, you ensure that every single dollar flowing in or out of your business is a clean, categorized digital record from the moment of its creation.

- **The Bookkeeping Layer (The AI Accountant):** This is where the magic of automation takes place. Instead of manually entering transactions into a ledger, you use an AI-powered bookkeeping platform like **Digits** or a modern cloud accounting tool like **QuickBooks Online**. These platforms connect directly to your Stripe and Mercury accounts via API.

    a. **Real-Time Categorization:** The moment a customer's subscription payment is processed by Stripe, the AI recognizes it as "Subscription Revenue" and books it accordingly. When you pay your monthly subscription for an AI tool via your Mercury debit card, the system recognizes it as a "Software Expense."
    b. **The Founder's Role:** Your job is not data entry; it is exception handling. The AI can automate over 99% of transactions. Your role is to spend 15 minutes once a week reviewing the handful of transactions the AI was unsure about, teaching it how to categorize them for the future.

- **The Reporting Layer (The Live P&L):** Because bookkeeping is happening in real-time, so is your financial reporting. At any moment, you can pull up a perfectly accurate, up-to-the-minute Profit & Loss (P&L) statement, balance sheet, or cash flow statement. Accounting ceases to be a historical artifact and becomes a live dashboard for strategic decision-making. You can see the immediate impact of a new marketing campaign on your revenue or a new tool on your expenses.

Advanced Strategy: Predictive Cash Flow Modeling

Knowing your exact financial position today is powerful. Knowing where you will be in six months is a strategic superpower. This is where you leverage an LLM as your personal financial analyst.

This is a systematic process:

1. **Export Your Data:** From your automated bookkeeping tool, export the last 12 to 24 months of detailed financial statements.
2. **Prompt Your AI Analyst:** Feed this clean, structured data into a sophisticated LLM like GPT-5 or Claude 4 Opus. Your prompt should be specific and goal-oriented.

> **Action Item: The Predictive Finance Prompt**
>
> *"You are a senior financial analyst at a top venture capital firm, specializing in SaaS businesses. I am the solo founder of my company. Attached are my complete financial statements for the past 24 months.
>
> Your task is to build a predictive cash flow model for the next 12 months. Your model must project three distinct scenarios:
>
> 1. **Aggressive Case:** Assume our current 12% month-over-month revenue growth continues.

2. **Base Case:** Assume revenue growth slows to a more conservative 6% month-over-month.
3. **Worst Case:** Assume revenue growth flattens to 0%.

For each scenario, provide a month-by-month projection of revenue, total expenses, net profit, and ending cash balance. Finally, provide a one-paragraph summary identifying any potential cash flow crunches and suggest strategic actions I could take today to mitigate those risks."*

3. **Act on a Projection, Not a Panic:** The AI will generate a detailed model that gives you a clear window into the future. If the model shows a potential cash shortfall in seven months under your "Base Case," you have seven months to act. You can make a calculated decision to reduce a specific expense, run a promotional campaign to boost near-term revenue, or secure a line of credit from a position of strength, not desperation. This process replaces guesswork and anxiety with data-driven foresight.

By building this automated financial stack, you transform one of the most feared aspects of running a business into one of your greatest strategic assets. You spend zero time on manual administration and 100% of your "finance time" on high-level strategy, steering your company with the clarity and confidence that only a real-time, predictive view can provide.

6.2 Data Analysis and Business Intelligence

In a traditional corporation, data analysis is a slow and frustrating process. A manager has a question, they file a ticket with a specialized business intelligence (BI) team, and they wait. Days or even weeks later, they receive a static report or a clunky dashboard that often answers their initial question but sparks five new ones, starting the slow cycle all over again. The solo founder cannot afford this latency. They require a fundamentally different approach: a living, breathing, autonomous BI system powered by an AI data analyst that works 24/7 to answer complex questions, monitor business health, and proactively uncover the hidden opportunities that drive growth.

The Architecture of an Autonomous BI System

This system is designed to turn the raw, chaotic data generated by your business into clean, actionable, strategic insights.

Step 1: Centralize Your Data (Build a Single Source of Truth) You cannot analyze data that is siloed across a dozen different applications. The foundational step is to create a central repository for all your key business data.

- **The Tools:** You don't need a complex, expensive data warehouse. You can use an automation workflow in **n8n** to pull data from all your sources on a regular schedule (e.g., every hour).
- **The Data Sources:** This includes user behavior data from your **Bubble** application database, payment and subscription data from **Stripe**, website traffic and conversion data from **Google Analytics**, and email engagement data from **Mailchimp**.
- **The Destination:** This data is then consolidated into a simple, cloud-based data warehouse like **Google BigQuery** or even a highly structured **Airtable** base for leaner operations. This creates a single, comprehensive view of your entire business.

Step 2: The AI Analysis and Visualization Layer With your data centralized, you can now deploy an AI to make sense of it. This is where you interact with your data in plain English.

- **The Tools:** This new category of AI-native BI platforms includes tools like **ThoughtSpot** or **Glean**. These platforms connect directly to your data warehouse.
- **Natural Language Querying:** Instead of writing complex SQL code, you can simply ask questions. "What is the average lifetime value of customers acquired in the last quarter?"

"Compare the churn rate of users on our 'Pro' plan versus our 'Standard' plan." "Show me a list of our top 10% of users by feature engagement." The AI translates your question into a query, fetches the data, and presents the answer in a clear visualization—a chart, a graph, or a table.

- **The Live Dashboard:** Any answer you find valuable can be "pinned" to a live dashboard. This becomes your mission control. At a glance, you can see real-time data on user sign-ups, revenue growth, customer churn, and marketing campaign performance.

Advanced Strategy: Proactive Insight Generation

A truly intelligent BI system doesn't just answer the questions you ask; it tells you what questions you *should* be asking. This is the difference between having a data calculator and having a data strategist.

- **Automated Anomaly Detection:** Your AI analyst can be programmed to monitor all your key metrics continuously. If it detects a statistically significant deviation from the norm, it can automatically alert you. You might receive a Slack message at the start of your day saying, "Alert: New user sign-ups from mobile devices in the UK have dropped by 40% in the last 48 hours. This is a 4-sigma event. It appears to be correlated with the new app update pushed two days ago." This allows you to identify and fix a critical bug before it impacts thousands of users.
- **Proactive Opportunity Surfacing:** The system's greatest power is its ability to find hidden correlations that a human might never see. After analyzing months of user data, it might generate an insight like: "I have identified a new user cohort with a 3x higher lifetime value. These are users who integrate our product with HubSpot within their first 7 days. We are not currently marketing this integration. A targeted campaign aimed at HubSpot users could be a significant growth lever." This is the AI acting as a true strategic partner, finding gold hidden inside your own data streams.

This entire BI system is built on a feedback loop. The insights it generates are not just interesting; they are actionable directives that feed back into your other automated systems. The insight about HubSpot users immediately informs your sales and marketing engines, which can now be re-tasked to target that specific segment. The data becomes the command, and the execution is automatic. This creates a data-driven, self-improving organization that learns and adapts at a velocity no human-run team could ever hope to match.

6.3 Legal and Compliance Automation

For many founders, the legal and compliance aspects of running a business are the most opaque and intimidating. They represent a world of dense contracts, arcane regulations, and expensive hourly fees. A single misstep can pose an existential threat to the company. The traditional approach is reactive: you hire a lawyer when you have a problem. The AI-first solo founder takes a different approach: they build a proactive, automated legal framework designed to minimize risk from day one, handling the vast majority of routine legal work automatically and freeing up capital for expert counsel only when it is absolutely critical.

Reality Check: AI is Not Your Lawyer

It is crucial to state this clearly: The AI tools and strategies described here are incredibly powerful for handling routine, standardized legal tasks and providing first-pass analysis. They are designed to make you more informed and efficient. They are **not** a substitute for professional legal counsel from a qualified human lawyer for high-stakes, unique, or contentious situations. The goal of this system is to automate the 95% of legal legwork so you can afford to pay for top-tier human expertise for the critical 5%.

The AI-Powered Legal Stack

An automated legal framework has three core functions: creating necessary documents, reviewing incoming documents, and monitoring the regulatory landscape.

1. AI-Powered Contract and Document Generation Every business needs a standard set of legal documents: Terms of Service, a Privacy Policy, Non-Disclosure Agreements (NDAs), and independent contractor agreements.

- **The AI First Draft:** Instead of starting from a blank page or a questionable online template, you can use a sophisticated LLM like **Claude 4 Opus** as your initial drafter. Its massive training data includes a vast corpus of legal text, allowing it to generate high-quality, context-aware first drafts.

    - **Action Item: The Legal Drafting Prompt**

      "You are a US-based corporate lawyer with expertise in technology startups. My company, 'DataView AI,' is a B2B SaaS product that provides data analytics. Please generate a comprehensive Privacy Policy that is compliant with both GDPR and CCPA standards. The policy should clearly explain what user data we collect, how it is used, our data retention policies, and the user's rights regarding their data."

- **The Platform Layer:** Once you have this strong first draft, you finalize it using a trusted legal tech platform like **LegalZoom** or **Clerky**. These services provide lawyer-vetted templates and ensure your documents are tailored to your specific jurisdiction and business type. For managing the signing process, tools like **DocuSign** automate the entire workflow.

2. AI-Assisted Contract Review When a potential partner, vendor, or enterprise customer sends you their contract, the review process can be daunting. An AI can act as your tireless paralegal, performing a first-pass review to flag key terms and potential risks.

- **The Workflow:** You upload the contract PDF into an LLM with a large context window (like Claude 4 Opus).

- **The Analysis Prompt:** *"You are a meticulous contract analyst. I am the founder of a small startup. Please analyze the attached 20-page Master Service Agreement from a potential enterprise customer. Your task is to:
    1. Provide a one-paragraph executive summary of the agreement in plain English.
    2. Identify any clauses that are non-standard or unusually restrictive, especially concerning intellectual property rights, liability caps, and data usage permissions.
    3. Extract all key dates, payment terms, and auto-renewal conditions into a simple table.
    4. Flag any language that seems vague or ambiguous and could lead to future disputes."*

This AI-driven analysis does not replace a final legal review for a major contract, but it arms you with incredible leverage. You can go into a negotiation already aware of the key points, and if you do engage a human lawyer, you can direct them to the specific clauses flagged by the AI, saving them hours of reading time and saving you thousands of dollars in fees.

3. Automated Regulatory Compliance Monitoring Keeping up with the constantly changing landscape of data privacy (GDPR, CCPA) and industry-specific regulations is a full-time job. A solo founder can build an AI "Compliance Agent" to do it for them.

- **The System:** This is an **n8n** workflow that you can build to run on a weekly schedule.
- **The Process:**
    1. The workflow is programmed to monitor the official websites and news feeds of key regulatory bodies (e.g., the European Commission's GDPR news page, the FTC's website).
    2. It scrapes any new publications, guidelines, or press releases.
    3. It feeds the text of any new document into an LLM with the prompt: *"Does the content of this new regulatory update have any potential impact on my global B2B*

SaaS business? If yes, provide a one-sentence summary of the change and list any recommended action items."

The founder receives a single, consolidated email digest each week that filters out all the noise and highlights only the regulatory changes that matter to their business. This transforms compliance from a source of reactive anxiety into a proactive, manageable, and automated process.

Strategic Scenario: The Self-Running Store

To demonstrate that backend automation is not limited to purely digital products, let's explore the case of "Artisan Weave." This venture proves that even a business with complex physical inventory and global logistics can be run by a single person with the right automated systems.

The Founder: Sonia Chen, a former supply chain consultant with a passion for preserving traditional textile arts.

The Product: Artisan Weave, a premium e-commerce brand that sources unique, handcrafted rugs, blankets, and tapestries directly from small artisan co-operatives in countries like Peru, India, and Morocco. She sells them directly to consumers worldwide via a high-end online store.

The Challenge: This business model is a solo founder's nightmare of backend complexity. It involves coordinating with dozens of non-technical suppliers across different time zones, managing the logistics of international shipping, tracking physical inventory for thousands of unique, one-of-a-kind items, and calculating the precise cost and profit for each individual sale.

The Business Outcome: As a solo founder, Sonia scaled Artisan Weave to **$3 million in annual sales**, managing a dynamic inventory of over 2,000 unique SKUs and shipping products to customers in over 40 countries, all while maintaining a healthy 35% net profit margin.

The Automated Backend: Sonia's Masterpiece

Sonia's success hinges on the four interconnected backend systems she built.

1. The Automated Supply Chain & Inventory Engine Sonia's core problem was coordinating with 50+ independent artisan groups. She solved this by building a simple, multi-lingual supplier portal on **Bubble**. Each artisan leader has a secure login.

- **The Workflow:** When a co-op in Peru finishes a batch of five unique rugs, their leader logs into the portal, uploads photos from their phone, and enters basic details (dimensions, materials, their cost).
- **The Automation:** The moment they hit "submit," a **Bubble** workflow triggers. It automatically adds the five new rugs as distinct products in her **Shopify** store, setting their inventory level to "1." Simultaneously, an AI (GPT-5) takes the artisan's simple description and rewrites it into a rich, evocative, SEO-optimized product description in Artisan Weave's brand voice.
- **Predictive Ordering:** An **n8n** workflow analyzes Shopify sales data daily. It uses a predictive model to identify which styles or regions are selling fastest. If it detects that "Peruvian Alpaca Throws" are selling out quickly, it automatically drafts a new purchase order and sends a notification to the relevant co-ops via the Bubble portal, suggesting they begin production on a new batch. This keeps her bestsellers in stock without manual forecasting.

2. The Autonomous Financial Engine E-commerce profitability is notoriously difficult to track. Sonia automated it.

- **Real-Time Profitability:** Her AI bookkeeping tool, **Digits**, is connected to Shopify, her payment processor (**Stripe**), and her business bank (**Mercury**). For every single sale, Digits automatically pulls the sale price from Shopify, the specific Cost of Goods Sold (COGS) for that unique item from the Bubble supplier database, the actual shipping cost from her shipping API (**Shippo**), and the transaction fee from Stripe.
- **The Margin Dashboard:** Her live P&L dashboard shows her not just revenue, but her exact gross margin and net profit, updated in real-time. She knows instantly which products are

most profitable and which marketing channels are delivering the highest-margin customers.

3. The AI-Powered Business Intelligence Analyst With thousands of unique products and customers, spotting trends manually is impossible.

- **Sonia's AI Analyst:** Sonia connected her centralized sales and customer data to an AI BI tool like **ThoughtSpot**. She can ask it complex questions in plain English.
- **Strategic Questions:** "What is the correlation between the primary color of a rug and its average time-in-inventory?" "Which country has the highest customer lifetime value after their first purchase?"
- **Proactive Insights:** Her AI analyst does more than just answer questions. It proactively discovered a powerful trend: customers in colder climates (like Canada and Northern Europe) who bought a wool blanket in the fall were 80% more likely to make a second, larger purchase (like a rug) within 90 days than any other customer segment. Armed with this insight, Sonia set up an automated email campaign specifically targeting this group with a curated selection of rugs, resulting in a 25% increase in repeat purchase revenue.

Sonia Chen's role is not that of an operations manager, a bookkeeper, or a data analyst. She spends her time traveling the world to meet new artisan partners—the creative, human foundation of her brand—and working on long-term brand strategy. She is the conductor of a complex global enterprise, but the backend systems she built are the orchestra, playing in perfect harmony to handle the immense operational load. Her business is a powerful testament to the fact that even complex, physical product businesses can be scaled to the multi-million dollar level by a single person.

Chapter Summary & Resources

This chapter has demystified the often-feared backend of a business. We have systematically replaced the manual, time-consuming tasks of finance, data analysis, and legal compliance with intelligent, automated systems. By building this "invisible backend," you create a resilient, data-driven, and scalable foundation for your enterprise. This is the internal machinery that enables you to operate with the professionalism of a large corporation without the associated costs or complexity, freeing you to focus on what truly matters: growth.

Key Takeaways

- An automated **finance stack** (e.g., Stripe, Mercury, Digits) provides a real-time P&L and enables predictive cash flow modeling, turning finance from a chore into a strategic weapon.
- An autonomous **Business Intelligence system** gives the solo founder a 24/7 AI data analyst that answers questions in natural language and proactively surfaces hidden growth opportunities.
- **AI tools can handle the majority of routine legal work**, such as generating standard contracts, performing first-pass reviews of vendor agreements, and monitoring regulatory changes to de-risk the business.
- Automating the backend is the critical step that allows a solo founder to **escape administrative drag** and focus their limited time and energy on high-value, creative, and strategic activities.

Action Items

- **Sketch Your Financial Data Flow:** On a piece of paper, map out the flow of money for your business idea. Which platform will you use for payments (e.g., Stripe)? Which for your business bank account (e.g., Mercury)? Which tool will you connect for automated bookkeeping (e.g., Digits)?
- **Ask One Strategic Data Question:** Assume for a moment that all of your business data were perfectly centralized and accessible. What is the single most important strategic question you would ask your AI data analyst right now? (e.g., "Which of my planned features is most likely to increase customer retention?").
- **Draft One Legal AI Prompt:** Practice using an LLM for a legal task. Write a detailed prompt to generate a standard Independent Contractor Agreement for a freelance designer you hypothetically need to hire for a one-off project.

Preview of Chapter 7

We have now architected a complete, automated organization—from the customer-facing front lines to the critical internal backend. The operational machine is built. But a machine, no matter how efficient, needs a product to create and sell. In **Chapter 7, Product Development Without Teams**, we enter the engineering lab. You will learn how to leverage AI to ideate, design, build, test, and scale software products as a single person, completing the final, critical piece of your operational puzzle.

Resources and Tools

- **Finance:** Digits, Pilot.com (for tax and high-level bookkeeping), Mercury (banking), Stripe (payments).
- **Business Intelligence & Data:** ThoughtSpot, Hex, Airtable (as a user-friendly database/warehouse).
- **Legal:** LegalZoom, Clerky (for standard documents), and advanced LLMs like Claude 4 Opus for first-pass reviews

Chapter 7: Product Development Without Teams

Introduction

Picture a modern software company. The scene that comes to mind is likely one of structured, collaborative chaos: a product manager whiteboarding user flows, a scrum master leading daily stand-up meetings, a team of engineers debating system architecture, and a separate QA department methodically hunting for bugs. This entire ecosystem, long considered the mandatory engine of innovation, is built on one core assumption: that creating complex, high-quality software requires a team of specialized humans. That assumption is now obsolete.

This chapter marks the final and most critical piece of our operational puzzle. In the previous chapters, we architected the autonomous business systems that will market, sell, and support your product. In this chapter, we build the product itself. We will dismantle the traditional product lifecycle and reassemble it with AI at its core, creating a new paradigm where a single founder can ideate, design, build, test, and scale sophisticated software products.

We will explore a new world where your creative partner is an AI, your lead engineer is a large language model, and your entire quality assurance team is a suite of automated agents. This is not about simply using AI as a coding assistant to write snippets faster. It is about leveraging AI as a full-fledged, end-to-end engineering partner, enabling you to build products with a velocity and quality that can rival, and often surpass, traditionally staffed development teams. Welcome to the one-person product studio.

7.1 AI-Assisted Product Design and Development

The journey from a raw idea to a functional, interactive prototype has traditionally been a long and fractured one, marked by handoffs between product managers, UX/UI designers, and engineers. Each handoff is a potential point of friction, misunderstanding, and delay. The AI-first solo founder bypasses this friction entirely, compressing the design and development process into a single, fluid, and rapid feedback loop where they act as the creative director and AI acts as the multi-disciplinary executor.

Phase 1: AI-Powered Ideation and User Experience (UX) Design

A great product is not built on a great idea; it is built on a deep understanding of a user's problem. Before writing a single line of code, the solo founder can use an LLM as a virtual product management and UX research team to ensure the product is built on a solid, user-centric foundation.

- **Developing Personas and User Stories:** Instead of brainstorming in a vacuum, you can have a structured conversation with your AI partner.

    - **Action Item: The User-Centric Design Prompt**

    *"You are a Senior UX Researcher at IDEO. My product idea is a mobile app that uses AI to create personalized travel itineraries based on a user's interests and budget. My target audience is young professionals aged 25-35 who value unique experiences over typical tourist traps.

    Your task is to:

    1. Create two detailed user personas: 'The Weekend Explorer' and 'The Sabbatical Planner'.
    2. For each persona, outline their primary goals, motivations, and frustrations with current travel planning tools.
    3. Write three 'user stories' for 'The Weekend Explorer' persona in the format: 'As a [user type], I want to [action] so that [benefit].'"*

This process forces you to think deeply about your end-user from the very beginning and provides a clear, documented set of requirements to guide development.

Phase 2: AI-Generated UI Mockups and Design Systems

With a clear user flow defined, the next step is translating it into a visual user interface (UI). This no longer requires hiring a freelance designer.

- **From Text to High-Fidelity Mockups:** Using text-to-UI platforms like **Galileo AI** or the generative features built into design tools like **Figma**, you can turn your user stories into polished visual designs. **Prompt:** *"Generate a UI mockup for a mobile app screen titled 'My Trip to Tokyo.' It should have a clean, airy aesthetic like Airbnb. The screen must display a daily itinerary in a scrollable list format, a small interactive map at the top, and buttons for 'Edit Interests' and 'Share Plan'."* Within minutes, you have a high-quality visual mockup that would have taken a human designer hours or days to create.
- **Instantaneous Design Systems:** To ensure visual consistency, you can ask an AI to create a complete design system for your product. **Prompt:** *"Generate a design system for my travel app. I want a color palette based on muted earth tones, a modern sans-serif typography pairing, and button styles with soft, rounded corners."* The AI will provide specific color codes, font names, and CSS values, creating a professional brand identity instantly.

Phase 3: AI-Powered Code Generation (The AI Co-Pilot)

This is the phase where the visual blueprint becomes a functional reality. The solo founder's role evolves from a manual typist of code to a high-level architect who directs their AI co-pilot.

- **The Tools:** This goes far beyond simple code completion. Modern tools like **GitHub Copilot Enterprise** (or its 2025 equivalent) function as true development partners. They are integrated directly into your code editor and can understand the entire context of your project.

- **The High-Level Prompting Workflow:** You don't ask the AI to write a single line; you ask it to build an entire feature. Taking the UI mockup from the previous phase, you can issue a series of high-level prompts.
    1. **Prompt for Structure:** *"Using React Native, create the file structure and boilerplate code for the 'Itinerary' screen based on the attached UI mockup."*
    2. **Prompt for Functionality:** *"Now, write the JavaScript function that will fetch itinerary data from a remote API endpoint and populate the list component. It needs to handle loading states and potential errors."*
    3. **Prompt for Interaction:** *"Make the list items tappable. When a user taps an item, it should open a detailed view modal with more information about that location."*

The solo founder acts as the lead architect, directing the AI to build components, connecting those components together, and reviewing the generated code for logic and correctness. This component-based approach allows a single person to assemble a complex application with breathtaking speed, turning weeks of traditional development work into a few days of prompt engineering and systems integration.

7.2 Quality Assurance and Bug Detection

In a traditional software company, Quality Assurance (QA) is a separate team and a distinct phase of development—a bottleneck that often occurs just before a major launch. This model is slow and inefficient. The solo founder cannot afford a separate QA phase; instead, they build an automated, AI-powered QA system that is woven directly into the development process. This system acts as a vigilant, tireless team of testers, working 24/7 to catch bugs, identify security flaws, and ensure a high-quality user experience from the very first line of code.

The Pillars of an Automated QA Strategy

A robust automated QA framework is built on three pillars that cover everything from individual code components to the full user experience.

Pillar 1: AI-Generated Unit & Integration Tests The foundation of software quality is a strong suite of automated tests that verify your code works as expected. Writing these tests is critically important but can be tedious. This is a perfect task for an AI.

- **The Concept:** A "unit test" checks a small, isolated piece of code (like a single function), while an "integration test" ensures that multiple pieces work together correctly.
- **The AI Solution:** Your AI co-pilot (like **GitHub Copilot**) is an expert test writer. After you've written a new function, you can prompt the AI directly in your code editor.

Action Item: The Test Generation Prompt

"I have just written this JavaScript function that calculates a user's total subscription cost based on their plan and the number of team members. Your task is to write a complete test suite for this function using the Jest testing framework. You must include tests for all valid inputs, as well as edge cases like zero team members, negative numbers, non-numeric inputs, and a test to ensure it handles large numbers correctly without overflowing."

- **The Value:** With a single command, you get a comprehensive safety net. Before you deploy any new code, you can run hundreds of these tests in seconds. If a test fails, you know you've introduced a bug and can fix it immediately, preventing it from ever reaching your users.

Pillar 2: Automated End-to-End (E2E) User Simulation While unit tests check the code's plumbing, E2E tests check the entire user journey. They simulate a real user clicking through your application to ensure the complete workflow is seamless.

- **The AI Solution:** Modern testing platforms like **Testim.io** or open-source frameworks like **Playwright** now incorporate AI to make E2E testing radically simpler. Instead of writing complex scripts, you can simply "record" a user journey. You perform the actions once—signing up, creating a project, uploading a file—and the AI observes your actions, automatically generating a stable, repeatable test script.

- **Visual Regression Testing:** These tools also bring the power of computer vision to QA. During a test, the AI takes a pixel-perfect screenshot of each page and compares it to a baseline "golden" image. If a new code change accidentally misaligns a button by two pixels, changes a color, or causes a layout shift on a specific mobile screen size, the visual regression test will fail. This catches subtle but unprofessional UI bugs that human testers often miss.

Pillar 3: Proactive Security and Quality Analysis The best way to fix a bug or a security vulnerability is to prevent it from being written in the first place. AI tools can act as a vigilant code reviewer that never gets tired.

- **AI Security Scanning:** Tools like **GitHub Advanced Security** or **Snyk** are integrated directly into your development workflow. They use AI models trained on vast databases of known vulnerabilities to scan your code in real-time. If you write a piece of code that is susceptible to a common attack like SQL injection, the tool will flag it instantly, explain the vulnerability, and often suggest the exact line of code to fix it.
- **AI Code Quality Review:** You can also use your LLM as a senior code reviewer. Before finalizing a feature, you can paste the code into the AI. **Prompt:** *"You are a Principal Engineer at Google, famous for your high standards for code quality. Please review the following Python code. Do not just check for errors. Look for 'code smells,' areas that could be refactored for better performance or readability, and ensure the code adheres to modern best practices."*

By integrating these three pillars into a **Continuous Integration/Continuous Deployment (CI/CD)** pipeline using a tool like GitHub Actions, the entire QA process becomes automated. Every time you commit new code, a workflow is triggered that runs all your security scans, unit tests, and E2E simulations. Only if every single test passes is the code automatically deployed to your users. This automated QA system provides an unparalleled level of confidence, allowing you to ship new features faster than your competitors while maintaining a higher standard of quality and security.

7.3 Feature Prioritization Using AI Analytics

In a traditional software company, the product roadmap is a battlefield. The sales team champions the features requested by their biggest clients, the marketing team pushes for features that will make a splash, and the engineering team advocates for refactoring technical debt. The result is often a roadmap built on compromise, intuition, and the influence of the loudest voice in the room. The solo founder cannot afford such subjectivity. Every hour spent building the wrong feature is a direct, unrecoverable loss.

To solve this, the solo founder replaces the chaotic battlefield with a calm, data-driven laboratory. They use AI to build a system that objectively analyzes user feedback and behavior, ensuring that every development cycle is spent on the single most impactful feature. This is achieved by supercharging a classic prioritization framework—RICE—with artificial intelligence.

The AI-Powered R.I.C.E. Framework

The RICE framework scores potential features on four criteria to determine their priority:

- **Reach:** How many users will this feature impact?
- **Impact:** How much will this feature move a key metric (like conversion or retention)?
- **Confidence:** How confident are we that this feature will achieve the desired impact?
- **Effort:** How much work will this take to build?

The final score is calculated as `(Reach × Impact × Confidence) / Effort`. The feature with the highest score is the top priority. Here's how a solo founder uses AI to score each component objectively.

Step 1: Create a Unified Feedback Funnel First, all user feedback must be centralized. Using an automation tool like **n8n**, you can create a workflow that pipes every piece of qualitative data—customer support tickets, feature request form submissions, survey responses, App Store reviews, and community comments—into a single, unified database in a tool like **Notion** or **Airtable**.

Step 2: Use AI for Thematic Analysis and to Score *Reach* An LLM like **Claude 4 Opus** can be programmed to read this entire database every day.

- **The Prompt:** *"You are a product analyst. Analyze all new user feedback entries from the last 24 hours. Group similar requests into common feature themes (e.g., 'Slack Integration,' 'Dark Mode,' 'Advanced Reporting'). For each theme, count the number of unique users who have requested it and update the master count in our feature database."*
- **The Result:** This process automatically generates an objective **Reach** score. You know with certainty that 'Slack Integration' has been requested by 250 users, while 'Dark Mode' has only been requested by 45.

Step 3: Use AI to Model *Impact* For each feature theme, you must estimate its potential impact on your North Star metric. Your AI BI tool (from Chapter 6) is perfect for this.

- **The Analysis:** You can ask your BI tool, *"Analyze the user segment that has requested 'Advanced Reporting.' What is their average LTV and churn rate compared to the platform average?"*
- **The Result:** If the AI reveals that these are your highest-value users and they are churning at a higher-than-average rate, you know the **Impact** of building this feature will be very high (e.g., a score of 9/10) because it will help retain your best customers.

Step 4: Use AI to Quantify *Confidence* Confidence is often the fuzziest metric. AI can add objectivity by analyzing the language of the requests.

- **The Prompt:** *"Analyze the sentiment and urgency of all 250 requests for the 'Slack Integration' feature. Categorize each request as 'Nice to Have,' 'Important,' or 'Critical/Deal-Breaker.' What percentage of users are explicitly stating they will churn or not purchase without this feature?"*
- **The Result:** If the AI reports that 60% of requests are "Critical" and use language like "we can't use your product without this," your **Confidence** score will be very high (e.g., 95%).

Step 5: Use AI to Estimate *Effort* Finally, you need an estimate of the development effort.

- **The Prompt:** Give your AI co-pilot a high-level technical brief. *"You are a senior engineering lead. Given our current tech stack, provide a rough estimate of the effort required to build a full, bi-directional integration with the Slack API. Provide the estimate in a range of 'developer-days'."*
- **The Result:** The AI might estimate the feature will take 5-7 days of focused work. This number becomes your denominator for the **Effort** score.

By running this process, you generate a simple, data-backed, ranked list of features. The product roadmap is no longer a matter of opinion. It is a living document, continuously and automatically reprioritized by the collective voice of your users and the analytical power of your AI. This ensures your most valuable resource—your own time—is always dedicated to building what matters most.

Strategic Scenario: The One-Person Software Conglomerate

The ultimate expression of AI-driven leverage is not just building a single successful product, but managing an entire portfolio of them. The story of "Studio AI" demonstrates how a solo founder can become a one-person software conglomerate, launching and maintaining multiple distinct, profitable products simultaneously.

The Founder: Javier "Javi" Rojas, a designer and self-taught developer who saw an opportunity not just to build one tool, but a suite of "micro-SaaS" products for a specific audience.

The Concept: Studio AI, a parent brand for a collection of small, targeted AI-powered tools for creative professionals. Each tool solves one specific, painful problem and is designed to be largely self-running.

The Product Portfolio:

1. **CopyCraft AI:** An AI copywriter trained specifically to generate high-converting product descriptions for e-commerce stores on platforms like Shopify.
2. **Visualyze AI:** An AI tool that takes a simple text prompt and generates a month's worth of on-brand social media visuals and ad creatives for platforms like Instagram and Facebook.
3. **TuneFlow AI:** An AI that generates high-quality, royalty-free background music in various genres for video creators and podcasters.

The Business Outcome: Javi simultaneously runs all three profitable products, achieving a combined **ARR of $1.5 million**. He manages the entire portfolio himself, working approximately 30 hours per week.

The Architecture of a One-Person Studio
Javi's success is not magic; it is a masterclass in system design and shared infrastructure.

1. The Unified "Studio" Infrastructure Javi's most brilliant decision was to not build three separate companies. He built a single, unified backend on **Bubble** that handles the core infrastructure for all three products. A user creates one "Studio AI" account, and from their central dashboard, they can subscribe to CopyCraft, Visualyze, or TuneFlow. Billing, user authentication, and customer data are all managed by this central Bubble app, connected to a single **Stripe** account. This "build once, serve many" approach drastically reduced his initial and ongoing development overhead.

2. AI-Powered Concurrent Product Management Javi acts as the "Studio Head," managing three product roadmaps at once.

- **The Unified RICE Model:** All user feedback from all three products funnels into a single Notion database. His AI-powered RICE prioritization system (as described in the previous section) runs across the entire portfolio. This allows him to see, for example, that the highest-impact feature across his entire business might be adding a new language model to CopyCraft, even if Visualyze users are being louder. He allocates his time based on objective data for the whole portfolio.
- **Parallel Development with an AI Co-Pilot:** Javi doesn't write code for three products; he directs his **GitHub Copilot** to write code for three products. He allocates his week in blocks: Monday is for improving CopyCraft's AI, Tuesday is for adding new visual styles to Visualyze, Wednesday is for enhancing TuneFlow's audio quality. Because the AI handles the bulk of the tedious coding, he can context-switch effectively, acting as the architect for three separate projects in the same week.

3. The Automated, Cross-Promotional Ecosystem This is Javi's primary growth lever. His **n8n** automation workflows create a synergistic ecosystem where the products sell each other.

- **Intelligent Cross-Selling:** The system analyzes user behavior. If a user on CopyCraft frequently generates descriptions for skincare products, the system flags them as a beauty e-commerce brand. A workflow is then triggered, sending them a personalized email: *"We see you're creating brilliant copy for your products with CopyCraft AI. Ready to create stunning social media ads to match? For the next 48 hours, get 30% off your first month of Visualyze AI."*
- **Bundled Subscriptions:** His Bubble backend allows for bundled pricing ("Get all three Studio AI tools and save 40%"), which is automatically offered to users who subscribe to any two of the

three products, dramatically increasing the average LTV per customer.

The Founder's Role: From Developer to Studio Head

Javi's daily work does not resemble that of a traditional founder. He does not spend his days buried in code or support tickets. He functions as the head of a creative studio. His primary tasks are:

1. **Greenlighting Projects:** Deciding on the next "micro-SaaS" tool to add to the Studio AI portfolio.
2. **Managing the Portfolio:** Reviewing the unified RICE roadmap to decide where to allocate his "development" time for maximum impact across the entire business.
3. **Directing the Symphony:** Tweaking the AI prompts and n8n workflows that form the connective tissue of his automated, cross-promoting ecosystem.

Javi's story shows the ultimate evolution of the solo founder. By leveraging a unified infrastructure, AI development partners, and intelligent automation, a single person is no longer limited to a single product. They can become a studio, a portfolio manager, a one-person software conglomerate, achieving a level of diversified, scalable success that was once the exclusive domain of large corporations.

Chapter Summary & Resources

This chapter concludes our journey into the operational core of the automated enterprise. We have demonstrated how the entire product development lifecycle—once the exclusive domain of large, specialized teams—can be effectively managed and executed by a single individual. By leveraging AI as a partner in design, a co-pilot in development, a vigilant tester in QA, and a data-driven analyst for prioritization, the solo founder can build sophisticated, high-quality products at an unprecedented velocity.

Key Takeaways

- The product design and development process can be compressed from months to days by using AI for UX research, UI mockups, and code generation.
- A robust, automated **QA system** using AI for test generation, user simulation, and security scanning allows for rapid and confident deployment of new features.
- An AI-powered **RICE model** transforms feature prioritization from a subjective debate into an objective, data-driven process, ensuring you always build what matters most.
- The solo founder is **not limited to a single product**; by using a unified backend infrastructure and AI development assistants, they can manage an entire portfolio of software tools.

Action Items

- **Design an AI-Assisted User Flow:** Take your primary product idea and use an LLM to act as your UX researcher. Prompt it to generate a detailed user flow for a key feature, from the moment the user decides to use it to the moment they achieve their desired outcome.
- **Create an Automated Test Prompt:** Write a specific, detailed prompt for an AI co-pilot to generate a suite of unit tests for a hypothetical but critical function in your app (e.g., "a function that processes a user's payment and updates their subscription status").
- **Run a Mini-RICE Analysis:** List three potential features for your product idea. First, do a quick, gut-level RICE score for each. Then, for each of the four components (Reach, Impact, Confidence, Effort), write down how an AI could help you get a more objective, data-driven score.

Preview of Part 3: The Scaling Playbook

In Part 2, we have assembled your entire AI-powered organization. You have the Foundation Stack, the automated customer-facing operations, the invisible backend, and now, the AI-assisted product development lifecycle. The machine is complete. In **Part 3, The Scaling Playbook**, we finally turn the key and start the engine. We move from building these autonomous systems to using them to generate revenue and scale your enterprise to massive heights, starting with **Chapter 8: The Million-Dollar Milestone**, where we will lay out the 90-day strategy to launch your product and achieve your first seven figures in revenue.

Resources and Tools

- **Design/UI:** Galileo AI, Figma (with its AI plugins like "Diagram" and "Magician").
- **Development:** GitHub Copilot Enterprise.
- **QA/Testing:** Testim.io (for AI-powered E2E testing), Playwright (for scriptable testing), GitHub Actions (for CI/CD pipelines).
- **Prioritization Framework:** Research the RICE and ICE scoring models for a deeper understanding of product prioritization principles.

Part 3: The Scaling Playbook

The "How": Actionable strategies to go from launch to million-dollar revenue and beyond.

Chapter 8: The Million-Dollar Milestone

Introduction

The machine is built. In Part 2 of this book, we assembled your AI Arsenal piece by piece. You have a Foundation Stack to power your operations, an autonomous engine to manage your customer interactions, an invisible backend to handle your finances, and an AI co-pilot to build your product. The engine is tuned and humming with potential. It is time to leave the garage and join the race.

Welcome to Part 3: The Scaling Playbook. This is where we translate the incredible potential of your automated enterprise into tangible business results: revenue, growth, and market dominance. This part of the book is not about building systems; it is about using those systems to execute a focused strategy for exponential growth.

Our first objective is a critical one: the **million-dollar milestone**. Achieving $1 million in Annual Recurring Revenue (ARR) is the first great checkpoint on the journey to a billion-dollar valuation. It is the market's definitive validation of your product and business model. It proves that you have achieved product-market fit, and it provides the financial fuel and strategic leverage for the next phase of scaling. For a solo founder, operating with the massive profit margins described by the Economics of One, a million-dollar business is a life-altering achievement.

This chapter provides the tactical, week-by-week playbook to get you there. We will define the most scalable business model for a solo founder and then lay out an aggressive 90-day strategy to take your validated idea, build an AI-assisted Minimum Viable Product (MVP), and secure your first paying customers. The million-dollar milestone is not a distant dream; it is a concrete target, and this is your plan to hit it.

8.1 Defining Your Scalable Business Model

Before you can execute a single line of code or launch a single marketing campaign, you must make the most important strategic decision of your entrepreneurial journey: choosing your business model. This choice will dictate the ultimate potential of your enterprise. For the solo founder, the ideal business model is not just one that can generate revenue; it must be one that is inherently designed for extreme scalability, high margins, and maximum automation. While countless models exist, three stand out as the primary contenders in the digital economy: Software as a Service (SaaS), the Marketplace, and the Platform.

1. Software as a Service (SaaS): The Gold Standard A SaaS model is one where customers pay a recurring fee, typically monthly or annually, for ongoing access to a software product. This is the default, gold-standard model for a solo founder for several powerful reasons.

- **Predictable Recurring Revenue:** The subscription model is the holy grail of business finance. It creates a predictable, stable stream of revenue (Monthly Recurring Revenue, or MRR) that allows for accurate financial forecasting and smooth, non-lumpy growth. This predictability is invaluable for a solo founder managing their own cash flow.
- **Exceptional Profit Margins:** The marginal cost of serving one additional SaaS customer is near zero. Once the core software is built and the automated systems are in place, the cost to support the ten-thousandth customer is virtually identical to the cost to support the hundredth. This leads to exceptional gross margins (often 80-90%+) that scale beautifully.
- **Hyper-Automation Friendly:** The entire SaaS customer lifecycle is perfectly suited for the automation we have discussed. From automated marketing funnels to self-serve onboarding, AI-powered customer support, and automated billing and upselling, a solo founder can genuinely run a global SaaS business with minimal manual intervention.

For solo founders, the most viable path is typically **niche B2B SaaS**. By focusing on solving a specific, expensive problem for a specific business audience (e.g., "AI-powered compliance reporting for small wealth management firms"), you can command higher prices, benefit from lower customer churn, and more easily target your automated sales and marketing efforts.

2. The Marketplace: The High-Risk, High-Reward Play A marketplace is a two-sided business that connects buyers with sellers of a product or service and takes a small percentage of each transaction (the "take rate"). Think of giants like Airbnb (connecting travelers with hosts) or Upwork (connecting businesses with freelancers).

- **The Challenge: The "Chicken-and-Egg Problem."** The fundamental difficulty of a marketplace is getting started. You need a critical mass of sellers to attract buyers, but you need buyers to attract sellers. Solving this problem typically requires immense capital and a manual sales effort to painstakingly build one side of the market before the other will show up.
- **The AI Exception:** For the first time, AI offers a potential solution to this dilemma. A solo founder could use generative AI to **simulate liquidity** on one side of the marketplace at launch. For example, to start a marketplace for graphic designers, an AI could generate hundreds of realistic, high-quality designer profiles and portfolios to attract the first clients. As real designers sign up, the AI-generated profiles are gradually phased out.
- **The Upside: Network Effects.** If you can solve the chicken-and-egg problem, the reward is immense. A successful marketplace benefits from powerful network effects—each new user adds value for all other users—creating a deep, defensible moat that is very difficult for competitors to assail.

For the solo founder, the marketplace model is an advanced maneuver. It is significantly harder to launch than a SaaS product, but if successful, its potential scale is enormous.

3. The Platform: The Billion-Dollar Endgame A platform is the final evolution of a software business. It's a model where a company builds a core service so successful that other developers and companies begin to build their own businesses on top of it, typically through an official App

Store or API program. Think of the Salesforce AppExchange or the Shopify App Store.

- **The Ultimate Leverage:** A platform is the most powerful and defensible business model in existence. As a solo founder, you are no longer just leveraging your own AI systems; you are leveraging the creative and developmental energy of thousands of third-party developers who are expanding your product's capabilities and ecosystem for you.
- **The Path to Platform:** You do not start by building a platform. You evolve into one. The path typically looks like this:
    1. Build a wildly successful niche SaaS product.
    2. Gain significant market traction and a passionate user base.
    3. Open up a robust, well-documented API.
    4. Nurture a community of developers who build integrations for their own needs.
    5. Formalize this by launching an official App Marketplace, creating a revenue-sharing model.

For the solo founder aiming for a billion-dollar valuation, this is the ultimate strategic goal. But it is a destination, not a starting point. The journey for 99% of solo founders should begin with the clean, scalable, and highly automatable model of niche B2B SaaS. Master that first, achieve your million-dollar milestone, and then you can begin the journey to becoming a platform.

8.2 The 90-Day Launch Strategy

You have an idea. You have chosen your business model. Now, it is time for execution. This section provides a tactical, week-by-week playbook for going from a standing start to a launched product with your first paying customers in a single 90-day sprint. This aggressive timeline is not a fantasy; it is a testament to the speed and leverage afforded by the AI-powered tools and frameworks we have assembled. This is where the machine starts to run.

Phase 1: Validation and Foundation (Weeks 1-2)

The goal of this phase is to validate your core assumption and lay the digital groundwork before writing a single line of product code.

- **Week 1: The 24-Hour Validation Cycle.** Your very first action is to run your core idea through the validation cycle from Chapter 3. Build an AI-generated smoke test landing page, define your core hypothesis, drive a small amount of hyper-targeted traffic to it, and rigorously analyze the signals. Do not proceed to Week 2 until you have a clear "Persevere" signal from the market. This single step will save you months of wasted effort if your initial idea is flawed.
- **Week 2: The Foundation Stack Setup.** Once validated, you build the scaffolding. This week is for infrastructure, not product.
    - Purchase your domain name.
    - Create your business bank account with **Mercury**.
    - Set up your core accounts: **Bubble** (for the app), **Webflow** (for the marketing site), **n8n** (for automation), **Stripe** (for payments), and get your API keys for **OpenAI** or **Anthropic**.
    - Build the basic, empty shell of your application: the user login/signup flow in Bubble and a "coming soon" page on Webflow.

Phase 2: Minimum Viable Product (MVP) Development (Weeks 3-8)

This is the six-week build sprint. The goal is not to build every feature you've ever dreamed of, but to build an MVP that solves **one problem** exceptionally well.

- **Weeks 3-4: The Core Feature Build.** Dedicate this entire two-week block to building the single most important feature of your product—the one that delivers the "wow" moment and proves your value proposition. Use your AI co-pilot extensively to write the back-end logic and front-end components. Your sole focus is on making this one feature work flawlessly.
- **Weeks 5-6: The "Wrapper" Features.** Now, build the necessary features that surround the core experience. This includes the user profile page, account settings, and, most

importantly, the subscription management and billing pages, fully integrated with Stripe.

- **Week 7: The Automated Onboarding Experience.** Your user onboarding is not an afterthought; it is a critical feature. Use **n8n** to design and build the automated email sequence that will guide new users from sign-up to activation, ensuring they understand how to use your core feature and experience its value as quickly as possible.
- **Week 8: The Automated QA Cycle.** Dedicate this entire week to quality. Run your full suite of AI-powered tests from Chapter 7: unit tests, integration tests, E2E user simulations, and security scans. Find and fix every critical bug. At the end of this week, your MVP should be stable, secure, and ready for its first users.

Phase 3: Launch and First Revenue (Weeks 9-12)

The product is built. This phase is about launching it into the world and acquiring your first ten paying customers.

- **Week 9: The Pre-Launch Hype.** Begin warming up your audience. Reach out personally to the people who signed up on your initial validation landing page. Offer them free lifetime access in exchange for being beta testers and providing testimonials. Use your autonomous marketing engine to start publishing valuable content related to the problem you solve.
- **Week 10: LAUNCH DAY.** The moment of truth. "Flip the switch" to make your payment forms live. Announce the launch to your email list, on your personal social media accounts, and in the niche online communities where your target users gather. A well-executed launch on a platform like **Product Hunt** can provide a significant initial surge of traffic and attention.
- **Week 11: Obsessive Listening.** Your first real users are now in the system. Your automated support agent is handling their basic questions, but your job this week is to listen with an intensity you will never have again. Watch user session recordings. Analyze where people get stuck. And most importantly, personally email your first ten paying customers to thank them, ask why they signed up, and what they hope to achieve.

- **Week 12: The First Iteration.** Take all the feedback and data from Week 11 and feed it into your AI-powered RICE prioritization model. Identify the single most impactful bug fix or small feature improvement you can make. Use your AI co-pilot to build and deploy it by the end of the week. Announce the update to your new users. This proves that you are listening and that the product is alive and improving, which is the single best way to build loyalty and turn your first ten customers into passionate advocates.

At the end of these 90 days, you have done what once took teams a year or more to accomplish. You have gone from a mere idea to a validated, launched, revenue-generating business with a built-in system for continuous improvement. The launchpad is built. The journey to the million-dollar milestone has officially begun.

8.3 Revenue Stream Diversification

You have launched your core product. The first stream of recurring revenue—the lifeblood of your business—has begun to flow. While nurturing and growing this primary engine is your top priority, the savvy solo founder understands the power of diversification. Building complementary, low-effort revenue streams is not a distraction; it is a strategic move that builds resilience, increases customer lifetime value (LTV), and captures value from your audience that your core subscription might miss. The key is that any new stream must be highly automated and leverage your existing systems and audience, adding to your bottom line without significantly taxing your time.

The Value-Ladder Framework

Think of your core SaaS product as the central rung on a ladder. Your goal is to add rungs both below and above it, creating multiple ways for a customer to give you money, depending on their level of commitment and need.

1. The Low-Effort Info Product: Monetizing Your Expertise You have built a product to solve a specific problem, which means you are now an expert in that domain. You can package this expertise into a digital information product—like an e-book or a short video course—and sell it as a low-cost, high-margin offering.

- **The AI-Powered Creation Workflow:** This does not need to take months. You can leverage the content already created by your autonomous marketing engine.

    Action Item: The E-book Generation Prompt

    *"You are a bestselling author and editor. I have provided you with the 50 most popular articles from my blog, which covers the topic of [Your Niche]. Your task is to analyze all of this content and repurpose it into a comprehensive, 20,000-word e-book titled 'The Definitive Guide to [Your Niche]'. You must:

    1. Structure the content into a logical sequence of 10 chapters.
    2. Rewrite and expand upon the blog content to create a consistent, authoritative voice.
    3. Generate a new, compelling introduction and a concluding chapter with actionable takeaways.
    4. Suggest five potential titles for the e-book."*

- **The Strategic Value:** This e-book can be sold for $39 on your website. It serves two purposes: it generates almost pure profit, and it acts as a powerful "tripwire" product for customers who are not yet ready to commit to your monthly SaaS subscription.

2. The Automated Affiliate Engine: Earning from Your Ecosystem
Your users see you as a trusted guide in your niche. When you ethically recommend other products and services that you genuinely use and believe in, you can earn affiliate commissions.

- **The Strategy:** Create a "/tools" or "/resources" page on your website. Use an AI copywriter to help you write authentic, detailed reviews of the products in your own tech stack (e.g., Bubble, Webflow, Mercury) and other complementary tools that your customers would find valuable. Include your unique affiliate links.
- **The Automated Workflow:** You can also build this into your product's automated onboarding. For example, if your product helps users create websites, your automated welcome email sequence could include a message like: *"Step 3: Choosing a great host. We build our own systems on [Hosting Provider] because of their speed and reliability. Here's a link to get started."* This provides genuine value to the user while creating a hands-off revenue stream for you.

3. The Premium Concierge Service: High-Ticket, Low-Volume This is the highest rung on your value ladder, designed for a tiny fraction of your most committed customers. It involves offering a high-priced, "done-for-you" service that leverages your expertise and AI tools to deliver incredible value with minimal time input from you.

- **The Concept:** Let's say your SaaS product is an AI that helps users optimize their online advertising campaigns. The core product is the self-serve tool. The premium service could be a "$1,000 One-Day Ad Account Overhaul."
- **The AI-Leveraged Delivery:** A customer purchases the service. They grant you temporary access to their ad account. You spend 90 minutes using a suite of your own advanced AI prompts and internal tools to perform a deep analysis, identify key areas for improvement, rewrite their ad copy, and generate a detailed, personalized strategy document. The value delivered is immense, but your time investment is small.
- **The Benefit:** This is not meant to be a scalable business in itself. By intentionally limiting it (e.g., "Only 3 slots available per month"), you create scarcity and urgency. It acts as a powerful cash-flow injection and provides you with deep insights from your most valuable customers, which can then inform your core product's roadmap.

By thoughtfully layering these automated revenue streams around your core product, you create a robust, multi-faceted financial ecosystem. This diversification makes your business more resilient to market shifts and significantly more profitable over the long term.

8.4 Strategic Scenarios: Solo Founders Hitting 7-Figure Revenue

The million-dollar milestone for a solo founder is not a theoretical unicorn. It is an achievable reality being demonstrated by a growing class of entrepreneurs who masterfully combine a niche problem with an automated system. Here are two distinct examples.

Case Study 1: The B2B Compliance Engine

- **Founder:** David Chen, a former paralegal who saw firsthand how small financial firms struggled with compliance.
- **The Problem:** Financial advisory firms with 5-50 employees are legally required to archive all client communications and ensure every outgoing email contains specific, up-to-date legal disclaimers. A failure can result in six-figure fines. This is a high-stakes, low-glamour problem.
- **The Product:** "ComplyBot," a simple, niche B2B SaaS product. It integrates directly with a firm's Microsoft 365 or Google Workspace account. Using a fine-tuned LLM, it scans every outgoing email in real-time. It checks for potential compliance violations, automatically appends the correct, jurisdiction-specific legal disclaimer, and saves a copy of every communication in a secure, encrypted, and instantly searchable archive for audit purposes.
- **The Path to $1.2M ARR:**
    - **Niche Focus:** David's masterstroke was ignoring the large banks and focusing exclusively on the underserved market of small-to-mid-sized advisory firms.
    - **ROI-Driven Outreach:** He used an automated sales stack (Apollo, Clay, Instantly) to target the managing partners of these firms. His message was brutally effective: "Are you confident your firm is 100%

compliant with SEC Rule 206(4)-7? Avoid a $100,000 fine for a $99/month subscription." The value proposition was undeniable.

- **Authority Marketing:** His autonomous marketing engine produced a steady stream of high-value blog posts and white papers on regulatory changes, quickly establishing ComplyBot as a thought leader in the space and driving high-intent inbound leads.
- **Simple Pricing:** David offered a simple, per-firm pricing model starting at $99/month. The product's "stickiness" was incredible—once integrated, no firm wanted to risk the compliance headache of leaving. With minimal churn, he steadily grew to over 1,000 paying firms in about 24 months, crossing the $1.2 million ARR mark.

- **Key Takeaway:** Solving a painful, expensive, and complex B2B problem, even in a "boring" niche, is one of the most reliable paths to seven figures. The ROI for the customer is so clear that the product sells itself.

Case Study 2: The Creator Economy "Pickaxe"

- **Founder:** Maria Flores, a former content creator who was burning out from the endless content treadmill.
- **The Problem:** Video podcasters and streamers create hours of valuable long-form content each week, but they lack the time and energy to repurpose it into the short-form vertical videos (for TikTok, YouTube Shorts, etc.) that are essential for audience growth.
- **The Product:** "VidStream AI." A user simply connects their YouTube channel or pastes a video link. The AI gets to work. It transcribes the entire video, uses sentiment analysis and topic modeling to identify the 5-10 most compelling and "viral" moments, automatically edits those moments into vertical clips, adds dynamic, animated captions, and assigns each clip a "virality score" to help the creator choose the best ones to post.
- **The Path to $2M ARR:**

    - **Community-Led Growth:** As a creator herself, Maria understood her audience. She launched VidStream AI on Product Hunt and in private creator communities. The product was inherently viral; creators would use it to make clips, post them, and then other creators would ask, "How did you make that?"
    - **Freemium Flywheel:** Maria offered a generous free plan that allowed anyone to process one video per month. This allowed her to build a massive top-of-funnel. Her paid plans ($29/$59/$99 per month) were tiered based on the number of videos processed, creating a clear upgrade path as a creator's channel grew.
    - **Smart Diversification:** Maria added two low-effort revenue streams. First, an affiliate page for other creator tools (cameras, microphones, editing software) that she genuinely recommended. Second, an AI-generated e-book, "The Science of Short-Form Virality," which she sold for $29 and also used as a lead magnet.
    - **The Viral Loop:** The product's core function was its marketing. The more people who used VidStream AI, the more clips were shared across social media, which acted as free advertising that drove more users back to the tool. This powerful, self-perpetuating loop allowed her to scale to over 5,000 paying customers and cross the $2 million ARR mark with virtually zero ad spend.
- **Key Takeaway:** In a growing "gold rush" (like the creator economy), one of the best business models is to sell the "pickaxes." By creating a tool that saves time and creates tangible value for a large, passionate community, you can leverage their collective success to fuel your own exponential growth.

Chapter Summary & Resources

This chapter marks the transition from building your machine to using it to achieve your first great objective: the million-dollar milestone. We have established that reaching seven figures in revenue as a solo founder is not just possible, but a concrete goal that can be reached with a systematic approach. By selecting a scalable business model, executing a disciplined 90-day launch plan, and intelligently diversifying your revenue streams, you lay the financial and strategic foundation for the entire journey to a billion-dollar valuation.

Key Takeaways

- The **million-dollar milestone** is the critical checkpoint that proves product-market fit, validates your business model, and provides the fuel for future scaling.
- For solo founders, a **niche B2B SaaS model** offers the best combination of predictable recurring revenue, high profit margins, and extreme automation potential.
- A structured **90-day launch plan**—focused on rapid validation, lean MVP development, and acquiring the first handful of loyal customers—is essential for building momentum.
- **Diversifying revenue** with low-effort, AI-powered streams like information products and affiliate marketing builds a more resilient and profitable enterprise.

Your 90-Day Launch Checklist

- **Week 1 Goal:** Validate your core idea with an AI-powered smoke test. Do not write a line of product code until you have a clear positive signal from your target market.
- **Weeks 3-8 Goal:** Build your MVP with a singular focus on solving ONE problem perfectly. Aggressively resist the temptation for feature creep during this phase.
- **Week 10 Goal:** Launch your product on a platform like Product Hunt to generate initial buzz and personally email your first 10 paying customers to thank them and solicit feedback.
- **Post-Launch Goal:** Choose ONE complementary revenue stream (e.g., an e-book). Use your AI content engine to create and launch a basic version of it within a single week.

Preview of Chapter 9

Reaching the million-dollar milestone is a monumental achievement. But with growth comes new challenges. The systems that work for one thousand users may start to strain under the load of ten thousand. How do you maintain high quality as you scale? How do you prevent your automated workflows from breaking under pressure? In **Chapter 9, Systems That Scale You**, we address the critical challenges of growth. You will learn how to build robust operational processes, automate quality control without a team, and deliver customer success at scale, ensuring your journey to ten million is as smooth as your journey to one.

Resources and Tools

- **Business Model Deep Dives:** Read Andrew Chen's essays on network effects and "the cold start problem" for a masterclass on marketplace dynamics.
- **Launch Platforms:** Product Hunt and BetaList are essential platforms for launching a new tech product to an audience of early adopters.
- **Community & Inspiration:** The Indie Hackers community and podcast are invaluable resources for real-world case studies and transparent conversations with founders who are on this exact journey.

Chapter 9: Systems That Scale You

Introduction

You have reached the million-dollar milestone. It is a monumental achievement, a testament to your vision and the power of the automated systems you built in Part 2. But with success comes a new, more dangerous set of challenges. The very growth you worked so hard for now threatens to overwhelm you. The ad-hoc processes that worked for one thousand users begin to fray at five thousand and snap completely at ten thousand. You find yourself working 80-hour weeks, not on strategy, but on putting out fires just to keep the business running. This is the scaling trap, and it is where many promising ventures stagnate and die.

The solution requires a fundamental shift in your role as a founder. You must evolve from being the **doer** of tasks to being the **designer of systems that do the tasks for you**. Your job is no longer to run the business; it is to build a business that runs itself, even at ten times the current scale. This chapter is about building that resilience.

In Chapter 8, we laid out the playbook to launch and secure your first million in revenue. In this chapter, we will provide the framework to ensure your success is sustainable. We will explore how to create robust processes that don't break under pressure, how to implement automated quality control systems that maintain excellence without a team, and how to deliver customer success at scale. This is how you build an enterprise that scales you, instead of an operation that crushes you.

9.1 Building Processes That Don't Break

The greatest single point of failure in any solo-founded business is the founder's own brain. In the early days, you can get by with having all the operational knowledge—how to handle a complex refund, how to onboard a new enterprise client, how to update a critical piece of infrastructure—stored as tacit knowledge in your head. This is fast and efficient, but it is incredibly fragile. If you get sick, need a vacation, or simply forget a crucial step, the entire business is at risk. To build a truly scalable enterprise, you must externalize this knowledge into a documented, automated system. This process of systematization is how you create a digital clone of your operational brain, ensuring resilience and consistency as you scale.

The "SOPs for One" Framework

A Standard Operating Procedure (SOP) is not a dusty binder on a shelf; it is a living, dynamic blueprint for every repeatable task in your business. The "SOPs for One" framework is about creating a digital command center for your company that is comprehensive, easily searchable, and directly connected to your automation workflows. It's about ensuring that for every process, there is a single source of truth that both you and your AI agents can rely on.

Step 1: AI-Assisted Process Documentation The biggest obstacle to creating SOPs is the tedious nature of writing them. AI can eliminate this friction almost entirely, turning a multi-hour task into a 15-minute review process.

- **The Tools:** Use AI-powered documentation tools like **Scribe** or **Tango**. These work as simple browser extensions or desktop apps that observe you as you work.
- **The Workflow:** To document a process, you simply activate the recorder and perform the task once. For example, to create an SOP for "How to Onboard a New Affiliate Partner," you would click through the steps: adding them in your affiliate management software, creating their unique tracking link, and adding them to the affiliate email list. The tool records every click and keystroke, automatically generating a beautiful, step-by-step guide complete with annotated screenshots and written instructions.
- **AI Refinement and Optimization:** This auto-generated draft is your raw material. You then elevate it using an advanced LLM, turning a simple guide into a strategic document.

Action Item: The Advanced SOP Refinement Prompt

*"You are a world-class operations consultant from McKinsey. I have provided an auto-generated SOP for a key business task. Your job is to refine this document into a strategic asset. You must:

1. Rewrite the instructions for maximum clarity, conciseness, and precision.
2. Add a 'Purpose' section explaining the strategic goal of this process.
3. Add a 'KPIs' section defining the key metrics for measuring the success of this process (e.g., 'Time to Onboard,' 'Partner Activation Rate').
4. Add a 'Risk Analysis' section identifying the step with the highest potential for error and suggest a way to re-engineer it for resilience.
5. Add a 'Related Automations' section that links to the n8n workflow that handles this task."*

Step 2: Creating the Central Brain (Your Company OS) All of these meticulously crafted SOPs must live in a single, centralized, and instantly searchable knowledge hub. A tool like **Notion** is perfectly suited for this. You can build a "Company OS" dashboard that acts as the single source of truth for your entire operation. Using Notion's database features, you can create a master SOP database where each entry is tagged with its status ('Documented,' 'Automated'), its owner (e.g., 'Founder,' 'AI Sales Agent'), and a 'Last Reviewed' date. This creates a dynamic, manageable system, not a static library of documents. This "brain" is also the core knowledge base that powers your AI Service Agent, ensuring it always has the most up-to-date information.

Step 3: From Documentation to Full Automation Documentation is the first step toward resilience, but automation is the ultimate goal. A documented process is good; a self-executing process is a scalable asset. For every SOP you create, the next critical question is: "How can I build an **n8n** workflow to perform these steps automatically?"

- **The Evolution of an SOP:** Consider the "New Customer Onboarding" SOP. The documented version shows you how to manually create a user in Bubble, a customer in Stripe, and add them to Mailchimp. The automated version is an n8n workflow triggered by a new user signup that does all of this via API calls. This workflow becomes a complex, intelligent process. For example, it first checks if the user's email domain belongs to a Fortune 500 company. If so, it tags them as a 'High-Value Lead' in your Notion CRM and sends you a personal Slack alert. If not, it proceeds with the standard onboarding sequence. The Notion SOP document now becomes the "schematic" for the automation, explaining the logic, branching paths, and purpose of the workflow.

Step 4: Automated SOP Maintenance A common failure point is that SOPs become outdated. You can build an n8n workflow that runs monthly, scans your Notion database for any SOP with a 'Last Reviewed' date older than 90 days, and automatically creates a task for you to review and update it. This ensures your company's central brain never becomes stale.

By building and maintaining this system of "SOPs for One," you are creating a digital clone of your operational brain—one that is perfectly documented, constantly improving, and increasingly autonomous. It is the foundational step in building a business that can scale far beyond your personal capacity.

9.2 Quality Control Without Quality Teams

There is a paradox at the heart of scaling: as a business grows, the quality of its product and service often declines. More users lead to more server load, more support tickets, more edge cases, and more potential points of failure. The personal touch and meticulous attention to detail that defined the early days get lost in the noise of scale. For the solo founder, solving this paradox is paramount. They must build systems that allow them to maintain, and even improve, quality as their user base grows tenfold. This requires an automated Quality Control system that acts as a vigilant, 24/7 QA team for the entire business, not just the software.

Pillar 1: Proactive System Health Monitoring You cannot afford to learn about problems from angry customers on social media. Your systems must tell you about issues before your users ever notice them. This requires moving beyond simple uptime monitoring to intelligent, AI-powered observability.

- **The Tools:** This involves using application performance monitoring (APM) platforms like **Datadog**, **New Relic**, or a more specialized AI-powered log analysis tool like **Mezmo**.
- **The AI-Powered Workflow:**
    - **Automated Health Checks:** An **n8n** workflow acts as a "digital patrol," running every five minutes to make test calls to your critical APIs (OpenAI, Stripe, etc.) and your own application's core endpoints. If any service returns an error or fails to respond within a set threshold, it immediately sends a high-priority alert to your phone.
    - **Intelligent Log Analysis:** Every action in your system generates a "log" entry. Manually reading these is impossible. An AI tool like Mezmo ingests these logs and learns the normal pattern of your business. It can then provide incredibly specific alerts. For example: **"AI Alert: Log analysis shows a 1,000% spike in 'Database Connection Timeout' errors originating from our European server cluster over the last 30 minutes. The issue appears isolated to users on the Android mobile app, version 2.1. This is a critical severity event."** This level of specificity allows you to pinpoint and fix the problem in minutes, not days.

Pillar 2: Automated Data Integrity Audits As your business grows, data flows between multiple systems (e.g., Bubble, Stripe, Mailchimp). This data can easily become out of sync, leading to billing errors or poor customer experiences.

- **The Solution: A Nightly Reconciliation Bot.** You can build a powerful workflow in **n8n** that runs every night while you sleep to audit your data's integrity.
- **The Process:** The workflow fetches key data from disparate systems and compares them. For example, it will fetch the total daily revenue reported directly by the **Stripe API** and compare it to the total daily revenue recorded in your **Bubble** application database. If these numbers don't match by more than a tiny tolerance, it flags a potential payment processing or data recording error and creates a high-priority ticket. It can also reconcile user statuses, ensuring that a customer who cancelled their subscription is correctly marked as "cancelled" across all of your marketing and support platforms, preventing them from receiving unwanted emails.

Pillar 3: AI-Powered Customer Experience Auditing How do you know if your customers are having a good experience without talking to every single one? You build a system to audit their experience automatically.

- **Automated Sentiment Analysis:** All user feedback is piped through an LLM to assign a sentiment score. You have a live dashboard tracking this score. If it begins to dip, you have an early warning that a product issue or a confusing new feature is causing widespread frustration.
- **Proactive Frustration Detection:** Using a session replay tool like **FullStory** or **LogRocket** with AI capabilities is a game-changer. These tools can be configured to automatically detect signs of user frustration. If a user starts clicking the same button repeatedly ("rage clicks") or encounters a JavaScript error, the system can automatically capture a recording of that user's session and create a ticket for you. You can watch a video of the exact moment the user got frustrated and see the bug or confusing UI element for yourself.
- **Automated "Golden Path" Auditing:** You can define a "golden path"—the ideal journey for a new user (e.g., Signup -> Create Project -> Invite Teammate -> Upgrade). Your AI BI tool can monitor the completion rate of this funnel. If the rate for a

specific step suddenly drops, it alerts you, indicating a new point of friction has been introduced into your most important user journey.

This multi-layered, automated quality control system is the immune system for your solo enterprise. It proactively detects and addresses issues before they can impact the customer experience, allowing you to solve the scaling-quality paradox and build a brand that is trusted for its reliability and excellence.

9.3 Customer Success at Scale

As your business grows, a subtle but critical shift must occur in your mindset. You must evolve from focusing on reactive *customer support* to proactive *customer success*. Support is about solving problems when they arise; it is a cost center. Success is about ensuring your customers achieve their desired outcomes with your product, making them so valuable that problems rarely arise in the first place. It is the single most important driver of long-term retention, negative churn (i.e., expansion revenue), and advocacy.

The challenge is obvious: how can a solo founder act as a dedicated Customer Success Manager (CSM) for thousands of accounts? The answer is to build an automated Customer Success Engine that delivers personalized, proactive guidance to every user at scale.

Pillar 1: The Automated, Hyper-Personalized Onboarding Journey
The first 14 days of a user's experience are the most critical predictor of their long-term success. A world-class onboarding journey is your highest-leverage opportunity to build a successful customer. This requires a system far more sophisticated than a simple five-part welcome email sequence.

- **The System:** This is an advanced **n8n** workflow that creates a dynamic, responsive onboarding experience.
- **The Workflow:**
    - **Personalized Tracks:** When a new user signs up, the workflow is triggered. It first enriches the user's data. By

analyzing their email domain (`@company.com`) or self-reported industry, it can place them into a specific onboarding track. An architect signing up for your project management tool will receive a different set of in-app tips and email tutorials than a software developer using the same tool.
  - **Behavior-Driven Triggers:** The system is connected to your application's database and tracks key user actions. If a user successfully completes Step 1 of your "Golden Path" (e.g., creating their first project), the system immediately sends a congratulatory email with a short guide for Step 2. Conversely, if a user *fails* to complete Step 1 within 24 hours, it triggers a different workflow. This one sends a helpful email titled "Having trouble getting started?" with a link to a 60-second tutorial video, proactively addressing their point of friction.

Pillar 2: The Proactive Health Check & Engagement System You cannot wait for customers to tell you they are unhappy; by then, it is often too late. An automated system can monitor the "health" of every customer and intervene before they churn.

- **The System:** A weekly n8n workflow calculates a "Customer Health Score" for every active user.
- **Calculating the Health Score:** This score is a weighted average of several key data points pulled from your various systems:
  - **Recency:** When was their last login date?
  - **Frequency:** How many sessions have they had in the last 30 days?
  - **Depth of Adoption:** How many of your product's key features have they actually used?
  - **Support Load:** Have they filed multiple support tickets recently?
- **The Automated Interventions:** The user's health score (e.g., a number from 1-100) places them into an automated engagement funnel.
  - **"At-Risk" Customers (Score < 40):** The system triggers a personalized outreach email. The LLM is

prompted: *"This user has a low health score. Based on their user profile, draft a friendly, non-salesy email that highlights a new feature or a recently published guide that is specifically relevant to their use case. The goal is to provide immediate value and entice them to log back in."*

    - **"Power Users" (Score > 90):** These users are your future advocates. The system triggers a different email, perhaps inviting them to a private beta for a new feature or asking if they would be willing to provide a testimonial in exchange for a service credit.

Pillar 3: The Automated Churn-Prevention Engine The last line of defense is to intervene at the precise moment a customer decides to leave.

- **The System:** The workflow is triggered when a user clicks the "Cancel Subscription" button inside your application.
- **The "Smart Offboarding" Flow:**
    1. **The Exit Survey:** Before the cancellation is finalized, a simple, one-question form appears: "We're sorry to see you go! What's the main reason for your cancellation?" The options are pre-defined (e.g., "It's too expensive," "I'm missing a key feature," "I found an alternative").
    2. **The Dynamic Offer:** The user's selection triggers a specific, automated, and highly relevant counter-offer. If they chose "Too expensive," the system immediately presents a pop-up offering a 50% discount for the next three months. If they chose "Missing a key feature," the system can check their request against your product roadmap and reply, "Good news! The [Slack Integration] feature you're looking for is scheduled for release next month. Would you like to pause your subscription for free and be the first to get access?"

This automated Customer Success Engine allows a single founder to deliver a level of proactive, personalized engagement that most human-run CSM teams cannot match. It is a system that scales intimacy, ensuring that every user feels seen and supported on their journey to success with your product.

Strategic Scenario: The 10-Hour Work Week

The ultimate goal of building systems that scale you is not just to grow a larger business, but to buy back your own time and freedom. The story of "ProcessKit" and its founder, Liam Carter, is a powerful illustration of how a deep commitment to process automation can create not just a profitable business, an enviable lifestyle.

The Founder: Liam Carter, a former operations consultant for large creative agencies. He was obsessed with efficiency and frustrated by the chaotic, ad-hoc way most agencies managed their projects.

The Product: ProcessKit, a niche B2B SaaS tool designed specifically for small creative agencies (5-20 employees). It provides a unified platform to manage the entire client lifecycle, from initial proposal and contract signing to project management, client feedback, and final invoicing.

The Business Outcome: As a solo founder, Liam grew ProcessKit to **$1.8 million in Annual Recurring Revenue (ARR)**. What makes his story legendary in founder circles is his work schedule: he consistently works no more than **10-15 hours per week**, spending the rest of his time on his passions for surfing and woodworking.

The "Secret": The Central Brain Liam's freedom is not the result of a simple product, but of an extraordinarily complex and elegant system he built to run the company for him. The heart of his business is a meticulously designed "Company OS" built entirely within **Notion**, which he refers to as the "Central Brain." This OS is a collection of over 200 interconnected Standard Operating Procedures (SOPs), with nearly 90% of them being fully automated by **n8n**.

The Architecture of the Central Brain Liam's core principle is: *"If I have to do a task more than twice, it gets an SOP. If an SOP has existed for more than a month, it must be automated."* His Notion workspace is built around a few key databases:

- **The SOPs Database:** Every single business process is documented here. Each SOP is an entry in the database, tagged by department (e.g., 'Finance,' 'Support,' 'Product'), status ('Documented,' 'In Automation,' 'Fully Automated'), and a 'Last Reviewed' date.
- **The Customers Database:** A lightweight CRM that is automatically synced with Stripe and his Bubble app data.
- **The Product & Marketing Databases:** Housing the AI-driven RICE roadmap and the content for the marketing engine.

An Automated SOP in Action: "Disputed Client Invoice" To understand the power of this system, let's look at how it handles a high-stakes, sensitive event: an agency's client disputing an invoice generated through ProcessKit.

1. **The Trigger:** An agency user clicks a "Dispute Invoice" button within the ProcessKit app. This single click triggers an n8n webhook.
2. **The SOP Blueprint:** The corresponding document, "SOP-FIN-07: Disputed Invoices," outlines the exact 10-step process the automation must follow to de-escalate the situation and provide clarity.
3. **The n8n Workflow (The Automation):** The workflow executes the SOP perfectly in seconds:
    - It immediately pauses all automated payment reminders for that specific invoice in Stripe.
    - It accesses the project's history in the Bubble database and gathers all relevant artifacts: the original signed proposal, every task and deliverable logged against the project, and all client communication records.
    - It packages all of this information into a single, neatly organized PDF report.
    - It uses **Claude 4** to draft a neutral, professional email to both the agency and their client. The email states, "To facilitate a fair resolution regarding invoice #1234, we have attached a complete project summary, including the original scope of work and all logged tasks. We

- encourage both parties to review this document together."
- Finally, it creates a "Disputed" ticket in Liam's personal support queue within Notion, containing a link to the generated report, just in case human intervention is needed.

This automated system handles the stressful, administrative work instantly and impartially. It de-escalates 90% of disputes by providing objective data to both parties, and Liam only needs to step in for the most complex cases.

How the System Enables Liam's Lifestyle Liam's work week is calm and focused because he doesn't work *in* his business; he works *on* the system that runs his business.

- **Monday (4 hours): CEO Time.** He reviews his key dashboards. He then reviews the AI-prioritized product roadmap and decides on the one small feature or improvement he will direct his AI co-pilot to build this week.
- **Wednesday (4 hours): Growth Time.** He focuses on non-scalable activities that he enjoys, like being a guest on a popular design podcast or having a long conversation with a power user about their agency's future needs.
- **Friday (2 hours): Review & Refine.** He reviews the weekly performance reports from all his automated systems and handles the handful of truly escalated tickets that require his attention.

Liam Carter's story is the ultimate embodiment of building systems that scale you. By dedicating himself to process and automation, he built a company that is not dependent on his constant presence. The Central Brain is the true operator of ProcessKit; Liam simply serves as its chairman and chief strategist.

Chapter Summary & Resources

This chapter provided the crucial framework for scaling beyond the initial launch phase. We have shifted the founder's role from being the primary doer to being the primary designer of systems. By creating robust, documented processes, implementing automated quality control, and building a proactive customer success engine, you create a business that is not just bigger, but stronger, more resilient, and less dependent on your personal effort. This is the key to achieving sustainable growth without sacrificing your time or your product's quality.

Key Takeaways

- To scale from $1M to $10M and beyond, you must shift from **doing tasks to designing systems** that do the tasks for you.
- A system of **"SOPs for One,"** documented with AI assistance and stored in a central "Company OS," creates a resilient and scalable brain for your business.
- An **automated Quality Control system** acts as your 24/7 QA team, proactively monitoring system health, data integrity, and customer experience to prevent problems before they impact users.
- Proactive **Customer Success**, driven by automated, personalized onboarding, customer health scores, and intelligent churn-prevention triggers, is the key to long-term customer retention.

Action Items

- **Document Your First SOP with AI:** Choose one simple, repeatable task in your daily life or current work (e.g., how you organize your downloads folder). Use a tool like Scribe or Tango to record yourself doing it once, then use an LLM to refine the generated text into a formal SOP document.
- **Design One Quality Monitor:** Sketch out a simple automated check that would be valuable for your business idea. For example: "A nightly n8n workflow that checks for any new 1-star reviews on my product's App Store page and, if found, creates a high-priority ticket in my Notion database."
- **Create One Customer Success Trigger:** Define one specific, positive behavioral trigger for your product idea. For example: "If a user has successfully used [Key Feature X] five times in their first week, then send them an automated email

congratulating them and suggesting an advanced tip for that feature."

Preview of Chapter 10

With robust, scalable systems now in place, your business is prepared for hyper-growth. The operational foundation is solid. The final piece of the scaling puzzle is strategy. How do you identify the opportunities that will not just grow your business, but 10x it? How do you expand into new markets or verticals as a single person? In **Chapter 10, The Growth Acceleration Framework**, we will equip you with the strategic models to identify and capture exponential growth opportunities, pushing your enterprise to the next level of the stratosphere.

Resources and Tools

- **Process Documentation:** Scribe (scribehow.com), Tango (tango.ai).
- **Knowledge Management:** Notion, Airtable.
- **System Monitoring & APM:** Datadog, New Relic, Mezmo (for log analysis).
- **Customer Experience Auditing:** FullStory, LogRocket.

Chapter 10: The Growth Acceleration Framework

Introduction

There are two types of growth in the world of business: linear and exponential. Linear growth is steady and predictable; it's the path of adding a fixed number of customers or a fixed amount of revenue each month. It is comfortable, manageable, and it will never, ever lead to a billion-dollar valuation. Exponential growth, on the other hand, is the explosive, compounding force that creates market-defining enterprises. It is the path of doubling your user base in a single quarter.

In the previous chapters, we built the robust, automated engine capable of handling immense scale. Now, it is time to strap a rocket booster to it. This chapter marks a critical shift in mindset, moving from the operational focus of building resilient systems to the strategic pursuit of hyper-growth. The goal is no longer just to improve the business, but to find and exploit the hidden levers that can produce a tenfold return on your effort—the **10x multipliers**.

This chapter provides the Growth Acceleration Framework, a mental model for thinking about and engineering non-linear growth. This is not a list of short-term marketing hacks; it is a systematic, data-driven approach to identifying and capturing game-changing opportunities. We will explore how to find your unique multipliers, how to expand into new markets without cloning yourself, and how to leverage the power of partnerships. You will learn to think like a growth strategist, using AI to discover the hidden pathways that can catapult your business from seven figures into the stratosphere.

10.1 Identifying Your 10x Multipliers

The Pareto Principle, or the 80/20 rule, states that for many outcomes, roughly 80% of the consequences come from 20% of the causes. For a solo founder, whose time is their most finite and precious resource, this is not just a quaint observation; it is the fundamental law of survival and success. You cannot afford to spend your time on the 80% of activities that produce minimal results. Your entire mission is to identify that critical 20% and focus on it with relentless, single-minded discipline.

A "10x multiplier" is an activity, channel, or feature that lies at the very heart of that critical 20%. It is a lever that, when pulled, produces a disproportionately massive impact on your business's growth trajectory. Identifying these multipliers is not a matter of guesswork; it is a science. It requires a systematic, data-driven audit of your business, powered by the AI Business Intelligence system you built in Chapter 6.

The Framework: The AI-Powered Growth Audit

At least once per quarter, you must step back from the day-to-day operations and become a growth scientist. Your goal is to analyze the three core pillars of your business—Acquisition, Customers, and Product—to find the hidden levers.

1. Analyzing Your Acquisition Channels: Where do your *best* customers come from? It is easy to be seduced by vanity metrics like website traffic or the number of trial signups. A true multiplier is a channel that delivers not just any customers, but highly profitable customers.

- **The AI BI Workflow:** You ask your Business Intelligence tool a series of increasingly specific questions.
    - *"Rank all my acquisition channels (Organic Search, Paid Ads, Social Media, Referrals) by the volume of new customers in the last 90 days."*
    - *"Now, re-rank those same channels by the **conversion rate from trial to paid subscriber**."*
    - *"Finally, and most importantly, re-rank those channels by the **average Lifetime Value (LTV) of the customers they produce**."*
- **Identifying the Multiplier:** The AI's analysis will cut through the noise. It might reveal that your social media efforts (high effort) generate a lot of low-converting trial users, while the SEO-optimized articles from your autonomous marketing engine (low ongoing effort) attract customers with a 3x higher LTV.

The 10x multiplier is not social media; it is **SEO-driven content**. The strategic action is to immediately re-task your marketing engine to focus 90% of its resources on creating more of the specific content that attracts these high-value users.

2. Analyzing Your Customer Segments: Who are your *best* customers? Not all customers are created equal. Some are more profitable, more loyal, and easier to support than others. Identifying and cloning your ideal customer is a powerful growth multiplier.

- **The AI BI Workflow:**
    1. *"Segment all paying customers by industry, company size, and geographic location."*
    2. *"For each segment, calculate the average LTV, the churn rate, and the number of support tickets filed."*
- **Identifying the Multiplier:** The AI might discover a stunning pattern. While you proudly serve customers across a dozen industries, the data shows that "e-commerce businesses with 10-50 employees based in North America" have a 5x higher LTV and a near-zero churn rate compared to any other segment. This is your "Ideal Customer Profile" (ICP) on steroids. The 10x multiplier is this **hyper-specific customer niche**. The strategic action is to ruthlessly refocus your entire business—from your website's messaging to your automated sales outreach—to exclusively attract and serve this one hyper-profitable segment.

3. Analyzing Your Product Features: What do your *best* customers do? The features within your product are not all equally valuable. Some are nice-to-haves, while others are critical drivers of long-term retention.

- **The AI BI Workflow:**
    1. *"Analyze the feature usage data for my highest-LTV customer segment."*
    2. *"Identify the top 3 features they use most frequently."*
    3. *"Now, analyze the behavior of customers who churned in their first 90 days. What key features did they consistently fail to adopt?"*

- **Identifying the Multiplier:** The AI may reveal a critical correlation: customers who adopt your product's "Automated Reporting" feature within their first three days have a 90% retention rate after one year. Customers who never touch this feature churn at a rate of 60%. The 10x multiplier is not just the feature itself, but the **early adoption of that 'sticky' feature**. The strategic action is to immediately re-engineer your automated onboarding journey to guide, incentivize, and ensure that every single new user successfully uses the "Automated Reporting" feature as part of their initial experience.

Identifying your 10x multipliers is a continuous process of discovery. By running this AI-powered audit every quarter, you can ensure that your limited time and resources are always focused on the few critical levers that produce exponential, not linear, growth.

10.2 AI-Driven Market Expansion

The traditional playbook for market expansion is a daunting prospect for any company, let alone a solo founder. It involves immense upfront investment, hiring local teams, navigating foreign regulations, and managing complex logistics. It is a high-risk, capital-intensive endeavor. For the AI-powered solo founder, this playbook is irrelevant. Using AI as your infinitely scalable market research, localization, and go-to-market team, you can enter new geographic or demographic markets with astonishing speed and minimal cost.

Phase 1: AI-Powered Market Identification The first step is to replace guesswork with data. You need a clear, evidence-based signal telling you which new market to enter.

- **Analyzing Your Organic Reach:** Before you look outward, you must look inward at your existing data. Your business is already global, even if you don't realize it.
    - **The AI BI Workflow:** Ask your BI tool: *"Analyze the geographic distribution of my website traffic and free trial signups over the last six months. Outside of my primary market (the USA), which three countries are*

showing the highest organic growth rate? Now, cross-reference this with payment data from Stripe to see if these countries also produce customers with a high LTV."

- **The Insight:** The AI might reveal that, for no apparent reason, you have a small but growing cluster of high-value paying customers in Australia. This is a powerful, data-driven signal that a latent demand for your product already exists there.

- **AI-Powered External Market Research:** Once you have a target market in mind (e.g., Australia), you can use an LLM to perform a deep market analysis that would traditionally take a consulting firm weeks to complete.

  - **Action Item: The Market Expansion Prompt**

    *"You are a senior market expansion consultant for a B2B SaaS company. My product is a project management tool for creative agencies. I am considering a dedicated launch in Australia. Your task is to generate a concise market entry report that includes:

    1. The estimated size of the creative agency market in Australia.
    2. A list of the top 3 local competitors and an analysis of their primary weaknesses.
    3. An overview of any significant cultural or business nuances I should be aware of in my marketing copy.
    4. A summary of key business regulations, including data privacy laws like the Australian Privacy Act."*

Phase 2: The Automated Localization Workflow Once you've decided to enter a new market, you can execute the localization plan in a matter of days.

- **Product & Website Translation:** This is the most obvious step, but it must be done with nuance. You can build an automated workflow that extracts all the text ("strings") from your **Webflow** site and **Bubble** app and sends them to a sophisticated LLM like **Claude 4 Opus** with a detailed prompt. The prompt doesn't just ask for translation; it asks for localization—adapting idioms, cultural references, and tone.
- **Marketing & Support Localization:** Your autonomous systems can be cloned and retasked. The marketing engine's AI is now prompted to research trending topics in the Australian creative industry. The AI Service Agent is given a new persona with local vernacular and trained on a knowledge base that includes Australia-specific FAQs.
- **Pricing & Payments:** Using **Stripe's** global capabilities, you can easily create a new pricing page that displays your subscription fees in Australian dollars (AUD) and accepts local payment methods, removing a critical point of friction for new customers.

Phase 3: Expanding into New Verticals This same framework for geographic expansion can be applied to enter new demographic or industry verticals, which is often an even more powerful growth lever.

- **The Opportunity:** Your AI BI tool might reveal that while your product is for "creative agencies," a surprising number of users are actually architecture firms.
- **The AI-Driven Pivot:**
    1. **Research:** You use an LLM to learn the unique vocabulary, pain points, and workflows of architects.
    2. **Clone & Specialize:** You create a "clone" of your Webflow marketing site. You then prompt your AI copywriter to rewrite all of the headlines and body copy to speak directly to architects. "Manage Client Projects" becomes "Manage Architectural Projects from Concept

to Completion." The customer testimonials are swapped out for ones from architects.

3. **Targeted Outreach:** Your automated sales engine is now directed to build a list of architecture firms in Apollo.io, and the hyper-personalized outreach emails now reference specific architectural challenges and projects.

This ability to rapidly research, localize, and launch into new markets—whether geographic or demographic—is a superpower unique to the AI-powered solo founder. It transforms market expansion from a massive, high-risk corporate gamble into a fast, low-cost, data-driven experiment that can unlock entirely new vectors for exponential growth.

10.3 Partnership and Integration Strategies

For the solo founder, the ultimate form of leverage is not just optimizing their own systems, but plugging into the vast, pre-existing ecosystems of other successful companies. The traditional approach to business partnerships—months of negotiations, complex legal agreements, and resource-intensive co-marketing campaigns—is a non-starter. The AI-first founder pursues a different strategy: **programmatic, API-driven partnerships** that are automated, scalable, and require almost no meetings to maintain. This is how you tap into other companies' audiences and platforms to fuel your own growth.

The Integration Flywheel: Your Most Powerful Growth Engine

By far the most potent partnership strategy for a solo SaaS founder is the product integration. An integration is a technical connection that allows your product to seamlessly share data and functionality with another application. This creates a powerful, self-reinforcing growth loop known as the "integration flywheel."

1. **Build:** You build a valuable integration with a large, established platform that your ideal customers already use daily (e.g., HubSpot, Salesforce, Slack, Shopify).
2. **Get Listed:** You submit your integration to their public "App Marketplace" or "Integration Directory."

3. **Acquire:** A fraction of that platform's millions of users will discover your product while searching for a solution within that marketplace. This becomes a high-intent, highly-qualified, and completely automated customer acquisition channel.
4. **Reinforce:** As more of their users install your integration, its value to the platform's ecosystem increases. This can lead to you being featured more prominently—in blog posts, newsletters, or on the marketplace homepage—which drives even more users, spinning the flywheel faster.

Phase 1: Identifying High-Leverage Integration Opportunities The key is to choose your integration partners with surgical precision, guided by data, not just brand recognition.

- **The AI BI Workflow:** Your first step is to analyze your own user base.

> **Action Item: The Integration Discovery Prompt**
>
> Ask your AI BI tool: *"Analyze the data from our user signup forms and any enrichment data we have. What are the top 5 software platforms that our highest-LTV customers use most frequently? Cross-reference this with platforms that have a popular, open app marketplace."*

The AI might reveal that 70% of your best customers are also heavy users of HubSpot. This is a clear signal. Integrating with HubSpot is not just a good idea; it's a 10x multiplier opportunity.

Phase 2: The AI-Assisted Integration Build Building integrations can be technically challenging, but AI can serve as your expert integration engineer.

- **API Documentation Analysis:** The API documentation for a large platform can be thousands of pages long. You can feed this entire document into an LLM like **Claude 4 Opus**. **Prompt:** *"You are a senior software engineer specializing in API* *integrations. I want to build an integration that syncs contact data between my app and the HubSpot API. Based on the attached documentation, outline the authentication method I need to use, list the key API endpoints for creating and updating contacts, and generate the boilerplate code in Python to make the initial API connection."*

- **AI-Powered Code Generation:** Your AI co-pilot can then write the specific functions required to handle the data synchronization, error handling, and user interface elements for the integration, turning a multi-week project into a multi-day one.

Beyond Technical Integrations: The Automated Affiliate Army A simpler, yet still powerful, form of partnership is an affiliate program. This allows you to build a scalable, commission-based sales force without hiring a single person.

- **The System:**
    1. **The Platform:** Use a dedicated affiliate management tool like **Rewardful** or **PartnerStack**. These platforms handle everything from affiliate signup to unique link generation, tracking, and automated commission payouts.
    2. **The Recruitment Engine:** Use your automated outreach stack (from Chapter 5) to find and recruit affiliates. **Prompt for your AI:** *"Identify the top 100 influential bloggers, YouTubers, and newsletter creators in the [my niche] space who have an audience that matches my Ideal Customer Profile. Draft a personalized email to each one, highlighting the value my product could bring to their audience and inviting them to join our affiliate program, which offers a recurring 30% commission."*

By building these programmatic partnerships, you are effectively grafting your business onto larger, more established distribution channels. It is a strategy that allows a solo founder to achieve a reach and scale that would be impossible to build from scratch.

Strategic Scenario: The Power of No

In the pursuit of exponential growth, it is easy to believe that the path forward is always one of addition—more features, more customers, more markets. But often, the most powerful growth accelerator is not what you do, but what you choose *not* to do. The story of "FocusWriter" and its founder, Anya Sharma, is a powerful testament to the strategic power of subtraction and focus.

The Founder: Anya Sharma, a minimalist and former software engineer who was deeply frustrated by the bloated, feature-packed writing software on the market.

The Product: FocusWriter, an ultra-minimalist, distraction-free writing application for professional authors, journalists, and academics. Its core purpose was to provide a beautiful, reliable, and lightning-fast environment for pure writing. It launched with a simple, one-time purchase price and a ruthless commitment to simplicity.

The Competitor: "WordSuite," a heavily venture-funded competitor with a team of 50. Their product was a classic "kitchen sink," packed with features: AI writing assistants, collaboration tools, mind mapping, templates for every conceivable format, and complex formatting options.

The Business Outcome: WordSuite raised over $50 million, struggled with high burn rates and a confusing product, and was eventually acquired for a fraction of its funding. Anya's FocusWriter, as a solo-founder, bootstrapped business, grew through relentless word-of-mouth to **$3 million in ARR** with an estimated 90% profit margin.

Anya's success was defined by three strategic "No's."

1. Saying No to Distracting Features As FocusWriter gained popularity, Anya was inundated with feature requests. Users wanted collaboration modes, AI writing assistants, and screenplay templates. Each request seemed reasonable on its own.

- **WordSuite's Approach:** They said "Yes" to everything. Their product became a labyrinth of menus and toolbars. It was slow, buggy, and its core writing experience suffered.
- **Anya's Approach:** Anya used her AI-powered RICE model not as a "to-do" list, but as a "not-to-do" list. She analyzed the requests and her user data. Her AI BI tool revealed a crucial insight: the feature requests were almost all from casual, low-LTV users who churned quickly. Her core user base—professional writers—had an incredibly high LTV and almost never churned. The data showed that what they valued most was the product's speed and reliability. The highest-impact activity was not adding a new feature, but further optimizing the performance of the core editor. She politely and publicly said no to the feature requests, explaining her commitment to a distraction-free experience.
- **The Result:** FocusWriter's simplicity became its most powerful feature and its deepest competitive moat. It was the only tool that truly respected the focus of a professional writer.

2. Saying No to the Wrong Customers Anya was approached by a large corporation that wanted to purchase 1,000 licenses of FocusWriter—a single deal worth over $100,000. However, they had a list of demands: custom enterprise features like SAML authentication, administrative dashboards, and advanced security compliance.

- **WordSuite's Approach:** They chased every large deal, frequently derailing their product roadmap to build one-off custom features for a single enterprise client.
- **Anya's Approach:** Anya said no. The potential revenue was tempting, but she ran the opportunity through her decision framework. Her AI financial analyst confirmed the short-term cash injection would be significant, but her AI strategist warned that the "Effort" score was massive. It would consume her development time for an entire quarter, distracting her from serving her core, scalable market of individual professionals. She politely declined the deal.
- **The Result:** In the quarter she would have spent building custom features, Anya instead shipped two small but meaningful

improvements to the core writing experience. These improvements were celebrated by her core user base and led to a surge of positive reviews, ultimately attracting over 2,000 new individual customers—worth far more in the long run than the single enterprise deal.

3. Saying No to Funding and Hiring As FocusWriter's revenue climbed, VCs took notice, offering Anya millions of dollars in funding to "build a team" and "aggressively capture the market" from WordSuite.

- **WordSuite's Approach:** They raised multiple rounds of funding, hired a large team, and were constantly under pressure from their board to justify their massive valuation and burn rate.
- **Anya's Approach:** She said no. Her automated systems were handling the business operations. Her profit margins were spectacular. She did not need the money, and she fundamentally understood that accepting VC funding and hiring a team would destroy her greatest competitive advantage: her ability to operate without the Execution Tax. She chose profitability, control, and product purity over growth-at-all-costs.
- **The Result:** Anya Sharma's success is a powerful story of strategic subtraction. She won not by out-building her competitor, but by out-focusing them. Every "no" was a data-driven decision that protected her time, her product's integrity, and her business's profitability, proving that for a solo founder, the discipline to say no is often the greatest 10x multiplier of all.

Chapter Summary & Resources

This chapter provided a strategic framework for accelerating growth beyond the first million-dollar milestone. We have shifted the focus from building systems to strategically deploying them to find and exploit exponential opportunities. By identifying your unique 10x multipliers, expanding into new markets with AI, leveraging automated partnerships, and maintaining a ruthless focus on what truly matters, you can build a business that doesn't just grow, but compounds.

Key Takeaways

- Exponential growth comes from identifying and focusing on **"10x multipliers"**—the small percentage of activities, channels, or customer segments that generate a disproportionate majority of your results.
- AI can act as a fully-staffed **market research and localization team**, allowing a solo founder to expand into new geographic or vertical markets with minimal cost and effort.
- **API-driven integrations** and automated affiliate programs are powerful, low-touch strategies for leveraging other companies' platforms and audiences to fuel your own growth.
- The strategic decision to **say "no"** to distracting features, the wrong customers, and misaligned opportunities is often the most powerful growth accelerator for a solo founder.

The Personal Growth Multiplier Worksheet

Take a moment to apply these concepts to your own business idea.

- **My 10x Multipliers:** What do you *hypothesize* will be your highest-leverage acquisition channel? Who is your most valuable customer segment? What is your product's "stickiest" feature that drives the most retention?
- **My Expansion Plan:** Identify one potential geographic or vertical market you could expand into. Use an LLM to run a one-paragraph mini market-research prompt for it.
- **My 'Say No' List:** To maintain focus, list three specific things (e.g., features, customer types, marketing activities) that you will commit to *not* doing in your first year.

Preview of Chapter 11

You now have the framework for building a resilient, scalable, and exponentially growing business. But the journey of a solo founder, particularly one managing a high-growth enterprise, is not without its perils. What happens when a key system fails unexpectedly? How do you manage the immense pressure and avoid personal burnout? In **Chapter 11, Crisis Management for Solo Entrepreneurs**, we move from growth strategy to survival strategy. We will build the plans and systems to ensure your business—and, more importantly, you—can withstand any storm.

Resources and Tools

- **Books:** *The 80/20 Principle* by Richard Koch; *Essentialism: The Disciplined Pursuit of Less* by Greg McKeown. These are foundational texts on the power of focus.
- **Partnership Platforms:** PartnerStack and Rewardful are leading tools for creating and managing automated affiliate and referral programs.
- **Concept: The Integration Flywheel.** Research this concept, particularly in the context of B2B SaaS growth strategies, to understand how product integrations can become a dominant customer acquisition channel.

Chapter 11: Crisis Management for Solo Entrepreneurs

Introduction

There is an undeniable truth at the heart of every entrepreneurial journey: something will go wrong. Not *if*, but *when*. A critical server will fail during your biggest sales day. A third-party API your business depends on will have a catastrophic outage. A security vulnerability will be discovered. For a company with a large team, a crisis is a stressful event. For a solo founder, it can feel like a personal apocalypse. When you are the single point of failure, the weight of a crisis—technical, financial, and emotional—falls squarely on your shoulders.

This chapter is the antidote to that fear. It is a framework for preparing for the inevitable challenges that come with building a high-growth business. Proactive crisis management is not about learning to improvise under extreme pressure; it is about building the systems and playbooks *before* a crisis hits, so that when the alarm bells ring, you are not panicking, but calmly executing a well-rehearsed plan.

The last chapter was about building the rocket ship for exponential growth. This chapter is about building the life support systems, the heat shields, and the emergency protocols. We will explore how to architect resilient, antifragile systems that can withstand shocks, how to create a practical disaster recovery plan for a worst-case scenario, and how to manage the most critical asset of all: your own mental health. This is how you build a business that is not just scalable, but survivable.

11.1 Building Resilient Systems

In the world of risk management, there is a concept known as "antifragility." A system that is merely resilient or robust can withstand a shock and return to its original state. An antifragile system, however, actually gets *stronger* when exposed to stressors, chaos, and failure. For the solo founder, whose business is an extension of themselves, building an antifragile enterprise is the ultimate goal. This is not achieved by adding layers of human redundancy, but by designing a smarter, more distributed, and self-healing technical architecture from day one.

Pillar 1: Decentralizing Your Core Infrastructure The most fragile business is one where everything runs on a single server in a single data center. A single hardware failure or a local network outage could wipe your entire business off the map. A modern, antifragile architecture is decentralized by default.

- **The Tools:** This is achieved by leveraging the native capabilities of modern cloud providers like **AWS**, **Google Cloud**, and platform-as-a-service providers like **Vercel**.
- **The Architecture:**
    - **Global Content Delivery Network (CDN):** Your first line of defense is a service like **Cloudflare**. It acts as a shield and a distribution network, caching your website and application front-end in dozens of data centers around the world. If your primary server in Virginia goes down, your users in Europe might not even notice, as they are being served a cached version from a server in Frankfurt.
    - **Multi-Region and Replicated Databases:** Never let your customer data live in only one place. Use a managed database service like **Amazon RDS** or **Neon** that has cross-region replication enabled. This means a live, up-to-the-minute copy of your entire database is running in a completely different geographic location. If a major outage takes down the entire US-East-1 region of AWS, your system can be configured to automatically failover and re-route all traffic to the replica running in US-West-2 within minutes.
    - **Serverless Functions:** Instead of building your application as a single, monolithic program running on one server, architect it as a collection of small, independent, "serverless" functions (using **AWS Lambda** or **Vercel Functions**). Each function performs a single task. This is inherently more resilient; a bug or a

failure in the "image processing" function will not crash the "user authentication" function.

Pillar 2: Mitigating Third-Party API Risk Your AI-powered business is a symphony of interconnected services. Your greatest dependency is likely on your primary LLM provider (e.g., OpenAI). If they have a major outage, your product's core functionality could break.

- **The Solution:** Build a "model-agnostic" abstraction layer. Instead of having your **Bubble** app call the OpenAI API directly, it calls a single, intermediary API endpoint that *you* control. This endpoint then calls the OpenAI API.
- **The "Fallback" Logic:** You can program this intermediary function with intelligent fallback logic. For example: *"Try to call the GPT-5 API. If the request fails or takes more than 5 seconds to respond, automatically retry the request with the Claude 4 Opus API. If both fail, return a graceful error message to the user: 'Our AI partner is currently experiencing high demand. Please try again in a few minutes.'"*
- **The Strategic Value:** This simple architectural choice makes your business dramatically more resilient to an outage from a single provider. It also gives you immense flexibility. If a new, better, cheaper AI model is released in the future, you only have to update this one single function, not your entire application codebase.

Pillar 3: The Automated "Circuit Breaker" System A truly resilient system can detect when it's in a failing state and take automated action to protect itself and its users.

- **The System:** This is an advanced monitoring and response system built in **n8n**, triggered by your health-checking tools (from Chapter 9).
- **The Workflow:** Your monitoring system detects a critical, ongoing failure (e.g., the Stripe API has been returning errors for 5 straight minutes). The **n8n** workflow immediately triggers a "circuit breaker" protocol:

1. It uses the **Webflow API** to instantly publish a prominent banner across your marketing site: "We are currently experiencing issues with payment processing. Our team is aware and working on a resolution."
2. It uses the **Bubble API** to temporarily disable the "Upgrade Now" button inside your application, preventing users from attempting a transaction that is guaranteed to fail.
3. It automatically pauses any marketing emails containing payment links.
4. It sends a single, consolidated, high-priority alert to your phone summarizing the failure and the automated actions that have been taken.

A resilient system is not one that never fails; it is one that is designed to fail gracefully, contain the damage, and recover quickly. By building these principles of decentralization, abstraction, and automated response into your architecture, you create a business that is far more robust and antifragile than many larger, more traditionally structured companies.

11.2 Disaster Recovery Planning

The resilient systems we just designed are your first and best line of defense; they are designed to *prevent* a crisis. A Disaster Recovery (DR) plan, on the other hand, is your last line of defense. It is your detailed, step-by-step playbook for what to do when, despite your best efforts, a true disaster strikes—a major data corruption, a malicious attack, or a complete cloud provider meltdown. Having a written, well-rehearsed plan is what separates a manageable incident from a business-ending catastrophe. It is the tool that allows you to act with clarity and precision when you are under the most extreme pressure.

The Solo Founder's Disaster Recovery Checklist

Your DR plan should be a simple, actionable checklist stored securely outside of your main business infrastructure (e.g., in a personal cloud storage account and on an encrypted physical drive).

Part 1: The Automated Backup Strategy (Your Insurance Policy) Data is the one asset that is truly irreplaceable. Your backup strategy should be multi-layered and fully automated, following the "3-2-1" rule: at least **3** copies of your data, on **2** different types of media, with at least **1** copy being off-site and immutable.

- **Application Code:** This is the easiest part. Your entire codebase should be in a version control system like **GitHub**. By its very nature, it is distributed and backed up.
- **Application & User Database:**
    - **Primary Backup:** Use the automated daily snapshot feature of your managed database provider (e.g., AWS RDS, Neon). These are fast to restore from.
    - **Secondary Off-Site Backup:** This is critical. Set up a weekly **n8n** workflow that creates an additional, full backup of your database and securely transfers it to a completely separate, low-cost cloud storage provider like **Backblaze B2**. This protects you from an account-level compromise or a catastrophic failure at your primary cloud provider.
- **Your "Central Brain" and Critical Documents:** Your Notion "Company OS," which contains all your SOPs and business knowledge, is a mission-critical asset. Set up a workflow to automatically export your entire Notion workspace as Markdown and CSV files once per week and save it to your secure Backblaze B2 bucket.

Part 2: The Crisis Communication Plan (Maintaining Trust) When things go wrong, communicating quickly, clearly, and honestly with your users is the key to maintaining their trust. You cannot be writing these communications from scratch in the middle of a crisis.

- **The Status Page:** Your most important communication tool is a dedicated status page, hosted by a third-party service like **Statuspage.io** or **Better Uptime**. Because it's hosted on separate infrastructure, it will remain online even if your entire company is down. All of your users should know where to find it.

- **Pre-Written Update Templates:** In your secure DR document folder, you should have pre-written, fill-in-the-blank templates for various crisis scenarios.

  > **Template Example: "Initial Outage Notification"**
  >
  > **Subject:** [Your Company Name] Service Disruption
  >
  > *We are currently experiencing a major service outage affecting [describe the affected service, e.g., 'user logins and data processing']. Our team is aware of the issue and is actively working to identify the root cause.*
  >
  > *We sincerely apologize for this disruption. We will post our next update here on our status page in [e.g., '30 minutes or less'].*

Having these templates ready allows you to communicate within minutes of a crisis, which builds immense confidence with your user base.

Part 3: The Recovery Runbook (Your Step-by-Step Guide) This is the most critical part of your DR plan. It is a highly detailed, step-by-step technical checklist for restoring service from a worst-case scenario. It should be written with the assumption that the person executing it is stressed, tired, and likely to make mistakes.

- **Example Runbook Entry: "Full Database Restore from Off-Site Backup"**
  1. [ ] Authenticate into the Backblaze B2 command-line interface.
  2. [ ] Execute command: `b2 download-file-by-name [bucket_name] [latest_backup_file.sql.gz]`.

3. [ ] Provision a new, temporary database instance on AWS RDS with [specify exact instance size and configuration].
4. [ ] Unzip the backup file: `gunzip latest_backup_file.sql.gz`.
5. [ ] Import the backup into the new instance using the command: `psql -h [new_db_host] -U [user] -d [database] < latest_backup_file.sql`.
6. [ ] Update the 'DATABASE_URL' environment variable in the Bubble application settings to point to the new database instance.
7. [ ] Run the automated E2E test suite to verify data integrity and application functionality.

"War Gaming": The Power of Practice A plan that has never been tested is not a plan; it is a theory. Once per quarter, you should schedule a two-hour "war game" exercise. You don't have to take down your live site. Simply open your DR plan and walk through it, step-by-step. Try to access your backups. Read through your recovery runbook. Is it still accurate? Do all the commands still work? This practice session is invaluable for building muscle memory and ensuring that when a real disaster strikes, you are ready to execute your plan with calm confidence.

11.3 Managing Overwhelm and Burnout Prevention

We have spent the last several chapters designing systems to manage every aspect of your business. We must now address the most critical, complex, and fragile system of all: you. The solo founder's journey is a marathon, not a sprint, and your mental and physical health is the fuel that will determine whether you finish the race. Burnout is not a personal failure or a sign of weakness; it is a systemic risk to your enterprise, as dangerous as any server outage or data breach. If the founder breaks, the entire automated empire they have built grinds to a halt.

Therefore, managing your personal energy, focus, and well-being is not a luxury or an afterthought. It is a core business function that must be systemized with the same rigor you apply to your financial or operational processes. The "hustle culture" that glorifies 100-hour work weeks and sleeping under your desk is a toxic relic of a bygone era. The modern, AI-powered founder wins not by outworking the competition, but by out-thinking and out-recovering them.

Designing Your Personal "Operating System"

Just as your business runs on a "Company OS" in Notion, you need to design a "Personal OS" to manage yourself. This system is built on three core components: hard boundaries, consistent rituals, and intelligent cognitive offloading.

1. Setting Hard Boundaries (Your Personal Firewall) The greatest threat to a solo founder's well-being is the insidious creep of work into every waking hour. You must build a firewall between your business and your life.

- **Time Boundaries:** Define your workday and be ruthless in defending it. This could be a traditional 9 AM to 6 PM, or it could be two 4-hour deep work blocks. The schedule itself doesn't matter; the act of having a defined stop time does. Use technology to enforce this. Set your internet router to automatically turn off Wi-Fi at 7 PM. Use an app that blocks work-related sites on your phone after hours.
- **Communication Boundaries:** You must control your inputs. Turn off all notifications on your phone and computer. Every buzz and banner is a tiny withdrawal from your cognitive bank account. Adopt a "pull" not a "push" system for information; you decide when it's time to check email, not the other way around. Set up an email autoresponder that clearly communicates your availability: "Thanks for your message. I check and respond to emails twice a day, at 11 AM and 4 PM."
- **Scope Boundaries:** This is the strategic art of saying no (from Chapter 10) applied to your personal energy. Every "yes" to a non-essential task, a low-value meeting, or a distracting opportunity is a "no" to your own well-being and a "no" to the 10x multiplier activities that truly matter.

2. Implementing Daily Rituals (Your Maintenance Protocol) Under pressure, self-care is often the first casualty. The only way to prevent this is to build non-negotiable health and wellness rituals directly into your daily schedule with the same gravity as a critical business task.

- **The "Deep Work" Block:** As championed by author Cal Newport, schedule a 2-4 hour block of uninterrupted, high-cognition work every single morning. This is when you work on your highest-leverage strategic tasks. Protect this time fiercely.
- **The "Shutdown" Ritual:** At the end of your defined workday, create a clear ritual that signals to your brain that work is over. This could involve reviewing your task list for the next day, closing all of your browser tabs, and literally saying a phrase out loud like "Shutdown complete." This prevents the low-grade hum of work-related anxiety from following you into your evening.
- **Physical Maintenance:** You are a "corporate athlete." Your brain is your primary asset, and it runs on the hardware of your body. Schedule your exercise, your meals, and your 7-8 hours of sleep in your calendar with the same seriousness as you would a product launch.

3. Leveraging AI for Cognitive Offloading (Your External Brain) One of the biggest drivers of burnout is **decision fatigue**—the deterioration of decision-making quality after a long session of making choices. As a solo founder, you make hundreds of decisions a day. You must delegate the low-stakes ones to your AI partner.

- **The AI Chief of Staff:** Create an automated workflow that prepares a "daily briefing" for you each morning. The AI reviews your calendar, your key metrics dashboard, and any urgent alerts, and synthesizes it into a 3-point summary to focus your attention.
- **The AI Decision Support System:** For any non-critical, reversible ("two-way door") decision, offload the initial analysis to your AI. Instead of spending an hour comparing three different software tools, you spend five minutes writing a detailed prompt: *"Compare these three options based on these five criteria and provide a recommendation with your*

reasoning." You still make the final call, but you save 55 minutes of valuable cognitive energy.

Your personal health is the engine of your enterprise. By building a robust Personal OS, you can ensure that you have the sustained energy, clarity, and focus required to navigate the long and demanding journey from zero to hero.

Strategic Scenario: The Phoenix Project

The story of "Scribe AI" and its founder, Dr. Evelyn Reed, is a powerful and cautionary tale about how hyper-growth, without the right personal systems, can be as dangerous as any market competitor. It is a story of hitting rock bottom and using AI to automate not just the business, but the founder's role within it.

The Founder: Dr. Evelyn Reed, a brilliant former linguistics researcher who left academia to build a tool she desperately needed.

The Product: Scribe AI, a sophisticated SaaS tool that provides transcription, summarization, and deep thematic analysis for long-form audio and video content. Its primary customers were academic researchers, journalists, and corporate market researchers who needed to extract insights from hours of interviews and recordings.

The Crisis: Success-Induced Burnout Scribe AI was an immediate, runaway success. Evelyn's deep understanding of the problem space led to a product that was far superior to its competitors. Within 18 months, she had scaled the business to **$2 million in ARR**. But she was drowning. She was working 100-hour weeks. Every escalated support ticket, every sales inquiry from a large university, every operational hiccup landed directly on her. She was personally analyzing user feedback, managing the marketing content, and making hundreds of micro-decisions every day. The joy she once felt in building her product had been replaced by a constant, low-grade panic. Her health was failing, she was deeply isolated, and she was on the verge of shutting down a multi-million dollar business because the personal cost had become too high.

The Turning Point: Firing Herself as Chief Everything Officer The breaking point came when a renewal negotiation with her largest customer—a major university—stalled for a week because her follow-up email was buried under 500 other unread messages. The client was furious. Evelyn realized her personal bandwidth had become the company's primary bottleneck. The business was no longer scalable because *she* was not scalable.

She made a radical decision. For 30 days, she instituted a complete freeze on all new feature development. She announced to her users that she was taking a month to focus on improving the "internal systems and reliability" of Scribe AI. In reality, she was rebuilding her own role from the ground up.

The Great Cognitive Offloading Evelyn spent the first week meticulously logging every single task she performed. She then categorized them into two buckets:

1. **Founder-Level Work (The 20%):** Tasks requiring her unique vision, strategic thought, or personal relationships (e.g., setting the product's long-term vision, talking to her top 10 customers).
2. **Operational Work (The 80%):** Tasks that were systematic and repeatable, even if they required intelligence (e.g., triaging emails, summarizing user feedback, monitoring system health, drafting social media posts).

She was horrified to realize she was spending almost all of her time on the 80% bucket. Her goal for the rest of the month was to build an AI system to handle every single task in that second category. She set out to fire herself as the "Chief Everything Officer" and hire an "AI Chief of Staff."

The Systems She Built:

- **The Triage Agent:** She built an n8n workflow connected to her email and support desk. An LLM processed every single incoming message. Newsletters were automatically summarized into a daily digest. Routine support questions were routed to her

AI Service Agent. Only emails that were from her top 20 customers or contained keywords like "urgent" or "legal" were flagged for her personal review. This single system cleared 50% of her daily cognitive load.

- **The Strategy Synthesizer:** All user feedback from all channels was piped into a central database. Every night, an AI would analyze the new entries, perform a sentiment and thematic analysis, and update a "Strategic Briefing" dashboard in Notion. When Evelyn started her day, she could see a one-page summary of what her customers were thinking and feeling, without having to read hundreds of individual comments.
- **The Decision Support System:** She instituted a new rule: for any non-critical decision, she was required to spend 30 minutes prompting an LLM to analyze the options before she was allowed to make a choice herself. This forced her to structure her thinking and prevented her from making impulsive decisions based on stress.

The Result: The Rebirth of the CEO After 30 days, Evelyn had successfully delegated roughly 80% of her former cognitive and operational load to her new automated systems. Her work week dropped from 100 hours of chaotic reactivity to 25 hours of focused, proactive strategy. With her newfound time and mental clarity, she was able to see the bigger picture again. She identified and built a key strategic partnership with a large academic publisher that tripled her user base. The business grew *faster* when she worked *less*.

Evelyn's story is a powerful lesson that burnout is often a system design problem, not a personal failing. By strategically offloading the cognitive burden of running the business to AI, she not only saved herself but built a more resilient, scalable, and valuable enterprise.

Chapter Summary & Resources

This chapter has been a sober but essential exploration of the risks inherent in the solo founder's journey. We have moved from growth strategy to survival strategy, creating the frameworks to ensure your business—and you—are resilient enough to withstand the inevitable storms. By architecting your systems to be antifragile, creating a detailed disaster recovery plan, and proactively managing your own mental and physical health, you transform your business from a fragile startup into a durable, long-term enterprise.

Key Takeaways

- A resilient business is **"antifragile"**—designed to withstand shocks through decentralized infrastructure, API abstraction, and automated "circuit breakers."
- A detailed **Disaster Recovery (DR) plan** is a non-negotiable insurance policy that turns crisis-induced panic into a calm, checklist-driven execution.
- **Founder burnout is a critical systemic risk.** Managing your personal health with hard boundaries, daily rituals, and AI-driven cognitive offloading is a core business function.
- Strategically **delegating the 80% of your cognitive load** that is automatable frees you to focus on the 20% of high-leverage activities that truly drive growth.

Your Personal Resilience Plan

Take a moment to create the first draft of your own resilience plan.

- **Technical Resilience:** What is the single biggest technical point of failure in your business idea (e.g., dependency on one API)? What is one thing you can do to make it more resilient (e.g., design a fallback system)?
- **Disaster Prep:** Write down the first three steps of your personal Disaster Recovery "runbook." What are the very first three things you would do in a "worst-case scenario" data loss or outage?
- **Burnout Prevention:** Define ONE hard boundary for your workday (e.g., "No work after 7 PM"). Schedule ONE non-negotiable self-care ritual into your calendar for next week (e.g., "Gym - Tuesday 8 AM").
- **Cognitive Offloading:** Identify ONE recurring, low-stakes decision you make. Write a prompt for an LLM to act as your "decision support system" for it.

Preview of Part 4: The Billion-Dollar Mindset

In Part 3, we have mastered the playbook for building and scaling a resilient, million-dollar enterprise. You now have the operational systems and strategic frameworks for success. But the journey from a million to a billion is not just an operational challenge; it is a psychological one. In **Part 4, The Billion-Dollar Mindset**, we will shift our focus inward. We will rewire your brain for massive scale, moving beyond the "how" of running a business to explore the "who" you need to become to command a billion-dollar enterprise. Our journey begins with **Chapter 12: Rewiring Your Brain for Scale.**

Resources and Tools

- **Books:** *Antifragile: Things That Gain from Disorder* by Nassim Nicholas Taleb; *Deep Work: Rules for Focused Success in a Distracted World* by Cal Newport.
- **Tools for Well-being:** Mindfulness apps like Headspace or Calm; website blockers like Freedom to enforce boundaries.
- **Concept: Decision Fatigue.** Research this psychological concept to better understand the cognitive science behind burnout and the critical importance of offloading low-stakes decisions.

Part 4: The Billion-Dollar Mindset

The "Who": Cultivating the psychological and strategic framework required for massive scale.

Chapter 12: Rewiring Your Brain for Scale

Introduction

The automated enterprise you have designed in the preceding chapters is, in theory, capable of scaling to a billion-dollar valuation. The systems can handle the load. The question we must now confront is a far more personal one: can *you*? The journey from a seven-figure business to a ten-figure one is not merely an operational or strategic challenge; it is a profound psychological one. The thinking that gets you to your first million in revenue is often the very thinking that will prevent you from reaching your first hundred million.

Welcome to Part 4: The Billion-Dollar Mindset. In this section, we shift our focus from the external systems of your business to the internal operating system of your brain. The automated workflows, AI agents, and resilient infrastructure are the hardware; your mindset is the software that runs on it. If that software is not upgraded to handle the demands of massive scale, the entire system will crash.

This is a journey of internal transformation. It requires you to fundamentally rewire your relationship with time, value, risk, and your own role in the enterprise you've created. It is about evolving from a builder and an operator into a visionary, a strategist, and a capital allocator. This chapter will provide the initial frameworks for this rewiring process. We will teach you how to shed the limiting beliefs of a small business owner and adopt the expansive, systems-first mindset of a true CEO—one who thinks not in thousands, but in billions.

12.1 From Freelancer to CEO Mindset

Every solo entrepreneur, regardless of their ambition, begins their journey with a piece of the "freelancer" mindset hardwired into their brain. It is the natural starting point, but it is also a dangerous trap. The freelancer mindset is what helps you survive in the early days, but it is the single biggest psychological barrier that will prevent you from achieving massive scale. The first and most critical step in rewiring your brain is to consciously identify and eradicate this mindset, replacing it with the perspective of a true CEO.

Defining the Two Mindsets

The difference between the two mindsets comes down to their relationship with time and value.

- **The Freelancer Mindset *trades time for money.*** It asks, "How much is my hour worth?" or "How much can I charge for this project?" Value is directly coupled to the founder's personal effort and the hours they work. This mindset leads to a linear, and therefore capped, income potential.
- **The CEO Mindset *trades capital for assets.*** "Capital" can be money, but for a solo founder, it is primarily their focused attention. "Assets" are the automated systems that generate value. This mindset asks, "How can I build a system that creates $100 of value every hour, even when I am sleeping?" Value is decoupled from the founder's time, leading to exponential income potential.

Many solo founders build a successful business that generates millions, but they remain trapped in a high-earning freelancer mindset. They have built themselves a very demanding, high-paying job, not a scalable enterprise. Here are the symptoms of this trap and how to escape them.

Symptom #1: The "I Can Do It Faster Myself" Trap This is the most common and seductive trap. As a highly skilled founder, you are an expert at many tasks. When a repeatable task arises, you face a choice: spend 5 minutes doing it manually, or spend 2 hours building an automation to handle it. The freelancer mindset, optimized for short-term efficiency, always chooses to do it manually. This is a fatal long-term error.

- **The CEO Mindset Shift: The 30x Rule.** The CEO understands that their time is the most valuable and expensive resource in the company. It must be protected for high-leverage, strategic work. They apply the 30x Rule: if a daily task takes you 5 minutes to do manually, you should be willing to spend up to 30 times that duration (150 minutes) to build a system that automates it forever. This is a capital investment of your time to create a long-term, time-saving asset. This is the discipline required to build the automated SOPs and n8n workflows we have discussed.

Symptom #2: The "Effort-Based" Pricing Mentality The freelancer mindset prices based on the effort required to deliver a service. This leads solo SaaS founders to chronically underprice their products. They look at a piece of software that costs them virtually nothing to deliver to a new user and feel that they cannot charge a high price because it wasn't "enough work."

- **The CEO Mindset Shift: Price on Value, Not Input.** The CEO prices the product based on the *value and outcome it creates for the customer*. If your automated compliance software saves a law firm $100,000 per year in potential fines and reduced labor, it is worth a $10,000 annual subscription. It does not matter if your marginal cost is zero. You are not selling your effort; you are selling an outcome.
- **The AI Application:** Use your AI strategist to escape your own pricing biases. **Prompt:** *"You are a pricing consultant from Simon-Kucher & Partners. My SaaS tool provides [value proposition] to [customer segment], saving them an estimated [quantifiable value]. Based on value-based pricing principles, recommend three pricing tiers and provide a clear justification for each."*

Symptom #3: The Focus on "Doing" vs. "Designing" The freelancer feels productive when their to-do list is empty. They spend their days *doing* the work: answering emails, tweaking copy, closing sales. The CEO feels productive when the *systems* they have designed are performing flawlessly.

- **The CEO Mindset Shift: Work *On* the Business, Not *In* It.** The founder of a scalable enterprise must elevate their role. At least 80% of your time should be spent on strategic "design" work: analyzing data to find 10x multipliers, designing new automated systems, talking to your most valuable customers to understand their future needs, and setting the long-term product vision. The entire purpose of your AI-powered stack is to liberate you from the "doing." You must have the discipline to let the systems do their job and resist the temptation to dive back into the operational weeds.

Making the transition from a freelancer to a CEO mindset is a conscious and often difficult process. It requires you to unlearn the very habits that may have made you successful in the first place. You must evolve from being the business's most valuable employee to being its most valuable asset allocator, where the primary asset you allocate is your own focused attention.

12.2 Decision-Making Frameworks for Exponential Growth

As your enterprise scales, the magnitude and impact of your decisions scale with it. The mental models that are sufficient for running a hundred-thousand-dollar business are dangerously inadequate for steering a hundred-million-dollar one. Linear, incremental thinking leads to linear, incremental results. To achieve the exponential growth required for a billion-dollar valuation, you must upgrade your decision-making software with mental models designed for thinking on a logarithmic scale. These frameworks allow you to navigate uncertainty, make bolder bets, and align your choices with long-term, non-linear outcomes.

Mental Model 1: Second-Order Thinking Most people operate on first-order thinking. They consider the immediate, direct consequence of a decision. Exponential thinkers obsess over the second- and third-order consequences—the ripple effects that will play out over months and years.

- **The Concept:** For any major decision, you must relentlessly ask the question, "And then what?"
- **Example:**
    - **Decision:** Should I acquire a small, struggling competitor for a low price?

- **First-Order Thinking:** "Yes, we will instantly gain 2,000 new users and remove a competitor from the market."
- **Second-Order Thinking:** "And then what? We will have to spend the next three months integrating their messy codebase, which will halt our own product roadmap. Their users are not our ideal customer profile and will likely churn at a high rate, dragging down our metrics. Their brand is not well-respected, and acquiring it could dilute our own premium brand positioning. The long-term consequences are a net negative."

- **The AI Application:** Use your LLM as a dedicated second-order thinking partner. **Prompt:** *"You are a strategic advisor trained by Charlie Munger. I am considering [Decision X]. Please perform a second- and third-order consequence analysis. What is likely to happen immediately? And based on that, what is likely to happen in 6 months? And based on that, what is the likely outcome in 18 months? Consider the impacts on our product, brand, financials, and my personal focus."*

Mental Model 2: The Regret Minimization Framework Popularized by Jeff Bezos, this framework is designed for making the large, bold, and often terrifying decisions that define a company's trajectory.

- **The Concept:** When faced with a difficult, irreversible ("one-way door") decision, project yourself forward to the age of 80. Looking back on your life, which choice will you regret more: having done the thing and failed, or having never done the thing at all?
- **The Bias Toward Action:** This framework is purpose-built to overcome the fear of failure that often leads to conservative, incremental choices. The pain of a failed attempt often fades with time, but the haunting question of "what if?" can last a lifetime. This model pushes you toward the bold bets that, while risky, are often the necessary ingredients for exponential success.

Mental Model 3: Thinking in Probabilistic Bets The most sophisticated thinkers do not see the world in black-and-white certainties;

they see it as a spectrum of probabilities. Every major decision is a bet. The goal is not to always be right, but to make bets where the potential upside massively outweighs the potential downside.

- **The Concept:** This is the mindset of a world-class poker player or venture capitalist. For any significant investment of your time or capital, you should analyze it as an "asymmetric bet."
- **The Framework:**
    1. **Identify the Asymmetry:** Look for opportunities where the potential downside is capped and survivable (e.g., losing one month of time or $10,000), while the potential upside is uncapped or massive (e.g., a 10x or 100x return).
    2. **Estimate Expected Value:** For a given decision, model the potential outcomes and assign them a rough probability.
- **The AI Application:** You can use an LLM to structure this analysis. **Prompt:** *"I'm considering spending the next month building an experimental integration with a new, emerging platform. Let's model this as a probabilistic bet.
    - The downside is 1 month of my time (my most valuable asset).
    - Worst Case (70% probability): The platform doesn't take off, and the integration gets zero traction. The effort is wasted.
    - Best Case (10% probability): The platform explodes, and my integration becomes the #1 app in their marketplace, leading to a 10x growth in new users.
    - Moderate Case (20% probability): The integration drives a modest but meaningful 20% increase in signups.
    - Analyze this as a bet. Is the potential upside asymmetric enough to justify the downside risk?"*

By upgrading your mental toolkit with these frameworks, you shift your perspective from that of an operator to that of a true chief executive. You learn to see through time, weigh risks like a professional investor, and develop the courage to make the bold, calculated bets that are the true drivers of billion-dollar enterprises.

12.3 Risk Management When You Are the Single Point of Failure

In any solo-founded enterprise, there is one risk that dwarfs all others: you. The founder is the central processing unit, the strategic visionary, and the ultimate operational backstop. This concentration of knowledge and control is a source of immense speed and agility, but it is also the business's greatest vulnerability. A technical disaster can be recovered from with backups, but what happens if the human operator has a disaster of their own—a serious illness, an accident, or any other unforeseen event that renders them unable to work for an extended period?

Managing this "key person risk" is not a morbid or pessimistic exercise; it is the ultimate act of a professional CEO. It is the process of transforming your business from a personal project that is dependent on your daily presence into a resilient, transferable asset that has value independent of its creator.

De-Risking Strategy 1: The "Dead Man's Switch" Protocol A "dead man's switch" is a mechanism designed to activate if an operator fails to perform a regular action. For a solo founder, this is an automated emergency protocol that ensures the continuity and transferability of the business in a worst-case scenario.

- **The Technical Setup:** This is a simple but powerful **n8n** workflow.
    1. The workflow sends you a simple, automated email once every 24 hours with a unique link that says, "Click here to confirm you are okay."
    2. If this link is not clicked for a pre-determined number of consecutive days (e.g., 3 to 7 days, depending on your risk tolerance), the workflow triggers the emergency protocol.
- **The Emergency Protocol:** The workflow automatically sends a pre-written, heartfelt email to one or two trusted individuals whom you have designated beforehand (e.g., a spouse, a sibling, or your lawyer). This email contains a secure link to an encrypted "Emergency Handover Kit" stored in a secure digital

vault like **1Password** or **Bitwarden**. The master password for this vault should be held separately, perhaps by your lawyer or in a sealed envelope in a physical safe.
- **The Emergency Handover Kit:** This is a meticulously prepared digital package containing everything a successor would need to understand and take control of the business. It includes a master list of all business accounts and passwords, the detailed Disaster Recovery Plan, the location of the Notion "Company OS," and a high-level document explaining the business model, the core automated systems, and instructions on how to either maintain, sell, or gracefully wind down the company.

De-Risking Strategy 2: The AI as Your "Virtual Successor" Your goal should be to create a business so well-systemized that a reasonably competent person, guided by your documentation and AI, could step in and keep it running. This is where your "Company OS" becomes a critical asset for de-risking.

- **The Central Brain as the Guide:** The entire operational logic of your business is documented in your Notion knowledge base. It is not just a collection of SOPs for you; it is a complete instruction manual for a successor.
- **The AI Tutor:** A new operator could use an LLM with the Company OS as its knowledge base to learn how to run the business. They could ask, "I am the new operator of this business. The founder is unavailable. Based on the Company OS, what are the three most critical daily financial checks I need to perform?" This turns your documentation into an interactive, intelligent guide.

De-Risking Strategy 3: Financial and Legal Firewalls

- **Incorporate Early:** From day one, your business should be a separate legal entity (an LLC or a Corporation). This creates a legal firewall between your business assets and your personal assets, which is a critical form of risk management.
- **Build a Cash Buffer:** Your business should maintain a sacrosanct cash reserve in its bank account equivalent to at least

six months of non-negotiable operating expenses. This buffer allows the business to survive a sudden revenue downturn or an unexpected large expense without going into a panic.

- **Establish Professional Relationships:** Have a relationship with a trusted lawyer and accountant *before* you need them in a crisis. A one-hour introductory call when things are calm is an invaluable investment.

By systematically building these layers of redundancy—operational, knowledge-based, financial, and legal—you are doing more than just protecting your business. You are professionalizing it. You are transforming it from a fragile entity entirely dependent on you into a durable, resilient, and ultimately more valuable asset.

Strategic Scenario: The Psychology of Betting Big

The journey to a billion-dollar valuation is rarely a straight line. It is often defined by a handful of critical inflection points—moments where a founder must make a bold, terrifying, "bet the company" decision to leap from a linear growth path to an exponential one. The story of "ConnectSphere" and its founder, Dr. Lena Hanson, is a deep dive into the psychology of such a moment, illustrating how the mental models for exponential growth can be used to overcome fear and unlock massive value.

The Founder: Dr. Lena Hanson, a brilliant but naturally cautious data scientist who had built a successful and comfortable business.

The Product (Phase 1): "Graphly," a niche B2B SaaS tool that helped academic and scientific researchers create complex, publication-quality data visualizations. The product was widely respected in its niche, profitable, and growing steadily to an impressive **$1.5 million ARR**. It was a perfect lifestyle business, but it had a clear market cap.

The Catalyst: The Existential Threat The comfortable world of Graphly was shattered when a major tech giant launched a new, free data visualization tool as part of their existing suite. Lena's AI-powered market intelligence agent immediately flagged the announcement and, within weeks, her BI system detected a troubling spike in churn, with departing users citing the new free alternative. Her business was facing an existential threat. Her first, fear-driven instinct was to compete head-on by adding more features—a battle of attrition against a giant that she knew she would inevitably lose.

The Mental Calculus of a High-Stakes Pivot This crisis forced Lena to confront her own cautious nature. Instead of panicking, she decided to systematically apply the decision-making frameworks she had studied.

1. The Second-Order Thinking Session: Lena sat down with her AI sparring partner to think through the long-term consequences of her options.

- **Path A (Compete on Features):**
    - *First-Order Consequence:* "We will build more features to try and match the competitor."
    - *AI-Assisted Second-Order Consequence:* "This will pull our focus away from our core strength of simplicity. Our product will become bloated. We will be in a feature race we cannot win, slowly burning through our resources and brand equity until we become an afterthought."
- **Path B (The Bold Pivot):** A new, terrifying idea had been forming in her mind. Her core technology—a powerful, proprietary graph-rendering engine—was far more advanced than the tool itself. What if she stopped selling a *tool* to researchers and started selling a *platform* to developers? She could open up her engine via an API and allow other companies to build their own data applications on top of it.
    - *First-Order Consequence:* "This is incredibly risky. We will have to rebuild our entire product, rebrand the company, and we will almost certainly lose a large portion of our current customer base."
    - *AI-Assisted Second-Order Consequence:* "And then what? We would be entering a market that is 100 times larger. We would move from selling a $20/month tool to selling a platform with enterprise contracts. We would create an ecosystem with a deep, technical moat. The

risk of failure is high, but the potential upside is astronomical. Conversely, the second-order consequence of *not* doing this is a slow, certain death."

2. The Regret Minimization Framework: The analysis was logical, but the fear was emotional. Lena then applied Bezos's framework. She imagined herself at age 80.

- **Regret of Inaction:** She pictured looking back and saying, "Graphly was a wonderful business for a few years, but we couldn't keep up. I always wonder what would have happened if I'd been brave enough to go for that platform idea." The imagined regret was heavy and filled with the bitterness of a missed opportunity.
- **Regret of Action:** She then pictured the pivot failing spectacularly, the business shutting down. It would be a painful memory, but she would know that she took her shot. The regret felt like a clean wound, a battle scar earned in the arena, not the dull ache of cowardice. The choice became emotionally clear.

3. The Probabilistic Bet: Finally, she modeled the decision as a financial bet with her AI analyst.

- **The Downside (Capped):** The potential loss was her current $1.5M ARR business and six months of her focused effort. The downside was known and finite.
- **The Upside (Uncapped):** The potential gain was a shot at building the "Stripe for data visualization," a business with a potential valuation in the billions. Even if she assigned a low probability of success—say, 10-20%—the "expected value" of the bet was massively positive. It was a classic asymmetric opportunity.

The Pivot and the Outcome With the clarity provided by these frameworks, Lena made the bold decision to commit fully to the pivot. She rebranded the company as "ConnectSphere" and spent six months in deep work, using her AI co-pilot to build out the new platform and its APIs. The launch was a phenomenal success, attracting a new, far more valuable customer segment of developers and technology companies. Two years later, ConnectSphere is at a $25 million ARR run rate and is seen as the foundational platform in its space.

Lena's story is a powerful lesson in the psychology of scale. The breakthrough was not technical; it was mental. By using structured decision-making frameworks, she was able to overcome her innate risk aversion and make the strategically sound, albeit terrifying, bet that was necessary to leap from a linear path onto an exponential one.

Chapter Summary & Resources

This chapter marked our journey into the most critical and complex territory of all: the founder's own mind. We have established that the leap from a successful business to a massively valuable enterprise is primarily an internal one. It requires a fundamental rewiring of your mental software—shedding the limiting beliefs of a freelancer, adopting the expansive frameworks of a CEO, and systematically de-risking your own role as the central pillar of the company.

Key Takeaways

- The **"Freelancer Mindset"** trades time for money and is the primary psychological barrier to scale; the **"CEO Mindset"** builds systems and assets that generate value independent of time.
- Exponential growth requires exponential decision-making, using mental models like **Second-Order Thinking**, the **Regret Minimization Framework**, and **Probabilistic Betting**.
- A solo founder must systematically de-risk their own role as the single point of failure by externalizing knowledge into a **"Company OS"** and creating emergency protocols like a **"dead man's switch."**
- The biggest constraints on a solo-founder's success are not external resources, but their own limiting beliefs and the quality of their decision-making frameworks.

The Mindset Self-Assessment

Take a moment to audit your current mindset.

- **Freelancer vs. CEO:** Review your task list from the last week. How many hours were spent "doing" operational tasks versus "designing" new systems? What is one "doing" task you can commit to automating next week?
- **Apply a Mental Model:** Think of one strategic decision you are currently pondering for your business or your life. Write a short paragraph analyzing it through the lens of Second-Order Thinking. What are the "and then what?" consequences?
- **Identify Your Asymmetric Bet:** What is one high-risk, high-reward "bet" you could make in your business right now? What is the capped, survivable downside? What is the uncapped, massive upside?
- **De-Risk Yourself:** Write down the name of the one trusted person you would designate to receive your "Emergency Handover Kit" if the need ever arose.

Preview of Chapter 13

We have now begun the process of rewiring your internal operating system for scale. You have the mindset of a CEO. The next step is to apply this powerful new mindset to your external strategy. How do you perform sophisticated competitive analysis when you don't have a strategy team? How do you time the market and recognize inflection points before others? How do you build a defensive "moat" around your business without an army? In **Chapter 13, Strategic Thinking at Solo Scale**, we will explore the high-level strategic frameworks that allow a one-person company to outmaneuver even the largest industry giants.

Resources and Tools

- **Books:** *Thinking, Fast and Slow* by Daniel Kahneman; *Thinking in Bets* by Annie Duke. These are masterclasses in the psychology of decision-making under uncertainty.
- **Mental Models:** The Farnam Street blog (fs.blog) by Shane Parrish is the single best resource for learning about a wide array of powerful mental models.

- **Security Tools: 1Password** and **Bitwarden** are best-in-class password managers that both include "Emergency Access" features for creating a secure digital vault.
- **Concept: "Key Person Risk."** Understanding this core business and insurance concept is essential for any founder, particularly a solo one.

Chapter 13: Strategic Thinking at Solo Scale

Introduction

Imagine a grandmaster chess match. On one side, a corporate incumbent: a team of strategists, market researchers, and data scientists surrounds the player, analyzing every possible move, running complex simulations, and debating the long-term implications of each decision. On the other side: you, the solo founder. It appears to be an impossibly unfair fight. How can a single person possibly out-think an army of analysts?

The answer is that you don't play their game. While the corporation is playing a slow, deliberate game of classical chess, the solo founder, armed with their AI co-pilot, is playing blitz chess on a thousand boards at once. Your advantage is not in deep, bureaucratic analysis, but in superior, real-time intelligence and the velocity to act on it before the opposition has even finished their first planning meeting.

In Chapter 12, we upgraded your internal "CPU"—your decision-making mindset. Now, we will build the advanced, external sensor array that feeds it world-class data. This chapter is about developing the strategic frameworks that allow a one-person company to achieve a level of situational awareness and foresight that can surpass that of its largest competitors. We will explore how to build an AI that acts as your personal intelligence agency, how to recognize market-shifting opportunities before they become obvious, and how to build a defensive moat around your business. This is how you learn to out-maneuver, not just out-work, the giants.

13.1 Competitive Intelligence for One-Person Companies

Traditional competitive intelligence is a slow and expensive affair. It involves commissioning static market research reports that are outdated the moment they are delivered. For the solo founder, this model is useless. In a rapidly evolving, AI-driven market, you don't need a snapshot from three months ago; you need a live, 24/7 intelligence feed that constantly monitors the entire landscape—your competitors, your market, and the bleeding edge of technology—and distills it into actionable strategic insights. You don't need to hire an army of analysts; you need to build one.

Building Your AI "Compete" Agent

This is not a single tool, but a sophisticated, automated system you can build using the n8n workflow engine as its core. The goal of this system is to ingest a massive amount of unstructured information from across the web and synthesize it into a concise, high-signal intelligence briefing delivered to you each morning.

Step 1: Deploying the AI's "Sensors" Your n8n workflow is the orchestrator, programmed to scrape and monitor a wide array of public data sources on a continuous, automated basis:

- **Direct Competitors:** It monitors their company blogs for new posts, their press release pages for announcements, and, most importantly, their careers page. A sudden increase in hiring for "mobile engineers" or "data privacy lawyers" is a powerful leading indicator of their next strategic move.
- **Social Media & Community Channels:** The agent monitors X/Twitter, Reddit, and key industry forums for mentions of your competitors' products, tracking sentiment and identifying common complaints or feature requests that represent opportunities for you.
- **Technology & Research Hubs:** It scans niche technology news sites, academic research portals like arXiv.org, and even patent databases for signals of emerging technologies that could disrupt your market or enhance your product.
- **Financial & Funding Data:** It monitors platforms like Crunchbase and PitchBook for news about your competitors' funding rounds, acquisitions, or financial performance, providing insight into their strategic health and priorities.

Step 2: The AI Analyst (The "Brain" of the Operation) A solo founder cannot possibly read and process this firehose of information.

This is where your LLM partner comes in. All of the raw, unstructured text data gathered by the n8n sensors is piped into a sophisticated model like Claude 4 Opus.

Hot Take: The Master Intelligence Prompt

*"You are 'Athena,' my Chief Strategy Officer. I have provided you with a stream of raw, unsorted data from the last 24 hours concerning my competitors, market trends, and new technologies in the [your niche] space. Your task is to produce a concise, 5-point intelligence briefing for me. For each point, you must:

1. State the key event or observation.
2. Analyze its potential impact on my business, clearly labeling it a 'Threat' or an 'Opportunity.'
3. Suggest one concrete, actionable strategic response.
4. Assign it a priority level: Low, Medium, or High.
5. Ignore all irrelevant noise and marketing fluff."*

The Daily Intelligence Briefing Every morning, this system delivers a summary that is more timely and strategically relevant than any corporate report. It might look like this:

- **Priority: High | Competitor Threat:**
    - **Event:** Competitor 'SaaSify' just acquired a small AI copywriting tool.
    - **Impact:** They are likely to integrate this into their core platform, adding a feature that directly competes with one of our key value propositions.
    - **Response:** Accelerate the development of our next-generation writing features and prepare a marketing campaign that highlights their superior quality.
- **Priority: High | Market Opportunity:**
    - **Event:** A new data residency law for Canada has just been announced.

    - **Impact:** All companies serving Canadian customers will need a solution to ensure their data is stored locally. This is a new, urgent pain point.
    - **Response:** Task the AI co-pilot to prototype a 'Canadian Data Residency' add-on for our product and launch a targeted ad campaign at Canadian tech companies.
- **Priority: Medium | Emerging Technology:**
    - **Event:** A new open-source model for real-time voice translation has gained significant traction on GitHub.
    - **Impact:** This could enable a powerful new feature for our product: real-time translation of customer support calls.
    - **Response:** Allocate a 4-hour deep work block this week to experiment with this model and build a proof-of-concept.

This AI "Compete" Agent transforms the solo founder from being information-blind to having a true information advantage. It filters the overwhelming noise of the market, distills it into actionable strategy, and provides a level of real-time situational awareness that even well-staffed corporate strategy teams, with their slow-moving reporting cycles, struggle to achieve.

13.2 Market Timing and Opportunity Recognition

In the world of technology, building a great product is not enough. The greatest fortunes and most dominant companies are created by founders who build a great product at the *exact right moment*. Market timing is the art and science of recognizing major technological and cultural shifts—inflection points—before they become obvious to the mainstream. For the solo founder, whose primary advantage is speed, the ability to see around the corner and get to the future first is a superpower. This is not about predicting the future with a crystal ball; it is about using mental models to recognize the present more clearly than anyone else.

Framework 1: The Technology S-Curve The S-Curve is a simple but powerful model that describes the lifecycle of every successful technology. Understanding where a technology is on this curve is critical for identifying opportunity.

- **Phase 1: The Ferment.** The technology is new, experimental, often clunky, and used only by a small group of enthusiasts and early adopters. Performance is low, and costs are high (think of the first personal computers or early VR headsets). This phase is characterized by rapid, unpredictable change.
- **Phase 2: The Takeoff.** This is the inflection point. The technology crosses a critical "good enough" threshold in performance and/or cost. It starts to solve a real problem for a broader audience, and adoption begins to accelerate exponentially. This is the moment of maximum opportunity (think of the iPhone's launch or the public release of ChatGPT).
- **Phase 3: The Maturity.** The technology is now mainstream. Innovation becomes incremental, focusing on minor improvements rather than breakthroughs. The market is saturated, and the dominant players are entrenched (think of today's smartphone or laptop markets). The solo founder's strategy is to use this model as a map. You must **avoid building a business in Phase 3**. The game is already over. Instead, your mission is to identify a technology that is currently in Phase 1 but is showing clear, data-driven signals that it is about to enter the explosive takeoff of Phase 2. Your AI "Compete" Agent is the perfect tool for this, as you can train it to watch for the confluence of signals that precede an inflection point: a 10x improvement in a key performance metric, a dramatic drop in cost, the entry of a major player, or a surge in developer interest.

Framework 2: "Jobs-to-be-Done" (JTBD) Theory Developed by the late Clayton Christensen, JTBD theory argues that customers don't buy products; they "hire" them to do a "job." This simple reframing is a powerful tool for opportunity recognition. By focusing on the customer's underlying goal, you can see opportunities that are invisible to competitors who are myopically focused on features.

- **The Classic Example:** People don't buy a quarter-inch drill bit; they hire it to create a quarter-inch hole. The drill is just one solution. A laser or a chemical process could be another.
- **Applying JTBD:** Instead of looking at your competitors' products, analyze the "job" your customers are trying to get done.

Your competitors might be stuck in a feature race, adding more and more complexity to their "drill." By understanding the underlying "job," you might realize that what the customer *really* wants is not a better drill, but a better way to hang a picture—leading you to invent the 3M Command Strip, a completely different and superior solution.

- **Using AI for JTBD Analysis:** Your AI can be an invaluable partner in this process. You can feed it all of your user feedback, support tickets, and interview transcripts.

Action Item: The "Jobs-to-be-Done" Prompt

"You are a product strategist trained in the Jobs-to-be-Done framework. I have provided you with 100 recent customer support conversations. Your task is to ignore the specific feature requests and surface-level complaints. Instead, analyze the underlying context to identify the 'job' the user was trying to get done when they encountered a problem. What is the real progress they were trying to make? Summarize the top 5 'jobs' that our customers are hiring our product for."

This analysis can reveal that the feature everyone is asking for is just a symptom of a much deeper, unserved need. Building a solution for that core "job" is how you create a breakthrough product, not just an incremental improvement.

The solo founder's role as a strategist is to be a master synthesizer. You use your AI systems to gather a storm of disparate signals from the market. Then, you apply powerful mental models like the S-Curve and Jobs-to-be-Done to find the pattern in the noise. This is how you time the market and recognize a billion-dollar opportunity while everyone else just sees chaos.

13.3 Building Moats Without Armies

A "moat," a term popularized by investor Warren Buffett, is a sustainable competitive advantage that protects a business from being attacked by competitors, much like a real moat protects a castle. Traditional moats are built with immense resources: economies of scale (being so big you can make things cheaper), powerful brands built over decades with billion-dollar advertising budgets, regulatory capture, or vast distribution networks powered by armies of salespeople. The solo founder cannot build these moats. Your defenses must be smarter, more modern, and self-reinforcing. You must build your moats out of data, intelligence, and community, not headcount.

Moat #1: The Data Network Effect This is the most powerful and important moat for any AI-first business. A data network effect occurs when your product gets smarter and more valuable for every user as more people use it. This creates a virtuous cycle, a flywheel that spins faster with each new user, making it nearly impossible for a new competitor to catch up.

- **The Flywheel in Action:**
    1. A new user signs up for your product and begins to interact with it.
    2. These interactions generate unique, proprietary data that no one else has.
    3. This data is automatically collected and used to continuously fine-tune your specialized AI model.
    4. The improved, smarter AI model provides a better, more accurate, or more personalized experience for all users.
    5. This superior product experience attracts more users, which generates even more proprietary data, which makes the model even smarter.
- **The Example:** Consider "Scribe AI," our case study on burnout. Every time a user corrects a word in an AI-generated transcript, that correction is a valuable piece of training data. After millions of such corrections, Scribe AI's transcription model becomes uniquely accurate for the specific jargon of its academic and research users. A new competitor starting with a generic, off-the-shelf transcription model would seem "dumber" and less

accurate to users, and would have no way to acquire the unique dataset needed to catch up. Your user base becomes your unwitting, always-on R&D team.

Moat #2: The Proprietary, Fine-Tuned AI Model In a world where any competitor can access powerful foundational models like GPT-5 and Claude 3, how can an AI feature be a defensible moat? The answer is that you don't compete on the general-purpose model; you compete on a highly **specialized, fine-tuned model** that is uniquely good at one specific task.

- **The Strategy:** You begin by using a powerful foundational model to get your product to market quickly. In the background, you use the proprietary data generated by your data network effect to continuously fine-tune a smaller, often open-source, model (like a model from the Llama or Mistral families).
- **The Result:** Over time, your specialized, in-house model can become both *better* and *cheaper* to run for your specific niche task than the giant, general-purpose models. It's like the difference between a general practitioner and a world-renowned heart surgeon. For that one specific job, your model is the best in the world. A competitor cannot replicate this because they do not have your unique training data. You have built a defensible, proprietary "AI brain" at the core of your business.

Moat #3: The Community The final modern moat is not technical, but human. A passionate, engaged community around your product creates a powerful defense based on belonging, shared knowledge, and high switching costs.

- **The Switching Cost:** When a user is deeply embedded in a community, the cost of switching to a competitor's product is not just about migrating data; it's about leaving a network of peers, a source of identity, and a valuable knowledge hub. Think of Midjourney's Discord server. It is not just a support channel; it is the vibrant, beating heart of the product itself, where users share creations, discover new techniques, and feel like part of a movement.

- **The Solo Founder's AI Community Manager:** You cannot personally manage a community of thousands. But you can build an AI agent to do it. An automated workflow can:
    - Welcome every new member to your Discord or forum.
    - Use an LLM to analyze discussions and identify emerging power users to highlight.
    - Spark engagement by automatically posting a "daily challenge" or a "weekly showcase" of the best user-generated content.
    - Answer common questions, freeing you up to engage in the most strategic, high-level discussions.

The solo founder's moats are not built from brick and mortar, but from compounding, self-reinforcing digital and social loops. A business protected by a data network effect, a proprietary AI model, and a vibrant community is a fortress that grows stronger and more defensible with every passing day.

Strategic Scenario: The Architect's Dilemma

One of the greatest psychological challenges for a visionary founder is the immense gap between their grand, long-term ambition and the tedious, necessary work of the present moment. You may dream of building a cathedral, but you must spend your days laying one brick at a time. The story of "Archis an" and its founder, Isabelle Dubois, is a masterclass in how to manage this tension and balance a 10-year vision with a 10-minute to-do list.

The Founder: Isabelle Dubois, a former architect who was frustrated by the fragmented and inefficient software used in her industry.

The Long-Term Vision (The "Cathedral"): Isabelle's grand vision was to create "Archis an," a fully integrated, AI-powered operating system for the entire lifecycle of a building. It would handle everything from generative architectural design and 3D modeling in the early stages, to project management and contractor collaboration during construction, and even automated compliance checks against local building codes. It was a massive, industry-defining vision that would take a decade or more to realize.

The Short-Term Reality (The "Brick"): She knew this vision was unbuildable in one go. To start, she had to build a tiny, unglamorous "brick": a simple SaaS plugin for existing architectural software that automated the single most tedious task she knew—generating project timelines and Gantt charts from a list of deliverables.

The Business Outcome: By creating a system to manage her dual focus, Isabelle successfully navigated this tension. Archis an grew from a simple plugin into a comprehensive multi-module platform, reaching a **$50 million ARR** run rate within seven years, with a clear path to achieving her initial grand vision.

The Systems for Balancing Vision and Execution

Isabelle's success was not an accident; it was the result of a disciplined personal operating system designed to hold both the long-term vision and the short-term reality in her mind at once.

1. The "Two-Track" Roadmap In her Notion "Company OS," Isabelle maintained two distinct but interconnected roadmaps.

- **The Vision Roadmap (The Cathedral Plan):** This was a high-level, aspirational document. It looked like a timeline stretching out ten years, with major "eras" and product pillars. "Era 1 (Years 1-2): The Project Management Suite." "Era 2 (Years 3-4): The 3D Design & Collaboration Module." "Era 3 (Years 5-7): The Automated Compliance Engine." Isabelle would allow herself to dream in this document, but she would only review and update it once per quarter. This prevented the grand vision from becoming a source of daily distraction.
- **The Execution Roadmap (The Brick-Laying Plan):** This was a detailed, tactical, 90-day sprint plan. It was managed rigorously by her AI-powered RICE model, which analyzed user feedback and data from her *current* product. This roadmap was focused exclusively on the next logical, data-driven step.

2. The "CEO Time Block" Isabelle structured her work week to reflect this two-track thinking.

- **20 hours/week ("Bricklaying"):** This was her focused, deep work time, dedicated exclusively to the tasks on the Execution Roadmap. This was when she directed her AI co-pilot to build the next feature for the timeline plugin, or responded to user feedback.
- **5 hours/week ("Architecture"):** Every Friday afternoon was her protected, non-negotiable "CEO Time." During this five-hour block, she was forbidden from doing any operational work. Her only job was to zoom out. She would review the Vision Roadmap, use her AI research agent to explore new technologies and competitive moves, and think about the long-term strategic direction of the company. This ritual ensured that the urgent tasks of the week never completely crowded out the important work of long-term thinking.

3. The AI as the "Vision Keeper" Isabelle used her AI sparring partner to bridge the gap between her daily work and her long-term ambition. Once a month, she would run a specific prompt.

The Alignment Prompt

*"You are my strategic advisor. Attached are my 10-year Vision Roadmap and my current 90-day Execution Roadmap. Your task is to analyze both.

1. Are my current short-term priorities still in alignment with my long-term vision?
2. Identify one small thing I can do in the next 90-day sprint that will not only add immediate value to my current users, but will also create a small technical or strategic building block for the [Next Major Module] from my Vision Roadmap."*

This process was invaluable. The AI might suggest, for example, that when building a seemingly simple "file upload" feature for the timeline tool, she should structure the database in a specific way that would make it compatible with the 3D modeling engine she planned to build in two years. This ensured her daily "bricklaying" was always contributing to the structural integrity of the future "cathedral."

The Compounding Effect This disciplined, systematic approach allowed Isabelle to make steady, compounding progress. The timeline plugin became a profitable, self-sustaining product. The revenue and user data from that "brick" then funded and informed the development of the next module. Each stage was both a viable product in its own right and a stepping stone to the next level of the vision.

Isabelle's story is the perfect illustration of the founder's dual role. You must be the visionary architect who dreams of the cathedral, capable of seeing a decade into the future. But you must also be the disciplined mason who is obsessed with laying one perfect brick at a time. The key to success is building the mental and operational systems that allow you to be both.

Chapter Summary & Resources

This chapter has equipped you with the high-level strategic frameworks necessary to think and act like the CEO of a major enterprise, even as a company of one. We have explored how to build an AI-powered intelligence agency to achieve superior situational awareness, how to use mental models to recognize market-shifting opportunities before they become mainstream, how to construct modern, digital moats without a massive budget, and how to balance a grand, long-term vision with the disciplined focus required for daily execution.

Key Takeaways

- A solo founder can achieve superior strategic awareness by building an **AI "Compete" Agent** that provides a daily, real-time intelligence briefing on competitors, markets, and technologies.
- Market timing is not about predicting the future, but about using frameworks like the **S-Curve** and **Jobs-to-be-Done** to recognize the present more clearly than your competitors.

- Modern, defensible **moats** for a solo founder are not built with headcount, but with self-reinforcing loops of data network effects, proprietary fine-tuned AI models, and passionate communities.
- Successfully navigating the founder's journey requires a system, like a **"Two-Track Roadmap,"** for balancing a grand, long-term vision with the disciplined, data-driven short-term execution needed to get there.

Setting Up Your AI Strategy Officer

Take the first steps to building your own strategic intelligence system.

- **Define Your "Sensors":** List five specific online sources (e.g., a key competitor's blog, a specific subreddit for your industry, a tech news site) that you would want your AI "Compete" Agent to monitor daily.
- **Draft Your Master Prompt:** Write a draft of the master prompt you would use for your AI analyst to synthesize the data from your sensors into a concise daily briefing. Use the prompt in section 13.1 as a template.
- **Apply a Framework:** Pick one emerging technology that interests you (e.g., quantum computing, decentralized physical infrastructure networks). Where would you place it on the S-Curve (Ferment, Takeoff, or Maturity)? Write one sentence justifying your reasoning.
- **State Your Two-Track Vision:** In one sentence, write down your ambitious, 10-year "cathedral" vision. Then, in another sentence, write down the one "brick"—the smallest possible MVP—that you would build first.

Preview of Chapter 14

You now have the mindset and the strategic frameworks of a solo CEO. You know how to think at scale. The final challenge is to project that thinking outward, to influence an entire industry without a traditional team or corporate structure. In **Chapter 14, Leadership Without Followers**, we will explore the new model of solo leadership. You will learn how to build a powerful personal brand, create and nurture a passionate community, and exert industry-wide influence as a company of one.

Resources and Tools

- **Books:** *Good Strategy Bad Strategy* by Richard Rumelt; *7 Powers: The Foundations of Business Strategy* by Hamilton Helmer (for a deep, academic dive on moats).
- **Concepts:** The S-Curve of Technology Adoption; Jobs-to-be-Done (JTBD) Theory.
- **Tools for Monitoring: n8n.io** (for building the agent), Feedly, and Google Alerts can serve as simple starting points for monitoring your defined sources.

Chapter 14: Leadership Without Followers

Introduction

Leadership, in the traditional business lexicon, is inextricably linked to management. It is defined by the size of the team you command, the org chart you sit atop, and the number of direct reports who look to you for guidance. This definition, born from the industrial era of command-and-control, is now obsolete. For the solo founder, a new model of leadership is required—one that is decoupled from headcount and authority.

This new leadership is not about managing followers; it is about generating **influence**, articulating a **vision** so compelling that it creates a movement, and building a **community** that scales your impact far beyond your individual capacity. It is the ability to shape the conversation in your entire industry, to inspire a passionate user base to become your most vocal advocates, and to drive meaningful change, all as a company of one.

In the last chapter, we developed the strategic frameworks to out-think your competitors. In this chapter, we will learn how to project that strategic thought outward to lead your market. You will learn the strategies to become the go-to expert in your niche, the playbook for building a passionate community that acts as your de facto team, and the systems for using AI to amplify your voice. You do not need a C-suite or a PR department to be a titan of your industry; you need a powerful vision and the AI-powered systems to share it with the world.

14.1 Influencing Industries as a Solo Player

In any market, there are participants and there are agenda-setters. The vast majority of businesses are participants; they follow trends, react to market shifts, and compete within the established rules of the game. The true industry leaders are the agenda-setters; they create the trends, they cause the market shifts, and they rewrite the rules of the game. For the solo founder, with your inherent advantages in speed and insight, your goal is to leapfrog the participant stage and establish yourself as the primary agenda-setter in your chosen niche. This is achieved not through a massive marketing budget, but through the strategic amplification of unique insights and decisive action.

Strategy 1: The "Proprietary Insight" Engine The most valuable currency in any industry is a new, non-obvious insight. While your competitors are recycling the same generic content, you are sitting on a goldmine of unique, proprietary data generated by your own business. Your AI BI system is the key to mining this gold and turning it into industry-defining thought leadership.

- **The AI-Powered Workflow:**
    1. **Discovery:** You task your AI BI tool to find a surprising, counter-intuitive correlation in your user data. For example, your analysis of "SyncUp AI" (our case study product) might reveal: "Our data shows that teams who keep their internal meetings to under 25 minutes have a 40% higher project completion rate than those with 60-minute meetings."
    2. **Amplification:** You feed this single, powerful data point into your autonomous marketing engine. The prompt for your LLM is not to write a simple blog post, but to frame a paradigm-shifting argument.

    The Thought Leadership Prompt

    "You are a thought leadership writer for a publication like Harvard Business Review. I have a proprietary data point: [insert insight]. Your task is to write a compelling, 2000-word article titled 'The 25-Minute Mandate: The Data-Backed Case for Radically Shorter Meetings.' Use my data as the centerpiece of a larger argument. Include a strong narrative, challenge conventional wisdom, and provide actionable advice for managers."

- **The Impact:** You are no longer just another voice in the conversation about "productivity." You are now the author of the

"25-Minute Mandate." You have introduced a new, data-backed idea into the ecosystem that forces everyone else—your competitors, industry analysts, and potential customers—to react to *your* framework. You are setting the agenda.

Strategy 2: Strategic Action as Marketing In the world of software, actions often speak louder than words. A single, decisive action can generate more influence and goodwill than a year's worth of content marketing.

- **Open-Sourcing a Tool:** You can build a small, elegant solution to a common problem your audience faces and release it for free as an open-source project on GitHub. This is not about giving away your core product, but about offering a valuable "public good." This act instantly establishes your technical credibility and generosity, building a deep reservoir of trust.
- **Publishing a Transparent Dashboard:** In an age of corporate opacity, radical transparency is a powerful form of leadership. Using a tool like Baremetrics or by building a simple page on your site, you can publicly share your key business metrics—your ARR, user growth, churn, etc. This makes your journey a public case study, attracting a loyal following of other entrepreneurs and potential customers who admire your authenticity.
- **Taking a Contrarian Stance:** Your AI "Compete" Agent can be tasked with identifying a widely-held industry belief that is based on flimsy evidence. You can then write a well-researched, data-backed article that methodically dismantles this sacred cow. This positions you as a courageous, independent thinker.

Strategy 3: Building in Public This is the ultimate form of transparent, authentic leadership. Instead of building your product in a secret lab and unveiling it in a grand launch, you share the entire journey in real-time on social media, a blog, or a newsletter. You share the highs and the lows, the product mockups and the user feedback, the revenue milestones and the painful lessons.

- **The Benefits for a Solo Founder:**

1. **It Builds Your "Team" Before You Launch:** People become emotionally invested in your story. They root for you. They feel like part of the journey and are eager to become your first, most passionate customers.
2. **It De-Risks Product Development:** You have a built-in, real-time feedback loop with your target audience. You are co-creating the product with them, dramatically increasing the odds of achieving product-market fit.
3. **It Forges an Unbreakable Bond:** This level of authenticity builds a degree of trust and human connection that a faceless corporation can never replicate. Your story becomes your brand.

The solo founder cannot compete on the traditional metrics of authority like headcount or years in business. Your authority must be earned through the consistent demonstration of superior insight and strategic action. By becoming the primary source of new ideas in your niche, you create an influence moat that is far more defensible than any marketing budget.

14.2 Building Communities Around Your Vision

The single greatest asset of a solo-founded enterprise is not its technology, its intellectual property, or its revenue. It is the passionate, engaged community of users that forms around its product and its vision. A community is not just a marketing channel or a support queue; it is your unpaid, deeply motivated, and fiercely loyal de facto team. They are your evangelists who spread the word, your R&D department that provides invaluable product feedback, your support agents who help new users, and your defensive moat that protects you from competitors. Intentionally cultivating this community is one of the highest-leverage activities a solo founder can undertake.

Step 1: Choose the "Watering Hole" A community must be built where your users already feel comfortable and are actively congregating. Forcing them to adopt a new, proprietary forum on your website is a recipe for a ghost town.

- **The Platform Options:**

    - **Discord:** Ideal for tech-savvy audiences, developers, creators, and gamers. It allows for real-time, fluid conversations and a high degree of organization with different channels.
    - **Slack:** Excellent for B2B communities where users are already living in Slack for their workday.
    - **Circle.so or similar:** A more modern, structured, and brandable forum-style platform that feels like a private social network.
    - **A Subreddit:** A viable option if your target audience is already deeply entrenched in the Reddit ecosystem.
- **The AI-Assisted Decision:** Use an LLM to help you make this critical choice. **Prompt:** *"You are a community strategy consultant. My target audience is [detailed description of your ideal customer]. Analyze the strategic pros and cons of using Discord, Slack, and Circle.so to build a community for this specific audience. Provide a clear recommendation and justify it based on factors like user demographics, conversation style, and monetization potential."*

Step 2: The Founder's Role as "Chief Instigator" In the early days (the first few hundred members), a community cannot be a passive democracy. It needs a leader to spark the initial energy and set the cultural tone. Your job is to be the Chief Instigator.

- **Daily Rituals for Seeding Engagement:**
    - Post a thought-provoking "Question of the Day" related to your niche.
    - Share your own work-in-progress and genuinely ask for feedback.
    - Create a "#wins" channel and be the first to celebrate a member's success.
    - Personally welcome every new member for the first 100 members. Your early, high-touch engagement sets the cultural DNA of the community—is it supportive, expert-driven, collaborative, or competitive? You are the role model.

Step 3: Empowering Superusers and Automating Management A community that relies solely on the founder for energy cannot scale. The goal is to systematically transition the community from being founder-led to being self-sustaining.

- **Identifying Your Champions:** Your AI BI tool can be pointed at your community platform's data. **Prompt:** *"Analyze our Discord community data for the last 90 days. Identify the top 5% of members based on a weighted score of their message count, the number of 'reactions' their messages receive, and the number of times they have provided a helpful answer in the #help channel."*
- **Empowering a Volunteer Team:** You can reach out to these identified "superusers" and offer them an official "Community Moderator" or "Community Helper" role. The perks are not financial, but status- and access-based: a special role color, access to a private channel with you, and early access to new features. This creates a loyal volunteer team that feels a deep sense of ownership.
- **The AI Community Manager:** As the community grows, you deploy an AI agent to handle the scalable management tasks. It can be programmed to automatically welcome new members and point them to the community guidelines, monitor for and flag spam or inappropriate content for the human moderators, and identify frequently asked questions that should be turned into a permanent guide.

Step 4: The Community-Product Feedback Loop Your community is your single greatest source of product feedback. You must create a frictionless, transparent system to capture and act on their insights.

- **The Workflow:**
    1. Create a dedicated `#feature-requests` and a `#bug-reports` channel.
    2. An **n8n** workflow monitors these channels in real-time.
    3. When a new feature is requested, the workflow sends the text to an LLM to be summarized, categorized (e.g., 'UI

Improvement,' 'New Integration'), and checked for duplicates.
4. The cleaned-up request is then automatically added as a new entry into your product roadmap database in Notion, linked to the community member who requested it.
5. When you change the status of that feature in Notion to "In Progress," the workflow automatically posts an update back in the original thread: "Great news! We've started working on this feature."

This automated, transparent loop is incredibly powerful. It makes your community feel heard and valued, transforming them from passive users into active co-creators of your product. A competitor can copy your features, but they can never copy the trust, history, and collective intelligence of the community you have built.

14.3 Thought Leadership Through AI-Amplified Content

In the modern business landscape, expertise is the new currency. The most influential leaders are not necessarily those with the largest teams, but those with the most insightful, valuable, and consistent ideas. "Thought leadership" is the strategic process of establishing yourself as the go-to expert in your niche. For a solo founder, this is not a vanity project; it is a critical growth strategy that drives inbound leads, builds brand equity, and creates a powerful influence moat. The primary obstacle is the immense time and effort traditionally required to produce high-quality content across multiple platforms. This is a problem perfectly suited for an AI-amplified system.

The "Atomization" Framework: Create Once, Distribute Forever
The common content trap is trying to create unique, original content for every single platform. This is a recipe for burnout and mediocre output. The "atomization" framework is a far more leveraged approach. You focus your limited creative energy on producing one high-value, long-form "pillar" piece of content, and then use an AI-powered system to slice, dice, and repurpose that pillar into dozens of smaller "atomic" pieces for distribution across all your channels.

The AI-Amplified Content Workflow

This system is designed to turn a single hour of your focused, creative work into a full week's worth of multi-channel, high-quality thought leadership content.

Step 1: The "Pillar" Creation (The Founder's 1-Hour Input) Your only manual task in this entire system is to create one "pillar" piece of content per week. This is where you must deliver your most unique, proprietary, and insightful thinking—the kind of analysis that only you can provide.

- **Examples of a Pillar:**
    - A 30-minute solo podcast or video where you discuss a proprietary insight discovered by your AI BI tool.
    - A detailed, 2,000-word blog post that presents a contrarian viewpoint on a major industry trend.
    - A live, one-hour webinar or Q&A session with your community.

Step 2: AI-Powered Transcription and Analysis The pillar content, in its raw audio or video format, is the input for your automated system.

1. It is first fed into a highly accurate AI transcription service (like Descript or a specialized API) to create a clean, readable text document.
2. This full transcript is then fed into a sophisticated LLM like Claude 4 Opus.

The Content Atomization Prompt

*"You are an expert content strategist and editor. I have provided the full transcript of my latest podcast on [topic]. Your task is to atomize this content. You must:

1. Provide a clean, edited version of the full transcript suitable for a blog post.
2. Write a concise, 250-word summary suitable for an email newsletter.
3. Identify the 7 most powerful, quotable, and counter-intuitive 'soundbites' from the text.
4. For each soundbite, write a short, engaging caption for a social media post."*

Step 3: The Automated Distribution Engine (The n8n Workflow)
The structured output from the LLM now triggers a massive, parallel content distribution workflow in **n8n**:

- **The Full Transcript** is automatically sent to your **Webflow** CMS, creating a new, SEO-optimized blog post.
- **The Newsletter Summary** becomes the body of a new email campaign in **Mailchimp**, which is then scheduled to be sent to your subscribers.
- **The 7 Soundbites and Captions** are piped to an AI image generator like **Midjourney** to create seven visually appealing quote cards. These are then scheduled across Instagram and LinkedIn using a social media scheduling API like **Buffer**.
- **The 7 Soundbites** are also used to create a 7-day X/Twitter thread, with one soundbite being posted each day.
- **The Original Audio/Video File** is sent to an AI video editing tool. This tool uses the soundbites as markers to automatically find and edit seven short, vertical video clips, complete with animated captions. These clips are then scheduled for distribution on TikTok, YouTube Shorts, and Instagram Reels.

From your single, one-hour creative session, your AI-powered system has generated and scheduled an entire week of content, creating a "ubiquity effect." You appear to be an omnipresent, prolific thought leader, when in reality, you have leveraged a system to amplify your one core insight across the entire digital landscape. This is how you scale your voice, build a powerful brand, and become the undisputed authority in your field.

Strategic Scenario: The Network Effect for Individuals

In the world of solo entrepreneurship, there is a hidden moat that is often more powerful than any technology or business model: a deep, authentic, and influential personal network. A powerful network provides the leverage of a large corporation—deal flow, partnerships, strategic advice, and distribution—without any of the overhead. The story of "Momentum" and its founder, Chloé Dubois, illustrates how a solo founder can systematically build this "network effect for an individual."

The Founder: Chloé Dubois, a brilliant product-focused founder and a self-professed introvert who was initially terrified by the idea of "networking."

The Product: Momentum, a B2B SaaS tool that helps other SaaS founders manage their user feedback, build public roadmaps, and communicate product updates. Her target customers were other founders like herself.

The Business Outcome: Chloé successfully grew Momentum to **$5 million in ARR**. But her most valuable asset was not the company's revenue; it was her personal network. She became one of the most respected "super-connectors" in the SaaS ecosystem, which in turn created an unassailable competitive advantage for her business.

The Mindset Shift: From "Getting" to "Giving" Chloé's initial attempts at networking were a failure. She attended conferences and tried to make small talk, always feeling like she needed to "get" something—a new customer, a piece of advice, an introduction. It felt transactional and inauthentic.

Her breakthrough came when she decided to flip the script entirely. She realized the most powerful networkers don't focus on what they can get; they focus relentlessly on what they can **give**. Her new, single-minded goal was to become the most helpful person in her ecosystem. To do this at scale, she built a system.

The "Helpfulness Engine": A System for Scalable Generosity Chloé re-tasked her AI "Compete" Agent to become a "Helpfulness Engine."

- **The AI Listener:** The system was programmed to monitor X/Twitter, Reddit, and private founder communities not for competitive intelligence, but for "cries for help." It was fine-tuned to identify posts from other founders asking for recommendations or advice, such as: "Does anyone know a great lawyer for a Series A funding round?" or "I'm struggling to get my user churn rate below 5%."
- **The Human Connector:** Each morning, the AI would present Chloé with a digest of 3-5 opportunities to be helpful. Chloé would then spend a focused 30-minute block providing genuine, no-strings-attached value. If someone needed a lawyer, she'd make a warm email introduction to the one she used. If someone was struggling with churn, she'd share a link to a private playbook she'd written. She never mentioned her own product unless it was directly relevant. Her only goal was to help.

The Compounding Returns of Social Capital Over the course of two years, Chloé's reputation underwent a profound transformation. She was no longer just another founder; she was the ecosystem's go-to "super-connector." This immense social capital began to pay compounding dividends that functioned like the departments of a large corporation.

- **Her Automated "Sales & BD" Department:** Founders she had helped would proactively send new customers her way. VCs would send promising startups from their portfolio to use her tool. When she wanted to build an integration with a major platform, she often already had a warm relationship with their founder, allowing a partnership to be sealed with a single email. Her customer acquisition became almost entirely driven by word-of-mouth and warm referrals from her network.
- **Her Personal "Board of Directors":** She cultivated a small, private group of other successful founders whom she had helped

in the past. This became her trusted advisory board. When she faced a difficult strategic decision, she could tap into a world-class brain trust for advice—for free.

- **The AI-Powered "Relationship CRM":** To manage her growing network, Chloé used a simple Airtable base as a personal CRM. Before meeting with or emailing a key contact, she would use an AI prompt: *"Summarize the last 5 X/Twitter posts from [Founder Name] and any recent news about their company, [Company Name]."* This allowed her to start every conversation with a relevant, personal touch, further strengthening her relationships.

Chloé Dubois's story redefines networking. It is not an extrovert's game of schmoozing at conferences. It is the systematic, introvert-friendly process of creating value for others. By building a "helpfulness engine," she created a powerful, self-reinforcing network effect around herself as an individual. This personal network became her company's most valuable asset and its deepest competitive moat, providing her with the strategic leverage of an entire corporate development department.

Chapter Summary & Resources

This chapter has redefined leadership for the solo founder. We have moved beyond the traditional model of managing followers and established a new framework based on influence, vision, and community. By systematically generating proprietary insights, building a passionate user base that acts as your de facto team, amplifying your voice with AI, and creating a powerful personal network, a single person can achieve the impact and authority of an entire executive suite.

Key Takeaways

- Solo-founder leadership is about **influence, not authority**. You lead your industry by becoming the primary source of new, data-backed ideas and by shaping the conversation in your market.
- An **AI-amplified content "atomization"** system allows a solo founder to create a ubiquitous thought leadership presence from just a few hours of creative work per week.

- A passionate **community** is a solo founder's greatest asset, acting as their evangelists, their R&D department, and their most durable competitive moat.
- A powerful personal **network**, built on a systematic "give first" mentality, can provide the deal flow, partnerships, and strategic advice of a large corporation.

Your Solo Leadership Playbook

- **Find Your Proprietary Insight:** What is one unique, non-obvious data point that your business (or your unique experience) could generate? (e.g., "My data shows that users who do X are 3x more likely to succeed.").
- **Design Your Content Atomization:** Take that one insight. List the five different "atomic" pieces of content you could repurpose it into (e.g., a blog post, a Twitter thread, a short video, a quote graphic, a newsletter section).
- **Choose Your Community "Watering Hole":** Where do your ideal customers already congregate online? (e.g., a specific subreddit, a professional Slack group). Commit to spending one week there just listening to their conversations.
- **Schedule Your "Give First" Action:** Put a single 15-minute block on your calendar for next week with the title "Help Someone in My Network" with zero expectation of getting anything in return.

Preview of Chapter 15

You now possess the frameworks to lead as a company of one. You can influence your industry, build a community, and leverage a powerful network. We have completed our exploration of the Billion-Dollar Mindset. Now, we must apply this mindset to the final, most concrete challenge: designing the business itself. In **Chapter 15, The Billion-Dollar Business Model**, we will deconstruct the specific industries, revenue models, and IP strategies that have a realistic path to a ten-figure valuation.

Resources and Tools

- **Books:** *Superconnector* by Scott Gerber and Ryan Paugh; *The 22 Immutable Laws of Marketing* by Al Ries and Jack Trout.
- **Community Platforms:** Discord, Circle.so, Slack.
- **Content Creation Tools:** Descript (for editing and clipping audio/video), HeyGen (for AI video creation), Midjourney (for visuals)

Chapter 15: The Billion-Dollar Business Model

Introduction

A billion-dollar mindset, a world-class strategic framework, and a flawlessly automated operational stack are all essential components of the journey. But they are not sufficient. The grandest vision will ultimately fail if it is built upon a business and revenue model that is fundamentally incapable of scaling to a ten-figure valuation. The very architecture of your business—the industry you choose to compete in and the way you choose to charge for your value—will define its ultimate potential.

This chapter answers the final, most practical question of the billion-dollar mindset: "What kind of business should I actually build?" It is about moving from the abstract ambition of a massive valuation to the concrete blueprint of a company that has a realistic path to achieving it. We will bridge the gap between your capabilities as an AI-powered solo founder and the vast market opportunities waiting to be seized.

We will deconstruct the specific characteristics of industries that are ripe for solo-founder disruption, identifying the lumbering, inefficient dinosaurs that a nimble, intelligent competitor can outmaneuver. We will then move beyond simple pricing strategies to design sophisticated revenue models that scale exponentially with the value you create. This is the capstone of your strategic education—the process of architecting a business that is, from its very DNA, designed to become a billion-dollar enterprise.

15.1 Industries Ripe for Solo Disruption

Your mission as a solo founder is not to engage in a fair fight. It is to find a battlefield where the rules are tilted so heavily in your favor that victory is almost a foregone conclusion. This means actively seeking out industries dominated by large, slow-moving incumbents bogged down by legacy technology and inefficient, human-powered processes. Think of yourself as a hunter of corporate dinosaurs. You are looking for markets characterized by three key vulnerabilities: high margins with operational bloat, chronic information inefficiency, and service-based bottlenecks.

1. Vulnerability: High Margins & Inefficient Bloat The first signal of a ripe industry is the presence of established players with massive gross margins. This proves that customers are willing and able to pay a premium for a valuable service. However, if those same players have enormous operational costs—thousands of salespeople, layers of middle management, expensive physical offices—their bloat becomes your opportunity.

- **The Target: Legacy Enterprise Software.** Think of the old-guard CRM, ERP, or HR software companies. They often lock customers into huge, multi-year contracts sold by massive enterprise sales teams. Their products are powerful but notoriously complex and expensive to maintain.
- **The Solo Founder's Attack Vector:** You can build a self-serve, AI-powered alternative that delivers the 20% of features that 80% of users actually need. By replacing the entire sales and support organization with the automated systems we've designed, you can offer your product for a fraction of the price and still operate with a spectacular 90% profit margin.

2. Vulnerability: Information Inefficiency & Asymmetry Look for industries where the primary value is derived from the difficult and time-consuming process of analyzing vast amounts of complex, unstructured information. These are industries where "expert knowledge" has traditionally been a moat. Large Language Models are a wrecking ball to this type of moat.

- **The Target: The Legal and Paralegal Industry.** At its core, much of legal work involves reading and synthesizing immense volumes of text: contracts, case law, discovery documents. This is a task that AI can now perform faster, more comprehensively, and more accurately than a human.
- **The Solo Founder's Attack Vector:** You can build a niche B2B SaaS tool that productizes a specific legal task. Imagine a tool that can analyze a 50-page commercial lease and, in seconds,

produce a one-page summary of all non-standard clauses and potential risks. You are not selling legal advice; you are selling informational leverage at a scale no traditional law firm can match. The same principle applies to market research, consulting, and financial analysis.

3. Vulnerability: Service-Based Bottlenecks The third category includes industries where the core value is delivered by a skilled human performing a repeatable service. These manual processes are bottlenecks by definition; a single human can only do so much work in a day. AI is the ultimate tool for "productizing" these services, turning a linear, time-bound service into an infinitely scalable product.

- **The Target: Creative Services and Agencies.** A traditional marketing agency employs teams of copywriters, graphic designers, and video editors to create campaigns for clients. This is a high-cost, low-scalability model.
- **The Solo Founder's Attack Vector:** You build a specialized, generative AI tool that performs the function of an entire agency. Instead of hiring a firm for $20,000 to create a social media campaign, a customer pays your SaaS $200 a month to generate a thousand unique social media visuals, write all the copy, and even produce short-form videos.

The Synthesis: The AI-Native Business Model The ultimate opportunity for a solo founder is not just to disrupt an existing industry, but to create an entirely new category of business that simply could not have existed before the current generation of AI. An **AI-Native** business is one where the AI is not just a feature that improves the product; the AI *is* the product.

- **Example: AI Agents as a Service.** Imagine a platform where a small business can "hire" a team of specialized, autonomous AI agents to run their operations. They could hire an AI agent to manage their customer support, an AI agent to run their bookkeeping, and an AI agent to handle their social media marketing, all for a monthly subscription fee. The solo founder is not selling a tool; they are selling a virtual, automated workforce.

By specifically targeting industries with these deep-seated vulnerabilities, the solo founder creates an asymmetric advantage. You are bringing a new, hyper-efficient, and intelligent business model to a fight against slow, inefficient, and unintelligent incumbents.

15.2 Revenue Model Design for Extreme Scale

How you charge for your product is one of the most important strategic decisions you will ever make. It is not a financial afterthought; it is a core product feature that communicates value, influences user behavior, and ultimately determines the scalability of your entire enterprise. The simple, flat-rate subscription model that gets you to your first million in revenue is often not the model that will carry you to a billion. To achieve extreme scale, you must design a revenue model that grows exponentially as your customers derive more value from your product.

Beyond the Simple Subscription: The Three Axes of Scalable Pricing While a basic subscription is a great starting point, the most successful and scalable AI-native businesses evolve toward more sophisticated models that perfectly align their revenue with the value they create. We will explore three such models.

1. Usage-Based Pricing (The Pay-as-you-go Model) In this model, customers are charged based on their consumption of a specific metric—API calls, hours of video processed, number of contacts analyzed, or words generated.

- **Why it's Perfectly Suited for AI Businesses:** The largest variable cost for many AI products is the cost of the underlying API calls to foundational models. By tying your pricing directly to usage, your revenue automatically and elegantly scales with your costs, protecting your profit margins at all times.
- **The Growth Flywheel:** This model is incredibly effective for product-led growth. It creates a frictionless entry point for new users, who can start with very low usage (and low cost). As their business grows and they find more value in your product, their usage naturally increases, and they seamlessly become a larger and larger customer without ever hitting a "pricing wall" or

needing to speak to a salesperson. Your revenue grows *in direct proportion to your customers' success.*

- **Example:** An AI-powered video editing platform that charges $0.10 per minute of video rendered. A casual user might spend $5 per month, while a professional creative agency could easily spend $5,000 per month, all within the same self-serve system.

2. Value-Based Pricing (The Outcome-as-a-Service Model) This is the most advanced and potentially the most lucrative pricing model. Instead of charging for features or usage, you charge for the direct, measurable business outcome your product delivers.

- **Why it's a Billion-Dollar Lever:** It completely reframes the sales conversation. Your product is no longer a "cost" to be minimized; it is a "profit center" to be invested in. Because you can prove a direct ROI, you can command prices that are an order of magnitude higher than competitors who are simply selling software.
- **The Prerequisite:** This model only works if your product can demonstrably and quantifiably impact a critical business metric for your customer (e.g., revenue generated, costs saved, leads converted).
- **Example:** An AI tool that optimizes a company's spending on cloud services like AWS. The pricing model could be: *"Our service is free to implement. We simply take a 15% share of the money we save you on your cloud bill each month."* If you save a client $200,000 in a year, you earn $30,000. The sale is incredibly easy to make because there is zero upfront risk for the customer and the value is guaranteed.

3. The Hybrid Model (The Best of Both Worlds) For many SaaS businesses, the optimal solution is a hybrid model that combines the predictability of a subscription with the scalability of a usage- or value-based component.

- **The Structure:**
    1. **Platform Fee:** A stable, recurring subscription fee (e.g., $199/month) that gives the customer access to the core

platform and a generous baseline allowance of usage. This creates a predictable revenue floor.

2. **Usage Tier:** Once the baseline allowance is exceeded, the customer pays for additional usage. This allows you to capture the massive upside from your most successful power users.
3. **Value-Based Add-ons (Optional):** You can offer specific, high-impact features as add-ons that are priced based on the value they generate.

- **Example:** Our automated sales outreach tool. The base subscription of $199/month includes 1,000 enriched contacts. Beyond that, the customer pays $0.10 per additional contact. They could also purchase a "Conversion Booster" add-on, an AI that optimizes their email copy, for which they pay an additional 1% of the value of any deals closed through that campaign.

Your revenue model is a strategic tool. Start with a simple, easy-to-understand subscription to achieve product-market fit. But as you scale, relentlessly seek to evolve your pricing to better align with the value you create. This is how you build a truly exponential revenue engine.

15.3 Intellectual Property Strategy for Solo Founders

In the traditional industrial economy, Intellectual Property (IP) was synonymous with patents for physical inventions and trademarks for established brands. In the AI-first economy, the landscape of what constitutes a valuable, defensible asset has been radically transformed. For the solo founder, your most precious IP is not a patent on a specific algorithm; it is the living, evolving ecosystem of proprietary data, specialized AI models, and unique automated processes that make your business intelligent and efficient. A sophisticated IP strategy is not just about legal protection; it is about systematically building a portfolio of defensible assets that increases your company's valuation.

IP Asset #1: Proprietary Data (The Crown Jewels) As we established when discussing moats, your unique, proprietary dataset is your single most defensible long-term asset. This is the data generated through user interactions, which you use to make your AI models smarter than anyone else's. Protecting it is paramount.

- **Legal Protection:** Your first line of defense is a well-drafted Terms of Service and Privacy Policy. It is critical to work with a qualified lawyer to ensure these documents give you the clear right to use anonymized, aggregated user interaction data to train your models and improve your services. This legal foundation is non-negotiable.
- **Technical Protection:** Your databases must be treated like a fortified vault. This means employing best-in-class security practices: end-to-end encryption, strict access controls, and regular, automated security audits of your infrastructure. A data breach is not just a privacy violation; it is the potential theft of your crown jewels.
- **Process Protection:** Implement automated data anonymization pipelines that systematically strip all Personally Identifiable Information (PII) from user data before it is added to your training datasets. This not only protects your users' privacy but also ensures you remain compliant with global regulations like GDPR.

IP Asset #2: Fine-Tuned AI Models (The "Secret Sauce") Your specialized, fine-tuned AI model, trained on your proprietary data, is a unique and powerful asset. While the base model you started with might be a commodity, your version of it is your secret sauce.

- **Protection via Trade Secrets:** This is the most effective strategy for protecting your models. Unlike a patent, which requires you to publicly disclose the inner workings of your invention, a trade secret is protected by keeping it confidential. Your model "weights" (the specific parameters of your trained model) and your unique fine-tuning methodology are treated as highly confidential, proprietary information.
- **Technical and Contractual Controls:** The model itself should be hosted in a secure cloud environment with access limited to you and you alone. If you ever need to hire a freelance machine learning expert to assist you, they must sign a robust Non-Disclosure Agreement (NDA) and a Proprietary Information and Inventions Agreement (PIIA) that clearly states that all work product belongs to your company.

IP Asset #3: Automated Processes (The "Operational DNA") The complex, interconnected web of your n8n workflows, your specific LLM prompts, and the overall architecture of your "Company OS" is a valuable form of intellectual property. This system represents your unique, hyper-efficient method of operation, which a competitor could not easily replicate.

- **Copyright and Trade Secrets:** The specific code you write and the detailed text of your prompts are automatically protected by copyright. The overall design and logic of your automated systems can be protected as a trade secret.
- **Documentation as a Record:** Meticulously documenting these proprietary processes in your Notion "Central Brain" serves a dual purpose. It de-risks the business by externalizing knowledge, and it also creates a clear, time-stamped record of your unique operational IP. This documentation becomes an incredibly valuable asset during the due diligence process of a future sale or investment round.

The Role of Trademarks and Patents

- **Trademarks:** These are essential and relatively inexpensive. As soon as you have validated your business idea and chosen a name, you should file for a trademark to protect your brand identity.
- **Patents:** For AI software, patents are often a poor strategy for a solo founder. The process is slow (often taking 3+ years) and extremely expensive. By the time a patent is granted, the underlying AI technology has often advanced so far that the patent is obsolete. Focusing on the more agile protection of trade secrets for your data, models, and processes is almost always a more effective approach.

Your IP strategy as a solo founder is a modern one, focused on building a multi-layered defense around the assets that truly drive value in the AI age.

Strategic Scenario: The Architected Exit

The ultimate test of a billion-dollar business model is its ability to create transferable value—value that can be realized in a massive exit. The story of "ClauseOS" and its founder, Ben Carter, is a masterclass in how to architect a solo-founded business from day one with the specific goal of a billion-dollar acquisition.

The Founder: Ben Carter, a former corporate lawyer who had spent a decade experiencing the immense inefficiencies of high-stakes contract review.

The Product: ClauseOS, an AI-native SaaS platform for the legal industry. It used a sophisticated, fine-tuned LLM to analyze complex legal contracts, instantly identifying risky clauses, non-standard language, and potential contradictions. It was a perfect attack on a ripe-for-disruption industry.

The Business Outcome: Ben built and ran ClauseOS as a solo founder for six years, growing it to a hyper-profitable **$50 million in Annual Recurring Revenue (ARR)**. He then sold the company to a major legal technology conglomerate in a landmark deal for **$1.2 billion**.

The "Secret": Designing for Acquisition from Day One Ben never intended to run ClauseOS for the rest of his life. From the moment he validated the idea, every strategic decision was made through the lens of a single question: "Will this make my company a more valuable and attractive acquisition target in five to seven years?"

Part 1: The Blueprint (Year 1)

- **Choosing the Battlefield:** Ben deliberately chose the legal tech space because he knew it was dominated by a few large, slow-moving incumbents (like Thomson Reuters and LexisNexis). These companies had massive distribution channels and vast customer bases but were struggling to innovate with AI. He correctly identified them not as his primary competitors, but as his most likely future buyers.

- **Architecting the Revenue Model:** He chose a hybrid pricing model: a base per-seat subscription for law firms, plus a usage-based fee for every document analyzed. He knew this would be highly attractive to an acquirer, as it demonstrated both a predictable recurring revenue base and a scalable, high-margin upside.
- **Building the IP Portfolio:** From the start, his IP strategy was meticulous. His Terms of Service were ironclad, granting him the right to use anonymized contract data to train his models. He protected his proprietary contract-analysis AI model as a trade secret and immediately trademarked the "ClauseOS" name and logo.

Part 2: The Build (Years 2-5) - Creating a "Business in a Box" Ben knew that a business that was dependent on its founder was a risky and therefore less valuable asset. His goal was to build a company that could run without him.

- **The Maniacal Focus on Documentation:** He built his "Company OS" in Notion with the obsession of a librarian. Every single SOP, every strategic decision, every data model, and every piece of technical architecture was flawlessly documented. He was not just building a company; he was building the company's instruction manual. He knew this would make the future due diligence process seamless.
- **Pristine, Auditable Financials:** His automated finance stack meant that from day one, his financials were perfect, real-time, and easily auditable. There were no messy spreadsheets or co-mingled personal and business expenses. This signaled a level of professionalism and maturity that is rare in early-stage companies.

Part 3: The Signal (Year 6) - Making the Business Discoverable Once ClauseOS reached a significant scale (around $30M ARR), Ben began to intentionally make his company more visible to his short list of potential acquirers.

- **Strategic Integrations:** He dedicated a development cycle to building deep, valuable integrations with the core products of his top three potential buyers. This was a brilliant strategic move. It got his company onto their corporate development radar in a positive, collaborative way, and it proved the technical compatibility of their platforms, de-risking a future acquisition.
- **Hiring the Specialist:** At the $50M ARR mark, Ben made his first and only "hire." He did not hire a VP of Sales or a COO. He retained a top-tier investment banker who specialized in SaaS M&A. He hired an expert not to help him *run* the business, but to help him *sell* it.

Part 4: The Exit - The Payoff The final stage was a masterclass in execution.

- **The Bidding War:** Because Ben had built strategic relationships with multiple potential buyers through his integration strategy, his banker was able to create a competitive bidding process, which dramatically drove up the final sale price.
- **Frictionless Due Diligence:** The acquirer's due diligence team was astounded. When they asked for financial records, Ben gave them a secure login to his live financial dashboard. When they asked for technical documentation, he gave them access to the perfectly organized "Company OS." The process, which often takes months and is fraught with tension, was completed in three weeks. This transparency built immense trust and confidence.
- **The Final Valuation:** ClauseOS was acquired for $1.2 billion, a staggering 24x multiple on its revenue. The acquirer's CEO later stated that they paid such a high premium not just for the revenue, but for the "perfectly architected, self-running machine" that Ben had built. They were buying a flawless, scalable asset, not just a product.

Ben's story shows that a billion-dollar exit is rarely an accident. It is the result of a deliberate, long-term strategy that informs every decision, from the choice of industry to the details of documentation.

Chapter Summary & Resources

This chapter provided the final and most concrete piece of the billion-dollar mindset: the architecture of the business itself. We have moved from abstract strategy to a tangible blueprint for building a company that is designed for extreme scale from its very inception. By selecting a ripe industry, designing a scalable revenue model, building a defensible IP portfolio, and planning for an eventual exit from day one, you are laying the foundational stones for a ten-figure enterprise.

Key Takeaways

- Billion-dollar opportunities for solo founders lie in **"ripe" industries** characterized by high margins, information inefficiencies, and service-based bottlenecks that can be dismantled with AI.
- Revenue models must evolve beyond simple subscriptions to **usage-based or hybrid models** that align your price directly with the value your customers receive, enabling exponential scaling.
- A solo founder's most valuable Intellectual Property is often their proprietary **data and fine-tuned AI models**, which are best protected as trade secrets rather than patents.
- Designing your business to be a **valuable, transferable asset** from day one—with clean financials, defensible IP, and meticulous documentation—is the key to a massive and successful exit.

The Billion-Dollar Model Checklist

- **Industry Analysis:** Choose one industry from Section 15.1. List the three biggest 'dinosaur' incumbents and identify one specific inefficiency in their business model that your AI-native product could solve.
- **Revenue Model Design:** Sketch out a hybrid pricing model for your business idea. What is the base subscription fee that provides predictable revenue? What is the usage-based component that allows for exponential upside?
- **IP Audit:** What will be your single most valuable and defensible piece of IP? Will it be your proprietary user data, your fine-tuned

AI model, or your brand? What is one step you can take now to legally or technically protect it?

- **Exit Brainstorm:** List the top three companies that would be the most logical acquirers of your business in 5-7 years. What makes you a strategic fit for them?

Preview of Part 5: The Future Fundable

In Part 4, we have cultivated the mindset and designed the business model for a billion-dollar enterprise. You have the internal psychology and the strategic blueprint. But what if you decide you want to accelerate your journey with outside capital? How does the world of venture capital view a hyper-efficient company of one? In **Part 5, The Future Fundable**, we enter the world of high-stakes fundraising. We will explore how VCs are adapting their investment criteria to this new paradigm and provide a complete playbook for raising capital as a solo founder, starting with **Chapter 16: Redefining Investment Criteria.**

Resources and Tools

- **Books:** *The E-Myth Revisited* by Michael E. Gerber (for a masterclass on the importance of systemization); *Built to Sell* by John Warrillow (for the mindset of building a transferable asset).
- **IP Resources:** The United States Patent and Trademark Office (USPTO.gov) website provides excellent free resources for understanding the basics of trademarks and patents.
- **Exit Strategy:** To understand the minds of acquirers, follow the M&A-focused publications and investment banking blogs that cover the SaaS industry.

Part 5: The Future Fundable

The "Finish Line": Navigating the investment landscape and structuring for a unicorn valuation.

Chapter 16: Redefining Investment Criteria

Introduction

Picture the classic venture capital pitch: two co-founders in hoodies, standing in a Silicon Valley boardroom, asking for millions of dollars to hire their first team of engineers. For decades, this has been the archetypal scene at the beginning of every great startup journey. That scene, and the entire set of assumptions behind it, is rapidly becoming a relic. Venture capital, an industry built on identifying the future, is now scrambling to adapt to a new reality that is rewriting its own rulebook: the rise of the hyper-lean, solo-founded, AI-powered powerhouse.

The old VC playbook, which prioritized the founding team above all else, is breaking down. A single, brilliant founder with a flawlessly automated enterprise can now achieve capital efficiency and profit margins that were previously unimaginable, posing a new and complex challenge for investors. How do you value a company with millions in revenue and zero employees? How do you underwrite the risk of a single point of failure? VCs who fail to answer these questions and adapt their models will inevitably miss out on the next generation of unicorns.

In Part 4, you cultivated the mindset of a billion-dollar CEO. In this final part of the book, we will teach you how to communicate your vision to the people who write the biggest checks. This is your complete playbook for making your solo enterprise "fundable," should you choose to accelerate your journey with outside capital. We begin by pulling back the curtain on the changing world of venture capital, revealing the new criteria and the new metrics that define the future of investment.

16.1 What VCs Look for in Solo-Founded Companies

For generations, the venture capital mantra has been "we bet on the team, the team, the team." The quality, experience, and resilience of the founding team were considered the single most important predictor of a startup's success. This was a logical bet in an era where the primary function of capital was to hire human talent to execute a vision. But in a world where a solo founder can leverage AI to execute with the power of a 100-person organization, that logic is being fundamentally challenged. The most forward-thinking VCs at firms like Andreessen Horowitz (a16z), Sequoia Capital, and Y Combinator are not abandoning their core principles, but they are radically redefining how they evaluate founders and the companies they build.

The New Criterion #1: The Founder as a "Systems Architect" The evaluation of a solo founder has shifted from assessing their ability to *manage people* to assessing their ability to *design intelligent systems.* The VC is no longer just betting on a leader; they are betting on an architect. They need to see evidence that the founder is not just a great product builder, but a 10x systems thinker who has constructed a resilient, scalable, and automated enterprise.

- **What They Will Ask:** During a pitch meeting, the questions will be different. Instead of, "How will you build out your engineering team?" they will ask, "Walk me through your automated CI/CD pipeline and your AI-powered QA process." Instead of, "Who is your VP of Sales?" they will ask, "Show me the n8n workflow that powers your hyper-personalized outreach engine."
- **How to Demonstrate It:** You must be prepared to pitch your automated "team" with the same passion and detail as you would a human co-founder. Have your system architecture diagrams, your Notion "Company OS," and your key n8n workflows ready to share. The VC needs to underwrite the quality and resilience of your systems as a proxy for the traditional team.

The New Criterion #2: "Spiky" Talent and Maniacal Product Focus The ideal founding team was once thought to be a balanced trio: the hacker, the hipster, and the hustler. For a solo founder, VCs are now looking for the opposite: a "spiky" individual. This is a founder who is not well-rounded, but is in the top 1% of the world at **one specific thing**, be it a deep, almost esoteric understanding of their customer's problem, a genius for product design, or a world-class technical ability in a niche field.

- **Why This Matters:** Since there are no co-founders to compensate for weaknesses, the VC must believe that the founder's core "spike" is so sharp and so powerful that it can create a gravitational pull for the entire business. The founder is expected to use AI and automated systems to fill in their gaps, allowing their unique talent to be fully leveraged. Sequoia's famous concept of "founder-market fit" is now being re-evaluated as "founder-problem fit"—a founder with a maniacal, almost irrational obsession with solving a single, specific problem.

The New Criterion #3: Evidence of Extreme Capital Efficiency In the past, raising a large seed round was often seen as a badge of honor, a signal of ambition. Today, VCs are far more impressed by the opposite: a solo founder who has achieved escape velocity with little to no outside capital. Capital efficiency has become the new status symbol.

- **The Key Metric:** VCs are laser-focused on your "leverage ratio": how much ARR and user growth have you generated per dollar burned? A founder who can walk into a pitch and say, "We reached $1 million in ARR with a total capital burn of only $50,000," is making a powerful statement. They are proving that their business model is inherently profitable and that their systems are incredibly efficient. This de-risks the investment significantly. It shows that any capital invested will be used for strategic acceleration, not just to cover operational costs.

The New Criterion #4: A Defensible, Compounding AI Moat With the commoditization of powerful foundational models, the most pressing question for any investor in an AI company is: "What is your defensible moat?" The fear that a startup is just a "thin wrapper" on top of an OpenAI API—and could be made obsolete by a single feature announcement—is very real.

- **What They Will Scrutinize:**
  - **The Data Moat:** They will dig deep into your data network effect. "How, specifically, does your product

get smarter with each new user? What is the proprietary dataset you are building that no one else can replicate?"
    - **The Model Moat:** "Have you moved beyond generic APIs to build a fine-tuned, proprietary model trained on your unique data? How much better is it at its specific task than a general-purpose model like GPT-5?"
    - **The Community Moat:** "How strong is the network effect of your community? How does it contribute to user retention and product development in a way that a competitor cannot easily copy?"

VCs are still in the business of backing exceptional founders in massive markets. But their definition of an exceptional founder has evolved. It is no longer a charismatic manager of people, but a brilliant architect of systems, a spiky talent with a defensible, AI-native moat, and a disciplined master of capital efficiency.

16.2 Metrics That Matter in AI-First Businesses

The traditional SaaS dashboard, with its trusted metrics of Monthly Recurring Revenue (MRR), Customer Acquisition Cost (CAC), Lifetime Value (LTV), and churn, remains the foundation of a healthy business. But for an AI-first company, this dashboard is incomplete. The unique economics and operational models of AI-native businesses require a new set of metrics that provide a deeper insight into their efficiency, defensibility, and scalability. The sophisticated solo founder must track, understand, and be prepared to speak fluently about this new dashboard.

Metric #1: Gross Margin & The Cost of Intelligence The beauty of traditional SaaS was its near-perfect gross margin, often exceeding 90%. The cost of goods sold (COGS) was primarily fixed server hosting fees. This is no longer the case.

- **The New Reality: Inference Costs.** For most AI companies, the single largest component of COGS is the variable cost of running AI models—the "inference costs" paid for every API call. This can be substantial and can fluctuate with user activity.
- **The New Metric: Gross Margin Adjusted for Inference Costs.** VCs will scrutinize this number carefully. They want to see a

founder who is obsessed with optimizing their "cost of intelligence." This means demonstrating a sophisticated strategy for:

  - **Model Tiering:** Using the cheapest, fastest model (like Claude 4 Haiku) for simple, high-volume tasks, and reserving the most expensive, powerful models (like GPT-5) only for the highest-value tasks.
  - **Caching Strategies:** Implementing systems that cache the results of common AI queries to avoid redundant and expensive API calls.
- **The Benchmark:** A healthy and well-optimized AI-SaaS gross margin is in the range of 70-80%. More importantly, VCs want to see a clear plan for how you will improve this margin over time as you scale and further optimize your models.

Metric #2: The Automation Ratio In the old world, headcount growth was often used as a lazy proxy for a startup's progress. In the new world of the solo founder, the opposite is true. The key metric is the Automation Ratio—a measure of a company's operational leverage.

- **The Concept:** This metric quantifies how much of the business is running without human intervention.
- **How to Measure It:**
  - **Revenue Per Employee:** For a solo founder, this is simply your ARR. An investor seeing a single founder with a $2 million ARR understands they are looking at a business with extreme leverage.
  - **Automated Task Resolution Rate:** This is a more granular metric. For example: "96% of our customer support tickets are successfully resolved by our AI Service Agent without any human involvement." Or, "98% of our new user onboardings are completed on a fully self-serve, automated basis."
- **What VCs Look For:** They want to see a founder who is maniacally focused on increasing this ratio over time. They want to invest in a business that is demonstrably becoming *more* automated and *more* efficient as it grows.

Metric #3: Data Network Effect Velocity Simple user growth is a vanity metric. What matters is the speed at which your core defensive moat is growing stronger.

- **The Concept:** This metric measures the velocity of your data flywheel. It's not just about how many users you have, but how much proprietary data they are generating and how quickly you are turning that data into a better product.
- **How to Measure It:**
    - **Data Acquisition Velocity:** This is the rate at which you are collecting unique, proprietary data points. "Our users correct 10,000 AI-generated transcripts per week, providing us with a constant stream of high-quality training data."
    - **Model Improvement Rate:** This tracks the tangible impact of that data. "Based on the training data collected in Q2, we were able to reduce the error rate of our proprietary fine-tuned model by 15%."
- **What VCs Look For:** They are looking for hard evidence that your data moat is not just a theory, but a compounding, accelerating reality. This is the ultimate proof of a defensible, long-term business.

While the foundational metrics of LTV and CAC are still essential, VCs will analyze them through this new AI-first lens. They will want to know how your automated marketing engine is driving down your CAC, and how your AI-powered customer success systems are actively increasing LTV by reducing churn and identifying upsell opportunities. Mastering and presenting this new suite of metrics is how you demonstrate that you are not just building a product, but a sophisticated, efficient, and defensible AI-native enterprise.

16.3 Demonstrating Scalability Without Traditional Teams

The single most significant point of skepticism a solo founder will face from a venture capitalist is the question of scalability. In their minds, trained by decades of pattern-matching, scale has always been synonymous with hiring. Their default question will be, "This is impressive at your current stage, but how does this scale? What happens when you have 100,000 users? Won't the entire system collapse under the weight of one person?"

Your job is to preemptively and decisively answer this question, not with a hiring plan, but with a systems architecture plan. You must prove that your automated enterprise is not a clever workaround for a lack of a team, but a fundamentally superior and more scalable model than a traditional, human-powered organization.

The Core Argument: Systems Scale More Efficiently Than People
Your argument must be built on a simple, powerful truth: adding people to an organization introduces non-linear complexity and diminishing returns. As we have discussed, communication overhead and the "Execution Tax" mean that a 100-person team is not 100 times more productive than a one-person team. A well-architected software system, on the other hand, can scale with near-perfect efficiency. The marginal effort and cost to serve the 100,000th customer can be virtually identical to serving the 10,001st. You must make this abstract concept tangible and believable by breaking it down department by department.

Proving Scalability: An Automated Department-by-Department Breakdown

When a VC asks how you will scale, you can walk them through your "automated org chart."

- **"Our Sales Team Scales Infinitely."**
  - **Traditional Model:** To 10x revenue, a company must hire, train, and manage a sales team that is roughly 10x larger. This is a slow, expensive, and complex process.
  - **Your Proof:** "My revenue is driven by a product-led growth model and an automated, hyper-personalized outreach engine. To 10x our sales outreach, I do not need to hire a single person. I simply increase the budget on my Apollo.io and Clay.com subscriptions and raise

the daily sending limit in my email platform. The entire system is architected to handle a volume of 100,000 personalized emails per month. The cost of this system scales linearly with output, but the human effort required from me remains zero."

- **"Our Customer Support Team Has Near-Infinite Capacity."**
    - **Traditional Model:** More users directly translates to more support tickets, which requires a proportionally larger support team.
    - **Your Proof:** "Our AI Service Agent currently handles 96% of all incoming user queries with a 98% satisfaction rate. This agent can handle one thousand concurrent conversations as easily as it can handle one. As we scale to 100,000 users, the number of human-escalated tickets—the 4% the AI cannot handle—will grow. However, this growth is linear and manageable. At that scale, I would be personally handling approximately 10-15 of the most critical issues per day, which is a highly leveraged use of my time."
- **"Our Engineering Velocity Is Accelerating."**
    - **Traditional Model:** As famously described in *The Mythical Man-Month*, adding more engineers to a software project often slows it down due to increased coordination and complexity.
    - **Your Proof:** "My primary development partner is an AI co-pilot. The underlying models powering this AI are improving on an exponential curve. This means my personal ability to build, test, and deploy high-quality features is actually *accelerating* over time, not slowing down. Furthermore, our entire infrastructure is built on serverless, auto-scaling components from providers like AWS and Vercel. We can handle a million concurrent users tomorrow with no architectural changes. Our cloud

bill would increase, but our high, software-based profit margins are designed to easily absorb that cost."

The "Stress Test" Model To make your scalability claims irrefutable, you should include a "Stress Test" slide in your pitch deck. This is a quantitative model that projects the operational and financial impact of 10x and 100x growth.

Metric	Current (10k Users)	Projected (100k Users)	Projected (1M Users)
Monthly Cloud Bill	$1,000	$9,500	$90,000
Monthly AI Inference Cost	$3,000	$28,000	$270,000
Human-Escalated Tickets/Day	2	20	200
Founder Time on Ops/Week	5 hours	10 hours	20 hours (or hire 1 ops lead)

This kind of proactive, quantitative modeling is the ultimate proof. It shows an investor that you have thought more deeply about the challenges of scale than most multi-person founding teams. It replaces their fear of your solo status with confidence in your systems-first approach.

Strategic Scenario: The New Due Diligence

The process of due diligence—the rigorous investigation a VC firm conducts before investing—has always been an intense, invasive, and often grueling process. For a solo-founded, AI-native company, this process is changing. VCs are learning that they must audit the systems as much as they audit the founder. The following is a realistic walkthrough of a modern due diligence process for a solo founder.

The Players:

- **The VC Firm:** A top-tier, forward-thinking firm FutureFund (F@F).
- **The VC Partner:** "Sarah Chen," a partner renowned for her deep expertise in AI and product-led growth.

- **The Founder:** "Javier Rojas," the solo founder of "Automata" (the rebranded name for his "Studio AI" portfolio of creative tools from our previous case study).
- **The Company:** Automata has three successful, niche SaaS products, a combined **$1.5 million ARR**, and is highly profitable. Javi is raising a strategic $3 million seed round to accelerate his vision.

Act 1: The Initial Pitch - The System is the Team In his first meeting with Sarah Chen, Javi spends less than 20% of the time talking about himself. He spends 80% of the time giving her a live tour of his "Company OS" in Notion. He shows her the automated RICE model that prioritizes his product roadmap, the n8n workflow that powers his cross-promotional marketing engine, and the real-time dashboard tracking the health of his AI Service Agent. Sarah's key takeaway, which she shares with her partners, is: "This isn't a founder with a product; this is a brilliant systems architect who has built a self-running company. The system *is* the team."

Act 2: The Technical Due Diligence - Auditing the AI The F@F technical diligence team begins its audit. Their focus is radically different from a traditional review.

1. **System Resilience Audit:** They don't just ask if he has backups; they review his detailed Disaster Recovery Plan and his automated "circuit breaker" protocols. They are impressed by the maturity of his thinking around risk.
2. **AI Moat Analysis:** This is the core of the technical diligence. They ask to see the performance metrics of his proprietary, fine-tuned AI models versus the off-the-shelf foundational models. Javi shows them data proving his specialized model for e-commerce copywriting ("CopyCraft AI") has a 25% higher conversion lift than a generic prompt to GPT-5. He also shows them the velocity of his data network effect—how the model's accuracy is improving month-over-month as more user data is collected.
3. **The "Bus Factor" Test:** They ask the tough question: "What happens if you get sick?" Javi confidently walks them through

his "Dead Man's Switch" protocol and his "Emergency Handover Kit" stored in a secure vault. He proves that the business is a transferable asset, not just a personal project.

Act 3: The Commercial Due Diligence - The New Metrics The firm's growth and finance teams then dig into the business itself.

1. **Gross Margin Scrutiny:** They don't just look at his 90% software margins; they perform a deep analysis of his AI inference costs. They are highly impressed to see that Javi uses a sophisticated model-tiering system—using cheaper, faster models for low-stakes tasks and expensive models for high-stakes tasks—to keep his blended AI COGS low and his true gross margin at a healthy 75%.
2. **Automation Ratio:** The metric of "$1.5 million Revenue Per Employee" is powerful. They dig deeper, analyzing the conversion rates of his automated sales funnels and the 97% automated resolution rate of his customer support. They conclude that the company's operational leverage is in the top 1% of all companies they have seen.
3. **Capital Efficiency:** The fact that Javi reached $1.5M ARR with zero outside capital is the ultimate proof of a sustainable, efficient business model. It signals that their $3 million investment will be used purely for strategic acceleration, not to simply cover the bills.

Act 4: The Investment Decision In the final partner meeting, Sarah Chen makes her case. "Automata is the template for the future of software companies. The 'team' is a suite of intelligent, automated systems, and the founder is the architect. The capital efficiency is an order of magnitude better than a traditional SaaS company, and the data moat is real and compounding. This is a bet on a founder who is a world-class systems thinker. This is the future, and we need to own a piece of it." The partners vote unanimously to lead the $3 million seed round at a premium valuation, recognizing that the quality of the automated enterprise justified the price. This new diligence process proves that for the modern solo founder, the quality of your systems is the quality of your company.

Chapter Summary & Resources

This chapter has pulled back the curtain on the evolving world of venture capital. We have seen how the rise of the AI-powered solo founder is forcing investors to discard old rules and adopt a new framework for evaluation. By understanding these new criteria, mastering the metrics that now matter, and preparing to prove the scalability of your systems, you can confidently and effectively engage with the investment community.

Key Takeaways

- VCs are shifting their evaluation of solo founders from their ability to **manage people** to their ability to **design resilient, automated systems**.
- Traditional SaaS metrics are now augmented by a new suite of AI-specific metrics, including **inference costs**, **automation ratios**, and **data network effect velocity**.
- A solo founder proves scalability not with a hiring plan, but with a **systems architecture plan** and a quantitative **"stress test"** that models exponential growth.
- The **new due diligence process** is a rigorous audit of your automated systems, your AI-powered moat, and your capital efficiency, all of which you must be prepared to defend with hard data.

The VC-Readiness Checklist

- **The Scalability Argument:** Can you, in one compelling paragraph, answer the question, "How will your business support 100,000 users?" Your answer should focus on systems, not people.
- **Your New Metrics:** What is one "new" metric you can start tracking for your business idea today? (e.g., "I will track my target 'automated support resolution rate'").
- **Due Diligence Weakness:** What is the single biggest weakness a VC would likely find in your business model or systems during a due diligence process? What is one tangible action you can take this month to strengthen it?

- **Your Founder "Spike":** What is your "spiky" talent? Are you in the top 1% of the world at product design, a specific engineering niche, or deep domain expertise? Be prepared to articulate this clearly.

Preview of Chapter 17

You now understand what investors are looking for in a modern, AI-first solo enterprise. You know the criteria they use and the metrics they value. The final step is to learn how to run the fundraising process itself. In **Chapter 17, The Solo Founder's Fundraising Playbook**, we provide a tactical, step-by-step guide to the entire fundraising journey, from deciding *when* to raise and building your pitch deck, to negotiating your term sheet and successfully closing the deal.

Resources and Tools

- **VC Blogs to Follow:** Andreessen Horowitz (a16z.com), Sequoia Capital's blog, and all essays and videos from Y Combinator are essential reading for understanding how the world's best investors think.
- **The Definitive Book:** *Venture Deals: Be Smarter Than Your Lawyer and Venture Capitalist* by Brad Feld and Jason Mendelson. This is the undisputed bible for understanding the mechanics of a venture capital deal.
- **Metrics Mastery:** The "SaaS Metrics 2.0" guide by David Sacks is a foundational read for any software founder. Look for emerging writing on "AI SaaS Metrics" from leading VCs

.

Chapter 17: The Solo Founder's Fundraising Playbook

Introduction

Fundraising is not the goal of building a great company; it is a tool. For many traditional startups, it is a blunt instrument, used out of necessity to fund the high cost of hiring a human team. For the AI-powered solo founder, it is a precision instrument, a scalpel to be used strategically to accelerate an already-profitable and efficient enterprise. You are not just building a business; you are creating a new type of asset class, and learning how to capitalize it correctly is a critical skill.

Because your business is hyper-efficient and likely profitable, you approach the fundraising process from a position of immense strength. Unlike the desperate founder who needs venture capital to make payroll, you have the single most powerful piece of leverage in any negotiation: the ability to walk away. You are raising capital to go faster, not to survive.

In the last chapter, you learned to think like a venture capitalist and understand the new rules of the game. In this chapter, you will learn how to play that game to win. This is your step-by-step playbook for the entire fundraising journey. We will cover the most important strategic decision—*if* and *when* to raise—before diving into the tactical execution of building a compelling pitch deck, valuing your company, and negotiating the terms that will set the stage for your next phase of exponential growth. This is your guide to securing not just capital, but a true strategic partner to join you on your billion-dollar journey.

17.1 When to Raise and When to Bootstrap

The decision to raise venture capital is one of the most consequential a founder will ever make. It is a true "one-way door" decision; once you take on outside investors, the nature of your company, your role as its leader, and the definition of success are permanently altered. The AI-powered solo founder, with a profitable and capital-efficient business, is in the unique and privileged position of being "fundable but not fund-dependent." This transforms the decision from a necessity into a genuine strategic choice. You must weigh the trade-offs with clarity and deliberation.

The Case for Bootstrapping: The Path of Control Bootstrapping means funding the growth of your company using only the cash flow it generates. For a solo founder with an AI-powered, high-margin business, this is not just a viable path; it is often the default and most desirable one. The advantages can be summarized by three C's:

- **Control:** As a bootstrapped founder, you are your only boss. You have absolute and total control over the product roadmap, the company's vision, and its ultimate destiny. You answer to no one but your customers. You can choose to optimize for profitability, for lifestyle, or for long-term, sustainable growth, without the pressure of a VC's timeline.
- **Concentration (of Ownership):** You retain 100% of the equity in your company. This has a profound impact on your personal financial outcome. A $100 million exit as a solo bootstrapper is a far greater personal windfall than a $500 million exit where, after multiple funding rounds, you only own 15% of the company.
- **Calmness:** Bootstrapped companies are insulated from the often-frenzied pressures of the venture capital world. There is no board of directors demanding you pursue "growth at all costs." This allows for more deliberate, long-term decision-making and a more sustainable work-life balance.

The Case for Raising Venture Capital: The Path of Speed Raising venture capital means selling a portion of your company's equity to investors in exchange for cash and strategic support. It is a decision to trade a piece of your ownership for a massive injection of fuel. The advantages can be summarized by three S's:

- **Speed:** VC funding is rocket fuel. It allows you to invest aggressively in growth channels to capture a market as quickly as possible. In a "winner-take-all" or "winner-take-most" market—where the first company to achieve scale builds an insurmountable lead—speed is the only variable that matters.

- **Scale:** Capital allows you to make big, non-linear moves that would be impossible to fund out of cash flow. This could include acquiring a smaller competitor, launching an aggressive international expansion into five countries at once, or investing in a major R&D project to build a deep technological moat.
- **Support:** The right VC partner provides far more than just money. A top-tier firm gives you access to their invaluable network of potential customers, strategic partners, and world-class executive talent. Their brand and credibility can open doors that would otherwise be closed to you.

A Decision Framework for the Solo Founder To make this decision, you must analyze your specific situation with the dispassionate rigor of a CEO. Here is a framework you can use with your AI sparring partner.

- **Action Item: The Raise vs. Bootstrap Prompt**

*"You are my strategic advisor. I am a profitable, bootstrapped solo founder with [$X] ARR, growing at [Y]% year-over-year. I am considering raising a [$A] million seed round at a [$B] million valuation. Analyze this decision using the following criteria:

1. **Market Dynamics:** Is my market a 'winner-take-all' market where speed is the primary competitive advantage, or is it a fragmented market where multiple profitable niche players can coexist?
2. **Capital Allocation Plan:** What, specifically, would I do with the [$A] million that I cannot already do with my existing profits? Provide a detailed, ROI-driven budget for the use of funds.
3. **Outcome Modeling:** Model my potential personal financial outcome in two scenarios: (A) I bootstrap the company to a $150M exit in 8 years, retaining 100% ownership. (B) I raise this round, experience

30% further dilution in future rounds, and the company exits for $750M in 6 years.

4. **Control & Vision Assessment:** What is the risk that a VC partner would pressure me to compromise my long-term product vision in pursuit of short-term growth metrics that might damage the brand?"*

The best time to raise money is when you do not need it. By first building a profitable, capital-efficient, and sustainable business, the solo founder earns the ultimate form of leverage. The decision to raise capital is no longer a desperate plea for survival, but a calculated, strategic choice to trade a portion of a valuable asset for the fuel to make it even more valuable, faster.

17.2 Pitch Deck Essentials for One-Person Companies

A pitch deck is more than a presentation; it is a meticulously crafted narrative designed to convince a sophisticated investor to join you on a multi-year, high-stakes journey. For the solo founder, the deck bears a double burden. It must not only tell a compelling story about a massive market opportunity and a brilliant product, but it must also proactively dismantle the investor's inherent skepticism about a one-person company. Every slide must be framed to highlight the unique strengths and superior scalability of your AI-powered, systems-first enterprise.

The 12-Slide Solo Founder Pitch Deck Template

This is the blueprint for your story. Keep it clean, visual, and data-driven.

Slide 1: Title. Your company name, your name and title ("Founder"), and a single, powerful sentence that encapsulates your billion-dollar vision. E.g., "ClauseOS: The AI-powered operating system for every legal contract in the world."

Slide 2: The Problem. Describe the painful, expensive problem you solve in a way that is clear, relatable, and emotionally resonant. Use a powerful statistic or a short, compelling story.

Slide 3: The Solution. Introduce your product as the elegant, inevitable solution. Crucially, this is where you introduce the AI-native approach. "We solve this by using a proprietary, fine-tuned language model to analyze contracts with superhuman speed and accuracy."

Slide 4: Why Now? This is a critical slide that most founders miss. Explain why your company is only possible *now*. It is likely because of a recent technological inflection point (e.g., the release of GPT-5, a 90% drop in GPU inference costs) or a major market shift. This demonstrates your market timing and strategic awareness.

Slide 5: Market Size (TAM, SAM, SOM). Prove that you are chasing a massive, venture-scale opportunity. Use clear data to define your Total Addressable Market, Serviceable Addressable Market, and your initial Serviceable Obtainable Market.

Slide 6: The Product. Show, don't just tell. This should be a link to a live demo or, even better, a crisp, 60-second video of your product in action, showcasing its "magic."

Slide 7: Business Model & The New Metrics. How you make money. Present your scalable revenue model (e.g., your hybrid subscription and usage-based pricing). This is where you flex your AI-native strengths by showcasing the "new metrics" from Chapter 16: your high gross margin (adjusted for inference costs) and your off-the-charts revenue per employee.

Slide 8: Traction. This is arguably your most important slide. It must show a stunning, "up and to the right" graph of your revenue or user growth. You must highlight your extreme capital efficiency. A simple statement like "Bootstrapped to $1.5M ARR in 18 months" is more powerful than any projection.

Slide 9: The Automated "Team" & Scalable System. This slide directly confronts the "solo founder" objection. Do not show a slide with empty boxes for your future hires. Instead, show a diagram of your automated systems—your "Company OS." Instead of headshots, use the logos of your core stack: Bubble, n8n, OpenAI, Claude, AWS. You are presenting your resilient, automated system as your world-class, infinitely scalable team.

Slide 10: The Defensible Moat. Clearly and concisely articulate your primary moat. Is it your data network effect, your proprietary fine-tuned model, or your passionate community? Provide a single data point to prove it (e.g., "Our model's accuracy improves by 2% for every 1 million data points processed").

Slide 11: The Vision & The Ask. Start with your grand, long-term vision. Then, get very specific. State exactly how much you are raising (The Ask) and provide a detailed plan for how you will use the capital (The Use of Funds). This should be focused on strategic acceleration (e.g., "$1M for proprietary data acquisition," "$500k for initial international market expansion"), not on hiring a large team.

Slide 12: The Founder. End with a single, powerful slide about yourself. This is not a summary of your resume. This is where you articulate your "spiky" talent—your unique, world-class expertise, your deep personal connection to the problem, or your non-obvious insight that gives you an unfair advantage to win in this market.

A pitch deck from a solo founder must be a masterclass in narrative efficiency. It must tell a story of a massive opportunity, prove traction with undeniable data, and build unshakable confidence in the scalability and defensibility of a new kind of enterprise—one run by a single, visionary architect.

17.3 Valuation Strategies for AI-Leveraged Businesses

Valuation is one of the most mysterious and intimidating parts of the fundraising process. The truth is that early-stage valuation is not a precise science; it is a negotiated story about the future potential of your company. A traditional software company's story is often based on comparable companies with similar revenue and team sizes. As a solo founder of a hyper-efficient, AI-powered business, there are no direct comps. You are a new class of asset. Therefore, you cannot rely on the old valuation narratives. You must craft a new, compelling story that justifies a premium valuation based on the unique and superior economics of your business model.

The Foundation: Standard SaaS Valuation Metrics You must first understand the basics. The most common valuation method for a SaaS company is a **revenue multiple**. An investor will take your Annual Recurring Revenue (ARR) and multiply it by a certain number (the "multiple") to arrive at a valuation. For example, a company with $2 million in ARR at a 20x multiple has a pre-money valuation of $40 million.
The size of that multiple is determined by a few key factors:

- **Growth Rate:** The faster you are growing, the higher the multiple.
- **Gross Margin:** Higher margins command higher multiples.
- **Market Size:** A company in a massive, winner-take-all market will get a higher multiple.
- **Churn Rate:** Lower churn and higher net revenue retention lead to a higher multiple.

The AI-Leverage Premium: Arguing for a Higher Multiple Your job is to convince an investor that your business deserves a significant premium on top of the standard market multiple. You are not just another SaaS company; you are a new, more efficient species. Your argument is built on three pillars.

1. The "Capital Efficiency" Premium

- **The Narrative:** "A typical venture-backed SaaS company at our stage must reinvest 80% or more of its revenue back into sales, marketing, and R&D just to maintain its growth rate, resulting in a net profit margin of near-zero or worse. Our business, due to its fully automated operational stack, has a 70% net profit margin *while* growing at the same rate. Every dollar of our revenue is fundamentally more valuable, more profitable, and more durable. Therefore, our revenue deserves a premium multiple compared to our capital-inefficient peers."

- **The Proof:** This is where your automated financial stack (from Chapter 6) becomes a powerful fundraising tool. You can show the investor your pristine, real-time P&L statement, demonstrating a level of profitability and efficiency they have rarely seen.

2. The "Compounding Asset" Premium

- **The Narrative:** "You are not just investing in a stream of revenue; you are investing in two distinct, compounding assets. The first is our software. The second, and more valuable, is our proprietary dataset. Our data network effect means that with every new user, our core AI model gets smarter, our product gets better, and our competitive moat gets deeper. This systematically de-risks the business over time and creates a compounding value that a traditional software company without this data flywheel does not have."
- **The Proof:** You must show the metrics that prove your data flywheel is spinning (from Chapter 16). Present the charts showing your "Data Acquisition Velocity" and the corresponding "Model Improvement Rate." This turns the abstract concept of a data moat into a tangible, measurable asset.

3. The "Frictionless Scalability" Premium

- **The Narrative:** "The growth of a traditional company is constrained by its ability to hire, train, and manage people. This creates immense operational friction and risk. Our growth is constrained only by the scalability of our cloud infrastructure and AI APIs, which is practically infinite. We can 10x our user base with near-zero marginal cost and without introducing the communication overhead and execution tax that cripples human-run teams. This lower-risk, more predictable scalability profile warrants a premium valuation."
- **The Proof:** This is where you present the "Stress Test" model from your pitch deck, showing that you have a credible, quantitative plan to handle massive growth without breaking your operational or financial model.

By mastering this new valuation narrative, you reframe the conversation. You are no longer just a solo founder asking for money; you are the architect of a new type of hyper-efficient, data-driven, and scalable enterprise. You are confidently articulating why your business is a premium investment opportunity that deserves a premium price.

Strategic Scenario: The Term Sheet Negotiation

Securing a term sheet from a top-tier venture capital firm is a moment of incredible validation. But the work is not over. The term sheet itself—the document that outlines the core terms of the investment—is the beginning of a critical negotiation that will define your relationship with your investors and the future of your company for years to come. The story of Chloé Dubois and her negotiation with an aggressive VC firm is a powerful lesson in how a well-prepared solo founder can secure a truly founder-friendly deal.

The Players:

- **The Founder:** Chloé Dubois, the solo founder of "Momentum," a profitable B2B SaaS company with **$5 million in ARR**.
- **The VC Firm:** "Apex Ventures," a top-tier firm with a reputation for brilliant partners and sharp-elbowed, investor-friendly terms.
- **The Situation:** Chloé has run a competitive fundraising process and has received a lead term sheet from Apex to raise $10 million at a $100 million pre-money valuation. The headline numbers are exactly what she wanted, but the details contain several problematic clauses.

Act 1: The "Good News, Bad News" Term Sheet The term sheet arrives, and Chloé's initial elation at the $100 million valuation quickly turns to anxiety as she and her lawyer review the fine print. Her lawyer flags three "off-market" and highly aggressive clauses. Chloé knows that this negotiation will be a defining moment.

Act 2: The Negotiation - The Battle of the Clauses Chloé prepares for her negotiation with the Apex partner. She doesn't just rely on her lawyer; she uses an LLM to model the long-term impact of each clause and to research industry-standard counter-proposals. She enters the negotiation not with emotion, but with data and logic.

Clause #1: The Liquidation Preference

- **Apex's Term:** "3x Participating Preferred." Her lawyer and AI explain that this is a predatory term from a bygone era. It means that in an exit, Apex would get 3 times their money back *off the top*, and then also get to participate as a common shareholder, effectively "double-dipping."
- **Chloé's Stance:** She calmly and respectfully explains that her business's proven profitability and extreme capital efficiency do not warrant such a risk-heavy term. She states that the market standard is clear.
- **Her Counter-Proposal:** "1x Non-Participating Preferred." This is the clean, standard term where investors get either 1x their money back or convert to common stock and take their ownership percentage, whichever is greater.
- **The Outcome:** The Apex partner, knowing their initial offer was an aggressive test, quickly concedes the point and agrees to the market-standard term. **Chloé's Leverage:** Her company's strong, profitable fundamentals.

Clause #2: The Board of Directors

- **Apex's Term:** A 3-person board, structured as: one seat for Apex, one seat for the Founder (Chloé), and one "Independent" director to be appointed solely by Apex. This structure would give Apex effective control of her company's board.
- **Chloé's Stance:** She argues that as the sole founder and operator, maintaining a balanced board that represents the long-term vision of the company is paramount.
- **Her Counter-Proposal:** She agrees to a 3-person board but insists on the standard, balanced structure: one seat for Apex, one seat for her, and one Independent director to be mutually agreed upon by *both* parties.
- **The Outcome:** The partner pushes back, but Chloé holds firm, explaining that board control is a non-negotiable point for her.

Ultimately, they agree to her proposal. **Chloé's Leverage:** Her indispensable role as the company's sole visionary and operator.

Clause #3: Founder Vesting and Acceleration

- **Apex's Term:** A new 4-year vesting schedule on all of Chloé's existing equity, with a "single-trigger" acceleration clause upon a change of control (i.e., an acquisition).
- **Chloé's Stance:** She agrees that a new vesting schedule is standard to ensure her long-term commitment. However, she explains that a single-trigger clause creates a perverse incentive for an acquirer to fire her immediately after a sale to reclaim her unvested shares.
- **Her Counter-Proposal:** She insists on a "double-trigger" acceleration clause. This is the founder-friendly standard, and it means her unvested shares only accelerate if she is terminated *without cause* following an acquisition. This protects her from being unfairly pushed out.
- **The Outcome:** This is a highly reasonable and standard request, and Apex agrees without much debate. **Chloé's Leverage:** Her deep preparation and knowledge of market-standard terms.

The Final Deal: The Power of Walking Away Chloé successfully negotiates a clean, founder-friendly term sheet. She was able to do so not because she was a master negotiator, but because she had built her leverage long before she ever walked into the room. Her leverage was her profitability, which gave her the power to walk away from a bad deal. It was the competitive tension she created by talking to multiple firms. And it was the deep preparation that allowed her to negotiate based on logic and data, not fear.

Chapter Summary & Resources

This chapter has provided a complete, tactical playbook for navigating the complex world of fundraising as a solo founder. We have moved from the high-level strategic question of *if* and *when* to raise capital, to the practical execution of building a pitch deck that highlights your unique strengths, and finally to the high-stakes negotiation of the term sheet that will define your future. This playbook is designed to empower you, ensuring that you can secure the capital you need on terms that you deserve.

Key Takeaways

- The decision to raise capital is a strategic trade-off between **speed and control**; the best time to raise is when you don't need the money, as profitability gives you the ultimate leverage.
- A solo founder's **pitch deck** must tell a compelling story that reframes the one-person "team" as a scalable, automated system and highlights the business's extreme capital efficiency.
- Valuation for an AI-first business is a narrative based on a **"premium" multiple**, justified by superior profit margins, a compounding data asset, and frictionless scalability.
- A successful **term sheet negotiation** requires deep preparation, creating competitive tension among investors, and understanding your key sources of leverage to secure founder-friendly terms.

The Fundraising Prep Kit

- **Draft Your "Why Raise?" Paragraph:** Write a single, compelling paragraph that clearly articulates why you are raising capital. It must be for strategic acceleration, not to cover operational costs. What specific, game-changing goals will the capital enable you to achieve?
- **Create Your "Automated Team" Slide:** Sketch out the slide from the pitch deck template that visually represents your automated systems as your core team. How will you make your operational excellence tangible and impressive?
- **Identify Your Top 3 Negotiation Points:** If you were negotiating a term sheet today, what are the three most important, non-negotiable terms for you? (e.g., maintaining board control, a 1x non-participating preference, double-trigger acceleration).

Preview of Chapter 18

You have the capital. You have the systems. You have the mindset. The final part of the playbook is about executing the long-term strategy to reach the ultimate goal. In **Chapter 18, Building for Billion-Dollar**

Valuation, we will explore the final strategic requirements for achieving unicorn status, including validating a massive market size, building long-term defensibility in the age of AI commoditization, and understanding the potential path from a private solo-run company to a public one.

Resources and Tools

- **Books:** *Venture Deals: Be Smarter Than Your Lawyer and Venture Capitalist* by Brad Feld and Jason Mendelson; *Secrets of Sand Hill Road: Venture Capital and How to Get It* by Scott Kupor.
- **Term Sheet & Legal Resources:** The Y Combinator website has a library of founder-friendly standard legal documents, including their famous "SAFE" (Simple Agreement for Future Equity), which is often used for seed rounds.
- **Practice:** Search for successful startup pitch decks online (many are publicly available through sites like Pitch Deck Hunt). Analyze how they craft their narrative, present their data, and build a compelling case for investment.

Chapter 18: Building for Billion-Dollar Valuation

Introduction

A million-dollar business is built on a great product that solves a real problem. A billion-dollar business is built on a great product that solves a real problem in a massive market, protected by an unbreachable moat. The journey from the first million to the aspirational ten-figure "unicorn" status requires a profound shift in strategic thinking. The operational tactics that got you here are no longer sufficient. You must now think and act with the discipline and vision of a late-stage CEO, focusing on the fundamental pillars that justify a massive valuation.

In the last chapter, you secured the capital and the strategic partners to accelerate your journey. Now, you must deploy that capital with the singular goal of creating a "venture-scale" outcome—a business so large, durable, and defensible that it can generate hundreds of millions in annual revenue and command a valuation in the billions.

This chapter provides the final strategic frameworks required to cross that threshold. We will explore the non-negotiable market size requirements and the data-driven techniques to prove you are operating in a vast ocean, not a small pond. We will then dive into advanced strategies for building true, lasting defensibility in an age where the underlying AI technology is becoming a commodity. This is the final stress test for your billion-dollar ambition, ensuring your enterprise is built not just for success, but for significance.

18.1 Market Size Requirements and Validation

For any venture capitalist, the first and most important filter for any potential investment is the size of the market. VCs are not in the business of funding profitable lifestyle companies; they are in the business of finding outlier companies that can grow so large that a single successful exit can return the value of their entire fund. This is only possible in markets that are measured in the tens of billions of dollars. The most critical question you must answer is not just, "Can I build a successful business?" but "Can I build a business that can plausibly generate hundreds of millions in annual revenue?"

The Language of the Market: TAM, SAM, SOM To communicate your market opportunity effectively, you must speak the language of investors. This is the TAM, SAM, SOM framework.

- **TAM (Total Addressable Market):** This is the total global demand for a product or service. It is the "big picture" number that shows the upper limit of the opportunity. For example, the global market for all cybersecurity software.
- **SAM (Serviceable Addressable Market):** This is the segment of the TAM that your specific product or service targets. It is your specific playground. For example, the market for AI-powered email security for small and mid-sized businesses.
- **SOM (Serviceable Obtainable Market):** This is the portion of your SAM that you can realistically capture in the next 3-5 years. This is your near-term target.

The Unicorn Litmus Test: To be considered a potentially "venture-scale" business, investors typically need to believe that your TAM is at least in the tens of billions, and your SAM is, at a minimum, $1 billion. Why? A simple rule of thumb is that a great company might capture 10% of its SAM. If your SAM is $1 billion, a successful outcome is a $100 million ARR business. This is the scale required to justify a billion-dollar valuation.

Methodologies for Calculating and Proving Your Market Size

A claim about market size is useless without a credible, data-driven methodology to back it up.

Method 1: The Top-Down Approach This method starts with a large, aggregate market number from a reputable industry report (e.g., from Gartner, Forrester, or Statista) and then narrows it down with a series of logical assumptions.

- **Example:** "Gartner reports that the global market for CRM software is $80 billion (TAM). We estimate that the segment for businesses with under 500 employees is 25% of that, making our SAM $20 billion. We believe we can capture 1% of this market in the next 5 years, for a near-term target (SOM) of $200 million."
- **Pros & Cons:** This approach is easy to calculate but is often viewed with skepticism by sophisticated investors, as the percentage assumptions can seem arbitrary.

Method 2: The Bottom-Up Approach (The Gold Standard) This is the far more credible and powerful method. You build your market size calculation from the ground up by identifying the number of potential customers and multiplying it by how much you can charge them.

- **The AI-Powered Workflow:** As a solo founder, you can use AI to make this analysis incredibly robust.
    1. **Find the Customer Count:** Use a B2B data platform like **Apollo.io** or prompt an LLM with access to business data: *"Using the most recent available data, what is the total number of law firms in the United States, Canada, and the UK with between 10 and 150 employees?"*
    2. **Determine Your Price:** This is your estimated Average Contract Value (ACV) per year. Let's assume it's $10,000.
    3. **The Calculation:** If the AI determines there are 150,000 such firms, your SAM is calculated as: `150,000 firms × $10,000/firm/year = $1.5 billion`.
- **Pros & Cons:** This method is far more believable because it is built on tangible, verifiable data points. It proves to investors that you have a deep and granular understanding of exactly who your customer is.

The Narrative of Expansion A critical part of the billion-dollar story is demonstrating how you will expand your market over time. You must show a logical path from your initial, focused beachhead to dominating a much larger ocean. The narrative should be: "We are starting with law firms, a $1.5 billion SAM where we have a clear, unfair advantage. However, our core contract analysis technology is directly applicable to the corporate legal departments of large enterprises and the real estate industry. These adjacent markets represent an additional TAM of over $25 billion." This shows a clear, multi-stage plan for massive growth.

18.2 Defensibility in the Age of AI Commoditization

You have found a massive market. You have achieved product-market fit. You are growing quickly. Now you must answer what is perhaps the single hardest and most important question for any AI-native company: **"Why can't someone else do this?"** In an era where the underlying intelligence from models like GPT-5 is becoming a powerful, accessible commodity, how do you build a lasting, defensible business? A clever feature is not a moat. A good prompt is not a moat. True, long-term defensibility for a solo founder must be architected into the very fabric of the business.

Advanced Moat #1: The End-to-End Workflow Moat Your greatest defense is often not the "AI" part of your product, but the complex, automated, end-to-end workflow you build *around* the AI. The goal is to move beyond solving a single task and instead solve an entire multi-step problem for your user.

- **The Narrative:** "Our product is not just an 'AI transcription service.' It is a complete, automated post-interview workflow for a journalist. It transcribes the interview (Step 1), automatically identifies the most newsworthy quotes (Step 2), uses our AI BI tool to fact-check names and dates against a knowledge base (Step 3), integrates with their CMS to create a draft article with the quotes embedded (Step 4), and schedules a series of social media posts to promote the article (Step 5). A competitor could easily replicate our transcription quality (Step 1), but they cannot easily replicate the deep, five-step workflow integration that solves the user's entire problem from end to end."
- **How to Build It:** This is the culmination of all the systems we have discussed. It is about using **n8n** to seamlessly stitch together dozens of microservices, API calls, and AI model prompts into a single, cohesive user experience that feels like

magic. The complexity and elegance of this automated workflow is the real moat.

Advanced Moat #2: The Human Preference Data Flywheel We have established that a data network effect is a powerful moat. The advanced strategy is to focus on capturing a type of data that is impossible for anyone else to acquire: data on **human preference**.

- **The Strategy:** The raw output of a generative model can often be replicated. What cannot be replicated is the data about which outputs *humans actually prefer*. You must design your product to capture these preference signals at scale.
- **Example:** Your AI tool generates three different versions of an email subject line for a marketer. The marketer consistently chooses Version C. That click is not just a data point; it is a valuable "human preference" signal. Over millions of such choices, you build a unique dataset on what constitutes "persuasive" marketing copy, as judged by professional humans.
- **The AI Application:** This preference data is then used to fine-tune your specialized model using a technique like Reinforcement Learning from Human Feedback (RLHF)—the same core technique that makes models like ChatGPT so powerful. Your fine-tuned model becomes uniquely good at generating content that humans actually *like* and *respond to*. A competitor starting from scratch can generate grammatically correct text, but they cannot generate text that is optimized by millions of human preference data points.

Advanced Moat #3: The Platform Ecosystem Moat As discussed previously, the ultimate and most durable moat is to evolve from a standalone product into a platform on which other businesses build.

- **The Strategic Importance:** When you have an ecosystem of hundreds of third-party applications and integrations built on your API, your defensibility becomes exponential. A customer's switching cost is no longer just the pain of migrating their own data; it is the pain of abandoning an entire ecosystem of tools that are critical to their workflow. You are no longer just a vendor; you are a foundational piece of their infrastructure.

- **The Solo Founder's Path:** You must be intentional about this from day one. This means architecting your product with a clean, well-documented, and public-facing API from the very beginning. It means actively nurturing a community of developers around your product, encouraging them to build integrations long before you have a formal "app store." This long-term vision transforms your business from a single castle into a fortified kingdom.

In the age of AI, a single feature is not defensible. True, lasting defensibility is a multi-layered system—a deep workflow, a proprietary data flywheel, and a vibrant ecosystem. This is how a solo founder can build a business that is not just successful today, but is built to last for the next decade.

18.3 Revenue Quality and Growth Sustainability

As your business matures and its revenue grows, the lens through which sophisticated investors and potential acquirers evaluate you will change. They will shift their focus from the sheer *quantity* of your revenue to its **quality** and **sustainability**. A billion-dollar valuation is not built on a foundation of lumpy, unpredictable, or low-margin income. It is built on a bedrock of high-quality, predictable, and efficiently generated recurring revenue. As a solo founder, your AI-powered business model is uniquely positioned to produce the world-class metrics that define revenue quality.

Metric #1: Net Revenue Retention (NRR) - The Holy Grail Net Revenue Retention is arguably the single most important metric for a mature SaaS business. It measures the change in recurring revenue from a cohort of existing customers over a year, accounting for both expansion revenue (upsells, cross-sells) and contraction (downgrades, churn).

- **The Unicorn Benchmark:** A good SaaS company has an NRR of over 100%. A great, venture-scale company will have an NRR of **120% or higher**.
- **Why it Matters:** An NRR of 120% means that if you stopped acquiring new customers today, your business would *still grow*

by 20% next year, purely from your existing customer base. It is the ultimate proof that you have a sticky product, happy customers, and a business that grows organically. It is a powerful engine of compounding growth.

- **The Solo Founder's AI Advantage:** Your automated systems are a machine for generating high NRR. Your proactive Customer Success Engine (from Chapter 9) identifies at-risk customers and reduces churn. Your AI BI tool (from Chapter 6) uncovers upsell opportunities by analyzing feature usage, which can then be actioned by your automated marketing engine. This creates a systematic process for driving expansion revenue.

Metric #2: The "Magic Number" - A Measure of Growth Efficiency This metric answers a simple question: for every dollar we spend on sales and marketing, how many dollars of new annual revenue do we create?

- **The Formula:** `((Current Quarter's New ARR - Previous Quarter's New ARR) × 4) / Previous Quarter's Sales & Marketing Spend`
- **The Unicorn Benchmark:** A "Magic Number" greater than **1.0** is considered excellent and indicates a highly efficient and sustainable growth engine. It means your go-to-market strategy is profitable and ready for more investment.
- **The Solo Founder's AI Advantage:** For a traditional SaaS company, "Sales & Marketing Spend" is a huge number, dominated by the salaries of their sales and marketing teams. For you, this number is incredibly small; it is simply the subscription costs of your automated tool stack (e.g., Apollo, Clay, marketing AI). Because your cost base is so low, you can achieve a Magic Number that is almost impossibly high, demonstrating a level of growth efficiency that will be incredibly attractive to investors.

Metric #3: The Rule of 40 - The Bar for Excellence The Rule of 40 is a high-level benchmark used to assess the health of a mature SaaS company by balancing its growth rate with its profitability.

- **The Formula:** `Annual Revenue Growth Rate (%) + Net Profit Margin (%) ≥ 40%`
- **Why it Matters:** This rule acknowledges that a company can choose to be highly profitable with slower growth, or grow extremely fast while being unprofitable. As long as the sum of these two metrics exceeds 40, the business is considered healthy and well-managed.
- **The Solo Founder's AI Advantage:** This is where the solo-founder model completely shatters the traditional benchmarks. A typical high-growth, VC-backed company might achieve the Rule of 40 with a 60% growth rate and a -20% profit margin. Your AI-powered business, with its massive operational leverage, can achieve it with a **60% growth rate and a 70% profit margin**, for a total score of 130. This is an almost unprecedented combination of high growth and high profitability, and it is the ultimate testament to the quality and sustainability of the business you have built.

By mastering and optimizing these three key metrics, you are not just building a fast-growing business; you are building a high-quality, efficient, and sustainable enterprise. You are telling a sophisticated financial story that proves your company is not a fleeting success, but a durable institution worthy of a billion-dollar valuation.

Strategic Scenario/Analysis: The Path to IPO

The ultimate destination for a venture-backed company is a liquidity event, with the most prestigious being an Initial Public Offering (IPO). An IPO for a solo-founded, AI-native company would be a landmark event on Wall Street, introducing a new class of hyper-efficient enterprise to the public markets. Let's perform a rigorous, theoretical analysis of what the S-1 filing—the official document a company files to go public—might look like for our case study company, "ConnectSphere."

The Company: ConnectSphere, founded by Dr. Lena Hanson. After her successful pivot, the company has become the dominant platform for developers building interactive data applications. **The Scenario:**

ConnectSphere has reached **$150 million in ARR**. Lena, while still the visionary founder, has now strategically hired a small, elite leadership team (a COO, a CFO) to prepare for the rigors of being a public company. They are filing their S-1 to go public.

An Analysis of a Hypothetical S-1 Filing

Section 1: The "Letter from the Founder" Lena's letter would set the tone for the entire document. It would not read like a typical CEO's letter. It would frame ConnectSphere as the pioneer of a new, more leveraged and intelligent model of company-building.

- **Key Themes:** It would emphasize the "systems-first" philosophy from day one. It would talk about the power of AI not just as a feature, but as a core operational principle that enables "compounding efficiency." It would position the company's extreme profitability not as a sign of underinvestment, but as a sign of a superior, more sustainable business model.

Section 2: The "Risk Factors" This section requires radical transparency about the potential risks to the business. Lena would need to address two unique risks head-on.

- **Risk: "Key Person" Risk.** This would be the number one risk flagged by analysts.
    - **The Mitigation Narrative:** The S-1 would dedicate a full section to this. It would detail the meticulously documented "Company OS" and the robust, automated SOPs that run the business. It would highlight the company's resilient, decentralized systems. It would also introduce the small, world-class leadership team she has hired, demonstrating a clear succession plan and proving that the company's operations are no longer solely dependent on her.
- **Risk: "AI Model Dependency and Commoditization."**
    - **The Mitigation Narrative:** The filing would acknowledge the reliance on third-party foundational models. However, it would immediately counter this by

presenting hard data on its key moat: the proprietary, fine-tuned models trained on its unique human preference dataset. It would include metrics showing that its specialized models are more accurate and 50% cheaper to run for its specific use case than any generic alternative, proving it has a durable technological advantage.

Section 3: The "Management's Discussion and Analysis" (MD&A) of Financials This is the heart of the S-1, where the company's financial story is told. ConnectSphere's metrics would be almost unprecedented for an IPO.

Metric	ConnectSphere	Traditional SaaS IPO Benchmark
Annual Recurring Revenue	$150M	-
Y/Y Growth Rate	80%	50-70%
Gross Margin	78% (adj. for inference)	75-85%
Net Profit Margin	**50%**	**-10% to -30%**
Rule of 40 Score	**130** (80% + 50%)	**40-60**
Net Revenue Retention	140%	110-125%
CAC Payback Period	3 Months	12-18 Months
Headcount	**25**	**500-1000**
Revenue Per Employee	**$6 million**	**$200k - $300k**

The Analysis: This financial profile would be the central story of the IPO. The combination of hyper-growth (80%) and massive profitability (50%) is the holy grail for public market investors, who are often tired of high-growth but cash-burning companies. The 140% NRR proves the product's stickiness. But the most staggering metric would be the **Revenue Per Employee of $6 million**, a figure that is **20 times greater** than the benchmark for a traditional software company at IPO. This single number would be the ultimate proof of the solo-founder, AI-first model's superior efficiency and leverage.

The Conclusion: The IPO of a company like ConnectSphere would be a watershed moment. Its S-1 filing would serve as the manifesto for a new era of enterprise. It would tell a story not about hiring hundreds of people to build a great company, but about the power of a leveraged founder and a small, elite team to build an intelligent, autonomous, and wildly profitable market leader.

Chapter Summary & Resources

This chapter has provided the final strategic elements required to architect a business for a billion-dollar outcome. We have moved beyond the early stages of growth to the mature, sophisticated thinking that defines a true market leader. By proving you are attacking a massive market, building a multi-layered, modern moat, and demonstrating world-class revenue quality and sustainability, you are building an undeniable case for a unicorn valuation.

Key Takeaways

- A billion-dollar valuation requires a credible, data-backed plan to capture a significant portion of a **multi-billion dollar market (SAM)**.
- Lasting defensibility in the AI age is not built on features, but on systemic moats like **end-to-end workflow ownership** and a **proprietary human preference data flywheel**.
- High-quality revenue, as measured by elite metrics like **Net Revenue Retention (NRR) > 120%** and a **Rule of 40 score > 100**, is essential to justify a premium valuation.

- The path to an IPO for a solo-founded company is paved with an unprecedented combination of **hyper-growth and massive profitability**, leading to industry-defining metrics like Revenue Per Employee.

The Unicorn-Readiness Scorecard

- **Market Size Sanity Check:** Run a quick, bottom-up calculation for your business's Serviceable Addressable Market (SAM). Is it plausibly over $1 billion? If not, what adjacent markets could you expand into to reach that scale?
- **Moat Assessment:** What is your single strongest, most durable competitive moat? Is it your unique workflow, your proprietary data flywheel, or your community? Write one sentence explaining why a well-funded competitor could not easily replicate it in 12 months.
- **Revenue Quality Projection:** What is your target Net Revenue Retention (NRR) for your business? What specific automated up-sell or cross-sell strategies will you implement to achieve it?

Preview of Chapter 19

We have now covered the entire journey, from the initial spark of an idea, through the building of the automated enterprise, the execution of the scaling playbooks, and the final strategic considerations for a massive valuation. You have the complete blueprint. The final chapters of this book look to the future. In **Chapter 19, The First Solo Billionaire**, we will synthesize everything we have learned to profile the most likely candidates to achieve this historic milestone, analyze the timeline for when it might happen, and explore what this profound shift means for the future of entrepreneurship.

Resources and Tools

- **Financial Metrics:** The "Meritech Cloud 100 Benchmarks" report is an excellent public resource for understanding the key financial metrics of top-tier SaaS companies.
- **S-1 Filings:** The U.S. Securities and Exchange Commission's (SEC) EDGAR database is a public repository of all S-1 filings.

Reading the S-1s of successful tech companies like Snowflake, Datadog, or Cloudflare is a masterclass in business strategy.

- **Book:** *The Intelligent Investor* by Benjamin Graham. While focused on public market investing, its timeless principles on what constitutes a high-quality, durable business are invaluable for any founder building for the long term.

Chapter 19: The First Solo Billionaire

Introduction

The emergence of the first solo billionaire will not be just another headline in the technology press. It will be a landmark event, a historical marker signifying a fundamental shift in the nature of economic value creation. Like Roger Bannister breaking the four-minute mile, it will shatter a long-held psychological barrier, proving that an individual, armed with the right vision and the right tools, can build an enterprise with the same scale and impact as a massive corporation. Once this barrier is broken, it will unleash a torrent of ambition and innovation from a new generation of entrepreneurs who now see the path as possible.

Throughout this book, we have systematically assembled the blueprint for this new kind of enterprise. We have cultivated the billion-dollar mindset, architected the automated operational systems, mastered the scaling playbooks, and explored the strategic frameworks required to compete at the highest level. We have built the "how."

This final chapter is about the "who," the "when," and the "what next." We will synthesize everything we have learned to create a detailed, data-driven profile of the archetypal founder who will achieve this milestone and the business they will likely build. We will analyze the powerful technological and economic forces at play to forecast a realistic timeline for when this event will occur. Finally, we will explore the profound implications this will have for the future of entrepreneurship, work, and investment. This is a look at the future you are now uniquely equipped to build.

19.1 Profiling the Most Likely Candidates and Industries

While the specific identity of the first solo billionaire remains unknown, we can construct a remarkably detailed archetype of this individual and their business by synthesizing the core principles established throughout this book. This person will not be a fluke or an accident of history. They will be the product of a perfect storm: the right founder profile, operating in the right industry, with a business model that is perfectly attuned to the leverage of modern AI.

The Profile of the Founder: The New Titan The individual who achieves this will not resemble the charismatic, team-building CEOs of the past. They will be a new kind of leader, defined by a unique set of traits.

- **The "Spiky" Systems Architect:** This founder will not be a well-rounded generalist. They will be "spiky," possessing a world-class, top-1% talent in one critical domain—be it product design, a specific engineering niche, or a deep, intuitive understanding of a complex industry. Their core genius will not be in managing people, but in designing and orchestrating complex, intelligent, and autonomous systems.
- **The AI-Native:** This person will think in AI. For them, large language models are not just a tool to be used, but a fundamental building block of reality. When faced with a problem, their first instinct will not be "Who can I hire to solve this?" but "What kind of AI agent can I build to solve this permanently?"
- **The Master of Leverage:** They will be fundamentally driven by a desire for efficiency and leverage in all its forms. This includes technical leverage (automation, AI), financial leverage (extreme capital efficiency), and social leverage (building a passionate community and a powerful personal network).
- **The Stoic Operator:** Given the immense pressure of running a high-growth solo enterprise, this founder will possess a high degree of emotional resilience. They will have a well-developed "Personal OS," allowing them to manage stress, avoid burnout, and maintain a calm, long-term perspective amidst the chaos of hyper-growth.

The Profile of the Business: The "Quiet Unicorn" The company this founder builds will look and feel different from the unicorns of the past. It will be a "quiet unicorn," characterized by its extreme efficiency and understated operational footprint.

- **The Industry:** The business will operate in an industry that is "ripe for solo disruption," as defined in Chapter 15. It will almost certainly be a niche within a larger, regulated, and inefficient B2B market like **financial services**, **legal technology**, or **biotech/pharmaceuticals**. These industries have massive margins and are filled with information-based bottlenecks that are perfect targets for AI-driven automation. An alternative, but equally likely, candidate is a "pickaxe" business for a massive new technology wave (e.g., a core developer platform for quantum computing or spatial computing).
- **The Business Model:** It will be an **AI-Native** business. The AI is the core, value-creating product, not just a feature. The revenue model will be a sophisticated **hybrid**, combining a predictable subscription base with a scalable, usage-based component that is directly tied to the quantifiable value the customer receives.
- **The Moat:** The company's primary defense will be a powerful, self-reinforcing **data network effect**, likely based on capturing proprietary "human preference" data. This unique dataset will be used to continuously fine-tune a **proprietary AI model**, making it the best in the world at its one specific task. This technical moat will be further protected by a vibrant, passionate **community** of power users and developers.
- **The Financials:** The company's financial profile will be unlike anything public markets have seen before. It will exhibit both hyper-growth (80-100%+ year-over-year) and massive profitability (a net margin of 50%+). Its Net Revenue Retention will be well over 120%, and its revenue per employee (just the founder) will be in the tens of millions, demonstrating an almost surreal level of capital efficiency.

In essence, the first solo billionaire will not be the creator of a viral social app or a consumer gadget. They will be a deeply knowledgeable systems architect who builds an automated, intelligent, and defensible machine that solves a single, expensive, and complex problem for a specific business niche.

19.2 Timeline Analysis: A Data-Backed Forecast

Predicting the exact date that a historical milestone will be achieved is a difficult exercise, but it is not pure guesswork. By analyzing the key accelerating and decelerating forces, and by grounding our forecast in the predictions of industry insiders, we can create a reasonable, data-backed timeline for when the first solo billionaire is likely to emerge.

The Accelerating Forces (Why It Could Happen Sooner) Several powerful, exponential trends are compressing the timeline and pulling this future closer to the present.

- **The Exponential Pace of AI Capability (Moore's Law for Intelligence):** The underlying power of the AI models available to a solo founder is improving at a staggering rate. The leap in capability from GPT-3 in 2020 to GPT-4 in 2023 and to GPT-5 in 2025 was not linear. Each new generation unlocks fundamentally new possibilities. This exponential improvement in the "power" a founder can wield means that what might have taken a decade to build in 2020 could be built in just a few years today.
- **The Deflationary Cost of Intelligence:** At the same time, the cost to use these powerful models is plummeting. The cost per million tokens (the basic unit of AI work) for top-tier models has decreased by over 90% in just a few years. This makes it economically feasible for a single, bootstrapped founder to build a business that performs trillions of cognitive operations, something that would have been unimaginably expensive just a short time ago.
- **The Maturation of the No-Code and Automation Stack:** The tools that form the founder's "automated team"—platforms like Bubble, n8n, and Webflow—are themselves becoming more powerful and integrated with AI, dramatically lowering the technical barrier to building and scaling a sophisticated software enterprise.
- **Venture Capital Acceptance and Investment:** As we explored in Part 5, the venture capital industry has woken up to this new reality. They are now actively seeking out and funding elite solo

founders, which will pour rocket fuel on the most promising candidates and accelerate their growth trajectories.

The Decelerating Forces (The Potential Roadblocks) Despite the powerful tailwinds, several factors could slow the timeline.

- **Regulatory Headwinds:** Governments around the world are still grappling with how to regulate artificial intelligence. The sudden introduction of strict new laws around data usage, model training, or AI liability could increase the compliance burden and slow down the pace of innovation, particularly for a solo founder without a legal team.
- **The Data Bottleneck:** While the models and compute are becoming commodities, the acquisition of a large, high-quality, proprietary dataset needed to build a true data moat remains a significant challenge that often takes years.
- **The Human Element:** The psychological and emotional resilience required to steer a hyper-growth company as a single individual is rare. The pool of potential candidates who possess the unique blend of technical, strategic, and psychological fortitude required is, by its nature, extremely small.

The Forecast: A Probabilistic Timeline When OpenAI's CEO Sam Altman first began publicly predicting the emergence of a one-person, billion-dollar company in 2023, he gave a rough timeline of "within a decade." Given the significant acceleration in AI capabilities since that prediction was made, it is reasonable to believe the timeline has compressed. We can therefore forecast the milestone in terms of probabilities:

- **Within 3 Years (by the end of 2028):** A **25% probability**. This would represent a near-perfect scenario, likely involving a founder who was already well on their way before 2025 and who is able to capitalize on another unexpected leap in AI capability.
- **Within 5 Years (by the end of 2030):** A **70% probability**. This appears to be the most likely timeframe. It allows sufficient time for the current generation of AI-native founders (those starting in the 2024-2025 timeframe) to build their products, achieve

product-market fit, and scale to the necessary revenue milestones to command a billion-dollar valuation.

- **Within 10 Years (by the end of 2035):** A **95% probability**. Barring a major, unforeseen event like a new "AI winter" or a global economic catastrophe, it seems almost inevitable that this milestone will be crossed within the next decade.

The exact date is less important than the clear and powerful trajectory. The race is already underway, and all technological and economic signals point to this being a near-term, not a distant-future, event.

19.3 What This Means for the Future of Entrepreneurship

The emergence of the first solo billionaire will be far more than just a record-breaking financial achievement. It will be a seismic event, a signal that the tectonic plates of the global economy are shifting under our feet. This new paradigm of individual leverage, powered by artificial intelligence, will create profound and permanent ripple effects that will reshape the core institutions of the business world: how we learn (business schools), how we invest (venture capital), and how we work (traditional career paths).

The Disruption of Business Education For the last century, business schools have been highly effective factories for producing the managerial class. Their core curriculum—focused on organizational behavior, human resource management, and corporate finance—was designed to train students to become efficient cogs, and eventually managers, in large, human-powered corporations. This model is now facing an existential threat.

- **The New Skill Set:** The skills that traditional MBA programs have long prized—managing large teams, navigating complex bureaucracies, allocating resources within a large organization—are the very skills being systematically devalued or automated by AI. The solo founder's required skill set is entirely different. It is not about managing people; it is about designing intelligent, autonomous systems.

- **The Future MBA Curriculum:** A business school that wishes to remain relevant in the 21st century must undergo a radical transformation. Its core curriculum would need to look something like this:
    1. **AI-Native Business Model Design:** Teaching students how to build businesses where the AI is the core product.
    2. **Prompt Engineering for CEOs:** Training students to use LLMs as a strategic sparring partner.
    3. **Automated Systems Architecture:** Focusing on designing and orchestrating complex, automated workflows using no-code tools and APIs.
    4. **Community and Ecosystem Building:** The new "organizational behavior" is about nurturing a passionate user base, not managing direct reports.
    5. **Solo-Founder Psychology & Resilience:** Training students in the mental models and personal operating systems required to withstand the immense pressures of solo entrepreneurship. Business schools that fail to make this profound shift will become institutions teaching an obsolete version of history, producing graduates who are perfectly trained for a world that no longer exists.

The Transformation of Venture Capital The traditional venture capital model is built on writing large checks ($5 million or more) to fund a startup's primary expense: hiring a team. The AI-powered solo founder, who can reach profitability with a fraction of that capital, breaks this model.

- **The Rise of the "Solo Capitalist":** The early-stage investment landscape will likely be reshaped by a new class of investor. These will be "solo capitalists"—often successful former founders themselves—who write smaller, more strategic checks ($250k - $1M) and whose primary value-add is not helping with hiring, but providing high-level strategic guidance and access to their personal network. The relationship will be more akin to a deep advisory partnership than a formal board structure.
- **VCs as Platform Providers:** Larger VC firms will need to adapt their value proposition. Instead of just offering a network of

recruiters, they may begin to compete by offering their portfolio companies access to proprietary assets, such as massive, pre-trained AI models or unique datasets that can help a startup build its moat faster. Their value will shift from human capital to intellectual and data capital.

The End of the Traditional Career Path For generations, the safest and most prestigious career path for an ambitious individual was to join a large, established corporation and diligently climb the ladder. The rise of the solo founder marks the beginning of the end for this model.

- **The Soaring Opportunity Cost:** The leverage now available to a single, talented individual has become so immense that the opportunity cost of taking a traditional corporate job is skyrocketing. Why spend five years climbing the ladder to become a middle manager overseeing a team of ten, when in that same five years you could build a profitable, automated, globally-scaled enterprise that you own 100% of?
- **The "Great Unbundling" of the Firm:** The solo founder represents the ultimate "unbundling" of the traditional corporation. A single person, acting as a conductor, can now orchestrate a vast network of specialized AI services, APIs, and platforms to replicate the output of a multi-hundred-person company. The most ambitious and creative minds of the next generation will increasingly opt out of the corporate world in favor of this new, more leveraged path. This will create a massive brain drain from large incumbents, accelerating their decline and creating a powerful, self-reinforcing cycle that further cements the dominance of this new entrepreneurial model.

19.4 Preparing for the Post-Solo Billionaire World

The first solo billionaire is just the beginning, the single wave that signals the coming tsunami. To truly think on a billion-dollar scale, we must use second-order thinking to explore the profound, long-term societal and economic shifts that this new paradigm will create. What happens when there are not one, but one thousand solo-founded unicorns? What happens when building a multi-million dollar automated business becomes a common career path? The answers to these questions reveal the next, even larger, set of opportunities.

Economic Shift #1: The Hyper-Personalization of Everything and the Rise of the Aggregator

- **The Second-Order Consequence:** As the cost and friction of building a software business plummets to near zero, we will witness an explosion of "micro-SaaS" companies. The market will fragment from a few large, one-size-fits-all software suites (like Microsoft Office or Adobe Creative Suite) into millions of hyper-specialized, AI-powered tools that do one specific job perfectly. There will not be one CRM; there will be a CRM designed specifically for independent florists in the UK, another for freelance wedding photographers in California, and so on.
- **The Next Billion-Dollar Opportunity:** The new mega-opportunity will not be in building another one of these niche tools. It will be in building the **platform that aggregates and bundles them**. The winning model will be an "App Store for Micro-SaaS" or a "Spotify for Business Tools." A user will pay a single monthly subscription to an aggregator, and an AI will then curate a personalized, dynamic bundle of dozens of these niche tools that are perfectly suited to their unique workflow. The opportunity shifts from product creation to platform-level curation and distribution.

Economic Shift #2: The Emergence of the "Automated Cooperative"

- **The Second-Order Consequence:** If a single, AI-leveraged individual can build a billion-dollar company, what can a small, elite team of three to five such individuals build? This new reality will give rise to a new type of organization: the automated cooperative.
- **The Future Organization:** Imagine a three-person team deciding to tackle a problem like curing a rare disease. One is a world-class biologist, one is a world-class AI systems architect, and one is a world-class capital allocator. They have no employees. They operate as a decentralized, equity-based entity,

orchestrating a vast network of AI agents, automated cloud laboratories, and outsourced clinical trial services to achieve their goal with a speed and capital efficiency that no large pharmaceutical company could ever match.

- **The Next Billion-Dollar Opportunity:** Building the picks and shovels for this new type of organization. This could include a new legal and financial platform designed for fluid, project-based equity allocation, or a new type of project management software built for orchestrating complex, hybrid human-AI teams.

Societal Shift #1: The Acceleration of the Post-Work Debate

- **The Second-Order Consequence:** The same leverage that empowers the solo founder will also automate a significant portion of traditional knowledge work. The economic value of performing routine cognitive tasks will continue its steady march toward zero.
- **The Societal Reckoning:** This will intensify the societal debate around the future of work, the meaning of a career, and the potential need for economic models like Universal Basic Income (UBI). The solo billionaire will become a potent symbol of an economy that can produce immense wealth with an astonishingly small number of human workers.
- **The Next Billion-Dollar Opportunity:** Building the infrastructure for a world where "work" is redefined. This could include hyper-personalized, AI-powered platforms for lifelong learning and reskilling, or new social platforms designed not for professional networking, but for helping people find purpose, community, and fulfillment outside of a traditional career structure.

Societal Shift #2: The Individual as a "Superpower"

- **The Second-Order Consequence:** We are entering an age where the leverage available to a single individual will be so immense that a lone actor could have the same level of impact—both positive and negative—as a small nation-state. This raises profound ethical and security questions.

- **The Next Billion-Dollar Opportunity:** Building the "trust and safety" layer for the age of individual superpowers. This will be a new, trillion-dollar industry. It could involve creating AI-powered security firms that can detect and mitigate risks from rogue actors, building platforms for establishing verifiable digital identity and reputation, or creating new forms of decentralized, AI-assisted governance to manage these powerful new technologies.

The post-solo billionaire world will be one of unprecedented opportunity and staggering complexity. The skills you have learned in this book—systems thinking, AI-native problem solving, and a deep understanding of leverage—are the very skills that will be required to build the next generation of groundbreaking companies that solve these new and profound challenges.

Chapter Summary & Resources

This chapter has served as a synthesis of our entire journey, projecting the principles of the AI-powered solo founder onto the future of business and society. We have created a detailed profile of the archetypal founder and business that will first achieve the historic solo billionaire milestone. We have analyzed the powerful technological and economic forces at play to forecast a likely timeline for this event. And finally, we have explored the profound, second-order consequences of this shift, identifying the next great wave of entrepreneurial opportunities.

Key Takeaways

- The first solo billionaire will likely be a **systems-thinking, AI-native founder** in a niche B2B market, leveraging a powerful **data moat** to build a defensible, hyper-profitable business.
- The milestone is likely to be achieved within the next **5 to 10 years**, driven by the exponential growth of AI capabilities and the deflationary cost of intelligence.
- The rise of the solo founder will fundamentally disrupt traditional **business schools, venture capital models, and corporate career paths**, forcing them to adapt or become obsolete.

- The second-order consequences of this paradigm shift will create the next wave of billion-dollar opportunities in areas like **platform aggregation**, infrastructure for new organizational models, and solutions for a **"post-work" economy**.

Key Predictions to Watch For

- **The "Quiet Unicorn" Signal:** In the next 12-24 months, watch for the first credible news story of a solo-founder company that has bootstrapped its way to over $10 million in ARR. This will be the key leading indicator that the trend is accelerating.
- **The VC Model Shift:** Look for the emergence of a new, high-profile "solo capitalist" fund that explicitly states its investment thesis is to write $250k-$1M checks into solo-founded, AI-native companies.
- **The "Micro-SaaS" Explosion:** Monitor marketplaces like Acquire.com. You will see a dramatic increase in the volume and valuation of small, profitable, AI-powered SaaS businesses being bought and sold.
- **Your "Next Frontier" Idea:** Based on the second-order consequences discussed, what is one new business idea that would only be possible in a world where AI-powered solo entrepreneurship is the norm?

Preview of Chapter 20

We have reached the end of our exploration of the mindset, the systems, and the strategies of the solo founder. We have analyzed the future. The only thing left is to make that future your reality. The final chapter of this book, **Chapter 20: Your Zero to Hero Action Plan**, is the culmination of everything we have learned. It is a single, consolidated, and actionable roadmap designed to guide you from where you are today to your first million in revenue and, ultimately, to your place as a titan of this new economy.

Resources and Tools

- **Futurism & Tech Analysis:** The Stratechery blog by Ben Thompson and ARK Invest's annual "Big Ideas" report are two of the best resources for high-level, strategic thinking about the future of technology and its economic impact.
- **Books on the Future of Work:** *The Second Machine Age* by Erik Brynjolfsson and Andrew McAfee; *AI Superpowers* by Kai-Fu Lee.
- **Concept: Second-Order Thinking.** Revisit this mental model from Chapter 12. It is the single most important tool for thinking clearly and strategically about the long-term consequences and opportunities of major technological shifts.

Chapter 20: Your Zero to Hero Action Plan

Introduction

We have reached the end of the blueprint. Over the course of this book, we have journeyed through the profound shifts in mindset, the powerful AI-powered systems, the aggressive scaling playbooks, and the sophisticated strategic frameworks required to build a billion-dollar enterprise as a solo founder. The theories have been explained, the case studies analyzed, the tools revealed. The only thing left is to translate this knowledge into action.

This final chapter is the bridge between the book in your hands and the future you are about to build. It is the culmination of everything we have learned, consolidated into a single, concrete, and actionable roadmap. It is designed to take you from where you are right now—at the starting line, filled with ambition—and guide you through the critical stages of your journey.

In the last chapter, we looked to the horizon and saw the inevitable future of entrepreneurship. This chapter brings our focus back to the present moment—to day one, week one, and month one of your personal quest. We will provide two distinct but connected roadmaps: a detailed, tactical 12-month plan to achieve your first million-dollar milestone, and a high-level, strategic 5-year path to unicorn status. This is the most important chapter in the book. It is not just information; it is your personal operating manual for building a billion-dollar enterprise. The age of the solo titan is here. This is your map. The journey starts now.

20.1 The 12-Month Roadmap to Million-Dollar Revenue

This is your tactical playbook. The goal is aggressive but achievable: to go from an idea to a $1 million Annual Recurring Revenue (ARR) run rate—which is approximately $83,333 in Monthly Recurring Revenue (MRR)—within 12 months. This timeline is only possible by ruthlessly leveraging the AI-powered systems and hyper-efficient strategies we have detailed throughout this book. This is your sprint to product-market fit and initial scale.

Quarter 1 (Months 1-3): Foundation, Validation & Launch Theme: From Zero to One. The entire focus of this quarter is to go from a mere idea to a live product with your first handful of paying, passionate customers. This quarter is a direct execution of the 90-Day Launch Strategy from Chapter 8.

- **Month 1: Validation & Infrastructure.**
    - **Week 1:** Execute the 24-Hour Validation Cycle (Chapter 3). Before you build anything, create an AI-generated smoke test landing page and validate that your core hypothesis has a positive signal from your target market. Do not proceed without this validation.
    - **Week 2:** Assemble your Foundation Stack (Chapter 4). Purchase your domain, and set up your core accounts: Bubble, Webflow, n8n, Stripe, Mercury, and your chosen LLM API providers.
    - **Weeks 3-4:** Build your "Central Brain" in Notion (Chapter 9). Your first task is to create the initial SOPs for the most critical manual processes you'll face in the early days, such as "SOP for responding to early user feedback" and "SOP for deploying a critical hotfix." Simultaneously, design your "Personal OS" (Chapter 11), defining your non-negotiable work boundaries and shutdown rituals to set a sustainable pace from the very beginning.

- **Month 2: Minimum Viable Product (MVP) Development.**
    - **Weeks 5-6:** Enter a state of deep work. Focus exclusively on building the single core feature of your MVP using your AI co-pilot (Chapter 7). Your goal is to create the "magic" moment that solves your customer's primary pain point with undeniable elegance.
    - **Weeks 7-8:** Build the necessary "wrapper" features: a clean user profile page, simple account settings, and a

fully functional subscription management portal integrated with Stripe. Use n8n to build your initial automated, behavior-driven user onboarding sequence (Chapter 9). This sequence should be designed to guide every new user to your "aha!" moment as quickly as possible.

- **Month 3: Launch & The First 10 Customers.**
    - **Week 9:** Pre-launch. Engage with the early access list you built during your validation cycle. Offer them a generous discount or free access in exchange for being your first users and providing testimonials.
    - **Week 10:** Launch Day. Announce your product on platforms like Product Hunt and BetaList, and in the niche online communities where you first validated the idea.
    - **Weeks 11-12:** Obsessively listen. Watch user session recordings with a tool like LogRocket. Analyze where users get stuck. Personally email your first 10 paying customers to thank them, ask why they chose your product, and understand their goals. Use this feedback to ship your first significant product iteration by the end of the quarter, proving to your early adopters that you are listening and responsive.

- **End of Q1 Goal:** Achieve **~$1,000 MRR**. The revenue is secondary to the proof point: you have built something people will pay for, and you have established a tight feedback loop with your first passionate users.

Quarter 2 (Months 4-6): Product-Market Fit & The Growth Loop Theme: From 1 to 100 Customers. The goal is to move from a promising product to a genuine business by finding a repeatable, scalable growth loop.

- **Month 4: Finding Your Multiplier.** With a few months of data, you can now move from intuition to analytics. Implement your

AI BI system (Chapter 6). Run your first comprehensive AI-Powered Growth Audit (Chapter 10). For instance, the AI might reveal that while your product is for "marketers," your first 20 paying customers are all *in-house marketers at B2B fintech companies*, not agency marketers or B2C marketers. This is a critical insight that dramatically narrows and defines your Ideal Customer Profile (ICP).

- **Month 5: Doubling Down.** This month is about ruthless focus. You will realign your entire business around the ICP identified in Month 4. Rewrite your Webflow homepage copy to speak their language. Change the product screenshots to reflect their specific use cases. Retask your automated sales and marketing engines (Chapter 5) to exclusively target this persona. Every decision should be aimed at winning this niche.

- **Month 6: System Hardening.** As user numbers climb, you must proactively strengthen your systems. Scale your AI Service Agent's knowledge base with the new questions you're receiving. Implement your automated Quality Control systems (Chapter 9), such as proactive system health monitoring and data integrity audits, to ensure quality and reliability do not degrade with scale.

- **End of Q2 Goal:** Achieve **~$15,000 MRR**. You have now validated a scalable growth loop and have achieved definitive product-market fit within a specific, profitable niche.

Quarter 3 (Months 7-9): Acceleration & Expansion Theme: From 100 to 500 Customers. The focus is on pouring fuel onto your validated growth loop and beginning to expand your surface area.

- **Month 7: Market Expansion Test.** Your BI tool shows a surprising number of organic signups from the UK. Run a low-cost localization test. This involves using the Stripe API to display pricing in GBP (£), using an AI to rewrite key landing page copy with British-English colloquialisms, and running a £100 targeted ad campaign on LinkedIn to see if the conversion rate improves. This data will inform your future global strategy.

- **Month 8: Revenue Diversification.** Build your first complementary, low-effort revenue stream (Chapter 8). Use your AI content engine to repurpose your blog content into a high-value e-book and sell it for $49. This adds financial resilience and captures customers not yet ready for the core subscription.

- **Month 9: Moat Construction.** Shift focus to long-term defensibility (Chapter 13 & 18). Launch a private Discord server for your paying customers to begin cultivating your community moat. Verify that your data network effect is operational and that you are systematically collecting the proprietary data needed to fine-tune your unique AI models.

- **End of Q3 Goal:** Achieve **~$50,000 MRR**. You have proven that your model can expand and you are consciously building a durable, defensible business.

Quarter 4 (Months 10-12): Achieving Escape Velocity Theme: From 500 to 1,000+ Customers. The goal is to cross the seven-figure threshold and solidify your position as a market leader.

- **Month 10: Optimizing the Economic Engine.** Focus on the advanced SaaS metrics (Chapter 18). For example, you notice that a single, non-critical AI feature is responsible for 40% of your OpenAI bill. You spend a week refactoring it to use a much cheaper, specialized open-source model. This single change increases your gross margin by 5 points overnight.

- **Month 11: Scaling Your Influence.** Your AI-amplified content "atomization" engine (Chapter 14) should now be running at full capacity, establishing you as the primary thought leader in your space. Your personal time should be focused on high-leverage influence activities like podcast interviews.

- **Month 12: Hitting the Milestone & Strategic Planning.** With your optimized growth engine running, you should cross the **$83,333 MRR** target. Your primary job this month is to look to the future, using an LLM to war-game potential threats and opportunities for the coming year and making the critical "Raise vs. Bootstrap" decision (Chapter 17).

- **End of Q4 Goal:** Achieve a **$1 Million ARR** run rate. You have successfully built and scaled a profitable, efficient, and market-validated solo enterprise.

20.2 The 5-Year Path to Unicorn Status

Reaching the million-dollar milestone is a monumental achievement. It proves you have built a real business. The journey from $1 million to a billion-dollar valuation, however, is a different game entirely. It requires a shift from tactical execution to grand strategy. This 5-year roadmap is a high-level strategic overview, outlining the key themes and milestones required to transform your successful business into a market-defining unicorn.

Year 1: The Machine & The Model (Achieve $1M ARR)

- **Theme: Building the Machine and Proving the Model.** This is the entire 12-month roadmap we just detailed.
- **Key Milestones:** Go from idea to a launched MVP. Achieve definitive product-market fit within a specific niche. Build and harden all of the core automated systems for marketing, sales, support, and operations. Validate a scalable and repeatable growth loop.
- **End-of-Year Status:** The business is a profitable, hyper-efficient, solo-run enterprise with a $1 million ARR run rate. It is a proven and validated foundation, ready for true scale.

Year 2: The Moat Deepening Year (Target: $5M - $10M ARR)

- **Theme: Achieving Dominance in Your Beachhead Market.** The focus of this year is on making your position in your initial niche unassailable.

- **Key Milestones:**

- **Data Moat:** This is the year you focus on capturing unique human preference data. You will redesign parts of your product to include explicit feedback loops (e.g., thumbs up/down on AI suggestions), which will provide the proprietary data needed for Reinforcement Learning from Human Feedback (RLHF), making your fine-tuned model uniquely intelligent.
- **Community Moat:** Your user community will evolve into a self-sustaining ecosystem. You will use your AI BI tool to identify and empower a team of volunteer moderators and superusers.
- **Brand Moat:** You will become the #1 recognized thought leader in your niche through your AI-amplified content engine.
- **The Funding Decision:** If you choose to raise a Series A this year, your 'Use of Funds' will be highly strategic, such as "$3M to acquire a unique proprietary dataset to accelerate our model's training," signaling a focus on asset acquisition, not just hiring.

- **End-of-Year Status:** You are the dominant, most-respected player in your initial market. You have a multi-layered, compounding moat that makes it incredibly difficult for a new competitor to challenge you.

Year 3: The Expansion Year (Target: $20M - $30M ARR)

- **Theme: From Niche Leader to Multi-Market Player.** This year is about proving that your business model is a repeatable playbook for disruption.

- **Key Milestones:**
  - **Geographic & Vertical Expansion:** Execute a full-scale launch into your top 2-3 international markets and 1-2 new industry verticals. When entering a new vertical, you will fine-tune a *new version* of your core AI model

on a dataset specific to that vertical, creating a more specialized and valuable product.

  - **Your First Strategic Hire:** You may choose to hire your first employee. This person will be your "Automator-in-Chief," an operations expert whose sole KPI is to increase the company's "Automation Ratio." They will manage the "Company OS" and be responsible for turning every remaining manual process into a resilient n8n workflow, freeing you to focus 100% on product vision and grand strategy.

- **End-of-Year Status:** Your business is now a multi-market enterprise, proving your model's adaptability and dramatically increasing your Total Addressable Market.

Year 4: The Platform Year (Target: $50M - $75M ARR)

- **Theme: From a Great Product to an Essential Ecosystem.** This is the year you build the ultimate moat by transforming your product into a platform.

- **Key Milestones:**

  - **Public API as a Product:** You will launch a robust, well-documented, public-facing API, treating it as a first-class product with its own marketing and support systems.
  - **Developer Ecosystem & App Store:** You will actively cultivate a community of third-party developers, launching an official "App Store" or marketplace that features their integrations. This creates an ecosystem that drives value and defensibility far beyond what you could build alone.
  - **Your First Acquisition:** Your AI BI tool might identify a small, one-person tool with passionate users that solves a problem adjacent to yours. You acquire the asset and plug it into your hyper-efficient marketing and

operational systems, instantly making it more profitable and accelerating your roadmap.

- **End-of-Year Status:** You are no longer just a product company; you are a foundational platform for your industry. Your value is now derived from the entire ecosystem you have created.

Year 5: The Path to Liquidity (Target: $100M+ ARR)

- **Theme: Preparing for the Endgame.** Your business is now a mature, highly valuable asset. This year is about preparing it for a major liquidity event.
- **Key Milestones:**
    - **Building the Executive Team:** You will hire a small, world-class executive team. Your CFO will be an expert in usage-based pricing models and AI cost optimization. Your COO will be an expert in managing distributed, automated systems, not large human teams.
    - **Financial & Operational Maturity:** Your financials and metrics must be flawless, predictable, and auditable. Your "Company OS" becomes the core of the due diligence data room.
    - **The Strategic Decision:** You, along with your board and advisors, will make the final strategic decision based on your ultimate vision: begin the formal process of preparing for an IPO in the next 18-24 months to continue building independently, or pursue a strategic acquisition by a major tech giant for a multi-billion dollar valuation.
- **End-of-Year Status:** Your company is a mature, highly profitable, and strategically invaluable market leader. You have completed the journey from zero to hero.

20.3 Tools, Resources, and Community Building

The journey of a solo founder is a paradox: you build alone, but you cannot succeed alone. Your success is built upon a support stack composed of three critical pillars: the digital tools that grant you leverage, the knowledge resources that grant you wisdom, and the communities that grant you solidarity. This is not an exhaustive directory, but a curated, "desert island" list of the absolute essentials—the platforms, books, and networks that will support you on your journey from zero to hero.

The Essential Tool Stack (Your "Can't Live Without" List)

This is the core operational stack that enables the one-person enterprise.

- **Intelligence Layer:**
    - **OpenAI API (GPT-5 & family):** The indispensable workhorse for raw analytical power, complex reasoning, and state-of-the-art code generation. This is your virtual CTO and engineering team.
    - **Anthropic API (Claude 4 Family):** The specialist for nuance. Use it for high-quality, long-form content creation, analyzing large documents, and powering any customer-facing communication where a thoughtful, empathetic tone is paramount.
- **Creation & Operations Layer:**
    - **Bubble:** The non-negotiable platform for building your core, data-driven web application. Its combination of a visual front-end builder, a robust database, and powerful logic workflows makes it the operating system for your product.
    - **Webflow:** The best-in-class tool for building your world-class marketing website, blog, and landing pages. Its design flexibility and powerful CMS are unmatched.

- Notion: The flexible, powerful "Central Brain" for your Company OS. It is where your SOPs, product roadmaps, and customer databases will live.

- **Automation Layer:**
    - **n8n.io:** The industrial-strength nervous system for your entire business. While other tools are simpler, n8n provides the power and complexity needed to build the truly autonomous, multi-step workflows that a billion-dollar enterprise requires.

- **Growth & Analytics Layer:**
    - **Clay.com:** Your "secret weapon" for sales. The single best platform for enriching lead data and enabling the hyper-personalized outreach that actually works.
    - **A Session Replay Tool (FullStory, LogRocket):** Essential for moving beyond quantitative data and qualitatively understanding your users' experience, finding their points of frustration, and auditing your product's quality.

The Essential Resources (Your Personal Board of Directors)

This is the knowledge you need to internalize to make high-quality strategic decisions.

- **The Foundational Books:**
    - ***The Lean Startup* by Eric Ries:** The bible of the build-measure-learn feedback loop, which is the core of your rapid, AI-powered iteration cycle.
    - ***The E-Myth Revisited* by Michael E. Gerber:** The classic text on the importance of building systems and working *on* your business, not just *in* it. The philosophical foundation for the "CEO Mindset."

    - ***Venture Deals* by Brad Feld and Jason Mendelson:** An essential, tactical guide to understanding the mechanics of a venture capital deal, ensuring you can negotiate from a position of knowledge.
    - ***Thinking in Bets* by Annie Duke:** A masterclass in probabilistic thinking and decision-making under uncertainty, which is the core job of a founder.

- **The Real-Time Knowledge Feed:**

    - **Stratechery by Ben Thompson:** The single best resource for high-level, strategic analysis of the technology industry.
    - **Lenny's Newsletter:** Deep, tactical, and incredibly valuable advice on product, growth, and marketing from a former leader at Airbnb.
    - **Y Combinator's Blog and YouTube Channel:** A timeless, free library of foundational startup advice on every topic imaginable.

The Essential Communities (Your Peer Group) Isolation is the silent killer of solo founders. You must intentionally embed yourself in communities of your peers.

- **Indie Hackers:** The global digital hub for bootstrapped and solo founders. It is an invaluable place to share your progress, ask for tactical advice, and find solidarity with thousands of others who are on the exact same journey.
- **Your Niche "Watering Hole":** Find the primary online community for your specific target audience (e.g., a specific Discord server, a professional Slack group). Becoming an active, helpful member is not just a marketing tactic; it is the best way to maintain deep empathy and understanding for the people you are serving.
- **Your Personal Mastermind:** This is the most powerful community you can build. Identify 3-5 other non-competing, ambitious solo founders from a larger community who are at a similar stage. Propose a private group with a standing monthly

call where you hold each other accountable, share your biggest challenges, and act as a personal board of directors for one another.

You are building alone, but you are supported by the collective intelligence and experience of the entire global tech ecosystem. By deliberately choosing and engaging with these essential tools, resources, and communities, you build a "support stack" that provides the knowledge, motivation, and camaraderie needed to complete the journey.

20.4 Final Framework: From Solo Founder to Industry Titan

We have covered a vast territory in this book—from mindset shifts and system architecture to scaling strategies and fundraising playbooks. To make these concepts actionable, we can distill the entire Zero to Hero philosophy into a single, powerful, and memorable framework. This is the engine of your journey. It is a continuous, three-stage loop: **Automate, Replicate, Compound.**

This is the one page you should print out and put on your wall. It is your strategic compass.

A - AUTOMATE (The Foundation)

- **The Principle:** The primary, foundational activity of the solo founder is the relentless conversion of manual effort into automated systems. You must develop a deep, visceral allergy to repeatable, low-leverage tasks. Your default response to any task that you have to do more than twice should be, "How can I build a system to do this for me?"
- **The Mindset:** This is the embodiment of the **"CEO Mindset."** You are a designer of intelligent systems, not a doer of tasks. You understand that your time is the most valuable and scarcest resource in your company, and you protect it fiercely for high-level strategic work.
- **The Action:** You apply the **"Rule of 30x,"** investing your time to build permanent solutions. You use your Foundation Stack—

AI, No-Code, and Automation—to build your "Company OS," the central brain that runs the day-to-day operations of your business without you.

- **The Outcome:** An enterprise with extreme capital efficiency, massive profit margins, and a founder who is liberated from the operational weeds to focus on the bigger picture. This is the mastery of Parts 1 and 2 of this book.

R - REPLICATE (The Scaling Engine)

- **The Principle:** Once you have built a proven, automated system that successfully serves one niche market, the path to massive scale is to replicate that system across new markets and new opportunities.
- **The Mindset:** This is the **"Growth Accelerator" mindset.** You are not just looking for incremental improvements; you are systematically searching for the 10x multiplier opportunities that can lead to non-linear growth.
- **The Action:** You use your AI systems as an infinitely scalable expansion team. You use AI to identify and enter new **geographic markets** by localizing your product and marketing. You use AI to enter new **industry verticals** by cloning and re-tasking your core business model. You use **API-driven partnerships** to replicate your distribution by plugging into existing, large-scale ecosystems.
- **The Outcome:** Your business grows from a single, successful niche product into a multi-market, diversified enterprise, dramatically expanding its total addressable market and revenue potential. This is the mastery of Part 3 of this book.

C - COMPOUND (The Billion-Dollar Moat)

- **The Principle:** The ultimate goal is to build self-reinforcing loops—flywheels—where the business grows stronger, more valuable, and more defensible with each passing day. This is the magic of compounding advantage.
- **The Mindset:** This is the **"Billion-Dollar Mindset."** You are no longer just building a product or a company; you are architecting

a durable, long-term asset. You are making strategic, second-order decisions designed to create a lasting legacy.

- **The Action:** You focus on building the three modern moats that compound over time: the **Data Network Effect**, where your product gets smarter with more use; the **Community**, where your network becomes more valuable with more members; and your **Personal Influence**, where your social capital grows with every helpful interaction and original insight you share.
- **The Outcome:** A business with an unassailable competitive advantage, a brand that is synonymous with its category, and a valuation that reflects its long-term, durable earning power. This is the mastery of Parts 4 and 5 of this book.

Automate to free your time. **Replicate** to scale your reach. **Compound** to build a lasting moat. This simple, three-stage loop is the engine that drives a solo founder from an idea to an industry titan. It is the core philosophy of your Zero to Hero journey.

Concluding Message & Call to Action

We have reached the end of the blueprint. We have journeyed together from the initial spark of an idea to the grand vision of a billion-dollar enterprise. We have deconstructed the mindset, architected the systems, and laid out the strategies required to thrive in this new age of individual leverage. The image we began with—of a single founder at a laptop, commanding a global, automated, and massively valuable company—is no longer a distant fantasy. It is a tangible, achievable reality. This book has provided the map.

The tools are more powerful and accessible than they have ever been in human history. The cost of intelligence is plummeting toward zero. A new class of investors is actively seeking to fund the hyper-efficient, solo-founded companies of the future. The historical excuses that have held back ambitious individuals for centuries—"I don't have a technical co-founder," "I can't code," "I don't have millions in capital," "I don't have a team"—have been systematically and permanently dismantled by artificial intelligence.

All of the external barriers have been removed.

The only remaining variable is you. The only remaining question is not "Can I?" but "Will I?"

Will you embrace the CEO mindset and stop trading your time for money? Will you put in the hard, focused work to design the systems that will grant you freedom and scale? Will you find the courage to make the bold, asymmetric bets required for exponential growth? Will you commit to the discipline of building a durable, resilient enterprise for the long term?

The blueprints are in your hands. The path is clear. The opportunity to build a business that provides not just immense wealth, but profound freedom, global impact, and deep creative fulfillment is the defining opportunity of our generation.

The age of the solo titan has begun.

Go build your empire.

About The Editor

Aditya Basu is a distinguished serial digital media entrepreneur and internet marketer, having been honoured with the Karmaveer Chakra (United Nations + iCongo Award) on three occasions. With more than twenty years of experience in digital brand building and online business models, Aditya has established himself as an influential figure in the industry. Furthermore, Aditya has served as a judge for the International Digital Emmy Awards on three occasions, from 2009 to 2011, demonstrating his expertise in his field. In recognition of his contributions, Aditya was included in the list of Top 50 Thinkers in India, published by MTC Global in Bangalore in 2014. He has also been featured as a speaker at esteemed platforms such as REX Talks (iCongo, New Delhi), RIDE (Raisoni University, Nagpur), eDC (IIT Delhi), and MAN Impact Accelerator (Mumbai).

Aditya's areas of expertise encompass content, media, digital media, marketing, and venture building, making him a sought-after resource for keynotes at industry events, moderating discussions, and providing consultation services to startups in the areas of content, media, communication, and marketing strategies.

In addition to his consulting activities, Aditya is actively engaged in the development of over a dozen digital media brands, spanning various sectors including startups, sustainability, personal finance, cinema, music, documentaries, and news. Most recently, Aditya launched "Startup Lessons," a project dedicated to empowering startups and entrepreneurs with the knowledge and skills necessary to successfully launch, attract investments, and scale their businesses.

In recent years, Aditya has expanded his portfolio by venturing into the realm of eBooks, printed books, audiobooks, and podcasts, further diversifying his contributions to the media landscape.

- **Book:** www.hopp.bio/02hero
- **Blog:** www.adityabasu.com
- **Hopp:** www.hopp.bio/adityabasu
- **Consultancy:** www.topmate.io/adityabasu
- **NexTechie:** www.medium.com/nextechie
- **Startup Lessons:** www.startup.tk
- **Sustainability Now:** www.sustainability.tk

www.ingramcontent.com/pod-product-compliance
Ingram Content Group UK Ltd.
Pitfield, Milton Keynes, MK11 3LW, UK
UKHW011514190726
13845UKWH00034B/1248

9 789334 371864